INDIFFERENT INCLUSION

To my father, Bill McGregor, 1927–2011.

INDIFFERENT INCLUSION

Aboriginal People and
the Australian Nation

Russell McGregor

Aboriginal Studies Press

The pages of this book are printed on paper derived from forests promoting sustainable management.

First published in 2011
by Aboriginal Studies Press

© Russell McGregor 2011

All rights reserved. No part of this book may be reproduced or transmitted in any form or by any means, electronic or mechanical, including photocopying, recording or by any information storage and retrieval system, without prior permission in writing from the publisher. The Australian *Copyright Act 1968* (the Act) allows a maximum of one chapter or 10 per cent of this book, whichever is the greater, to be photocopied by any educational institution for its education purposes provided that the educational institution (or body that administers it) has given a remuneration notice to Copyright Agency Limited (CAL) under the Act.

Aboriginal Studies Press
is the publishing arm of the
Australian Institute of Aboriginal
and Torres Strait Islander Studies.
GPO Box 553, Canberra, ACT 2601
Phone: (61 2) 6246 1183
Fax: (61 2) 6261 4288
Email: asp@aiatsis.gov.au
Web: www.aiatsis.gov.au/asp/welcome.html

A Cataloguing-in-Publication entry is available from the
National Library of Australia
www.trove.nla.gov.au
ISBN: 9780855757793 (pb)
ISBN: 9780855757823 (ebook PDF)
ISBN: 9780855757854 (ePub)

Printed in Australia by McPherson's Printing Group

Front cover (composite): House interior courtesy www.tournorfold.co.uk; Ewald Namatjira, *MacDonnell Ranges*, © estate of the artist 2011, licensed by Aboriginal Artists Agency Ltd; Martin Boyd pottery tumbler, courtesy of the National Museum of Australia, photo by George Serras; Cover of Australian Geographical *Walkabout* Magazine, September 1950, the Australian National Travel Association.

Contents

Illustrations	vii
Acknowledgments	viii
Preface	xi
Notes on Terminology	xiv
Abbreviations and Acronyms	xv
Prologue: The Crimson Thread of Whiteness	xvii

CHAPTER 1	Preserving the National Complexion	1
	Managing miscegenation	2
	Hiding heredity	8
	Opponents	13
	Continuities and discontinuities	14
CHAPTER 2	Primitive Possibilities	18
	Reappraising the primitive	20
	Refiguring the federation	27
	Humanitarians and activists	31
	A new deal	34
CHAPTER 3	Aboriginal Activists Demand Acceptance	37
	Conditional citizenship	39
	Virile, capable and black	41
	Representation and rights	47
	Citizen soldiers	50
CHAPTER 4	Restricted Reconstruction	55
	Postwar world order	57
	Challenging white Australia	60
	An anthropologist discovers citizenship	64
	Appreciating the Aboriginal	69

CHAPTER 5	To Live as We Do	76
	Stranded individuals	78
	Avoiding 'Aborigines'	81
	Mobilising civil society	88
	Attenuated identities	93
CHAPTER 6	Assimilation and Integration	98
	Assimilation through tradition	101
	An expedient slogan	107
	Definitions and redefinitions	112
CHAPTER 7	Enriching the Nation	119
	Respect and redemption	120
	Sporting heroes	123
	Indigenous wisdom	129
	Appreciation and appropriation	134
CHAPTER 8	Fellow Australians	141
	Voting rights	144
	Drinking rites	147
	Right wrongs, write yes	151
	Special assistance or minority rights?	158
CHAPTER 9	After the Referendum	162
	Dream time in Canberra	164
	Land rights	169
	An Aboriginal nation	173

Epilogue: Unfinished Business	183
Notes	188
Select Bibliography	220
Index	223

Illustrations

Plates between pp. 134–135

Plate 1	Three generations of 'breeding out the colour'
Plate 2	Margaret Preston, *Still Life: Fruit (Arnhem Land motif)*
Plate 3	The Day of Mourning, 1938
Plate 4	Albert Namatjira, *Mt Hermannsburg*
Plate 5	Frontispiece for *One People*, 1961
Plate 6	Welcome home parade for Lionel Rose, 1968
Plate 7	William Ricketts, *Earthly Mother*
Plate 8	Playing cards designed by Lloyd Piper
Plate 9	Faith and Lilon Bandler at a 1965 demonstration
Plate 10	Right Wrongs Write Yes for Aborigines
Plate 11	Yolngu Bark Petition, 1963
Plate 12	Instalment of Doug Nicholls as *Bapu Mamus*, 1970
Plate 13	Aboriginal Tent Embassy, 1972

Acknowledgments

My first thanks are to my wife, Christine Mitchell, for her love, support and forbearance over the years consumed by the writing of this book. Always a level-headed critic of my writing, Christine balanced encouragement of my efforts with advice on how my intentions could best be realised. I thank also my daughter Caitilin and my son Lachlan for their assistance and affection. Thanks, too, to my brother, William McGregor, in the Department of Linguistics at the University of Århus, Denmark, for the encouragement he has given me over many years.

My debts to colleagues in academia are numerous. At my home institution of James Cook University, I owe special thanks to Rosita Henry; also to Claire Brennan, Maureen Fuary, Shelley Greer and Greg Manning. Among scholars from other institutions, Warwick Anderson, Bain Attwood, Tom Griffiths, Rani Kerin, Henry Reynolds, Tim Rowse and Paul Turnbull have profoundly influenced my historical practice and my understanding of the issues examined in this book. I also thank Judith Brett, John Chesterman, Ann Curthoys, Bronwen Douglas, Geoff Gray, Anna Haebich, Allison Holland, Robert Kenny, Marilyn Lake, Andrew Markus, John Maynard, Dirk Moses, Fiona Paisley, Sue Taffe, Jinki Trevellian and Christine Winter for the contributions they have made in ways too varied to list here. Some of these people, I am sure, would disagree with some (perhaps many) of my interpretations, but all have helped shape both my ideas and how I have expressed them in this book.

For their helpfulness, often beyond the call of duty, I thank the librarians and archivists at the Australian Institute of Aboriginal and Torres Strait Islander Studies, the Eddie Koiki Mabo Library at James Cook University, the Fisher Library at the University of Sydney, the National Archives of Australia, the National Library of Australia, the South Australian Museum

Anthropology Archives, the State Library of New South Wales and the University of Sydney Archives.

Earlier versions of parts of this book were presented as conference papers and published as journal articles and chapters in edited collections. The predecessor publications are: '"Breed out the colour" or the importance of being white', *Australian Historical Studies*, vol. 33, no. 120, 2002; 'Develop the north: Aborigines, environment and Australian nationhood in the 1930s', *Journal of Australian Studies*, no. 81, 2004; 'Avoiding "Aborigines": Paul Hasluck and the Northern Territory Welfare Ordinance, 1953', *Australian Journal of Politics and History*, vol. 51, no. 4, 2005; 'Assimilation as acculturation: AP Elkin on the dynamics of cultural change', in Tim Rowse (ed.), *Contesting assimilation*, API Network, Perth, 2005; '27 May 1967: The 1967 referendum: an uncertain consensus', in Martin Crotty and David Roberts (eds), *Turning points in Australian history*, UNSW Press, Sydney, 2009; 'Another nation: Aboriginal activism in the late 1960s and early 1970s', *Australian Historical Studies*, vol. 40, no. 3, 2009; 'Arguing about assimilation: Indigenous policy and advocacy in Australia', in Bain Attwood and Tom Griffiths (eds), *Frontier, race, nation: Henry Reynolds and Australian history*, Australian Scholarly Publishing, Brisbane, 2009. My thanks to the editors and referees of these articles and chapters for helping to discipline my arguments.

For the same reason, I thank the anonymous referees of the manuscript that became this book, and the staff of Aboriginal Studies Press, especially Rhonda Black and Rachel Ippoliti. Thanks also to Susan Jarvis for her editorial assistance.

Preface

In 1938, while settler Australians celebrated their 150-year occupancy of the continent, Aboriginal activists Jack Patten and Bill Ferguson asserted the claims of the Indigenous inhabitants: 'We ask — and we have every right to *demand* — that you should include us, fully and equally with yourselves, in the body of the Australian nation.'[1] For the next three decades, the quest for national inclusion headed the Aboriginal agenda. As understood at the time, inclusion in the nation entailed more than legal equality, important though that attainment was. It required Aboriginal people to be treated with respect and dignity, to be welcomed as full participants in the life of the community. This book recounts that multifaceted quest for national inclusion up to the early 1970s.

Over that period, inclusiveness of Aboriginal people increased, but inclusion was hesitant, often grudging and always incomplete. Against their acceptance as members of the nation stood a formidable array of assumptions and prejudices. Most of all, inclusion was inhibited by the sheer indifference of settler Australians. The fate of a tiny Indigenous minority, burdened with a plethora of negative stereotypes, was for the majority a matter of little consequence.

Yet public attitudes did shift, and exposition of those shifts takes my narrative beyond the narrowly political domain of parliaments, policies and protests. Adopting a broader canvas, this book explores the ways in which factors such as demonstrations of Aboriginal artistic talents and sporting prowess contributed to the acceptance of Aboriginal people into the national community, even as acceptance was compromised by entrenched assumptions of Indigenous ineptness. Acceptance, it must be conceded, is a rather amorphous achievement, and it is impossible to precisely calibrate the degree of acceptance at a particular point in time. Nonetheless, broad indicators of the level of acceptance, and of the willingness of the majority to extend acceptance, can be extrapolated from the historical record.

Social inclusion still retains positive connotations in Aboriginal affairs. Not so for another term that was commonly used to designate that process in the period under consideration: 'assimilation'. Today, assimilation is commonly demonised as little more than an attempt to destroy Aboriginal cultures and provide spurious justification for child theft. That the cultural destruction and child removals took place is not in question, but the meanings of assimilation were not exhausted by these practices, which were in fact opposed by many assimilationists. In the middle decades of the twentieth century, the word 'assimilation' encompassed a wide range of proposals for securing an Aboriginal future, and drew support from an equally diverse array of people — both Indigenous and non-Indigenous. To understand the prominence and credibility of assimilation at the time, we must look beyond the governmental policies and practices that went under the 'assimilation' label. 'Assimilation' was analogous to the more recent slogan in Indigenous affairs, 'reconciliation', with both words being interpreted and inflected in myriad, often discordant, ways and both denoting far more than merely the actions or ambitions of governments. One of the purposes of this book is to promote a more nuanced understanding of what assimilation meant in mid-twentieth-century Australia.[2]

I do not attempt to convey the lived reality of how Aboriginal people experienced their exclusion from, or inclusion in, the Australian nation. Exposition of those experiences may best be left to Indigenous writers. Nor do I attempt to offer a comprehensive account of the incremental changes in legislation by which Aboriginal people acquired formal legal equality. That has already been done by others.[3] Rather, I seek to elucidate the ideas and ideals that propelled the quest for Aboriginal inclusion in the nation in the middle decades of the twentieth century, the impediments to that quest and its stumbling successes. This is a book about the transformation of the Australian nation as it made faltering steps to come to grips with the endurance of the Indigenous people and as Indigenous people themselves strove to secure a place within the nation.

To illuminate the changing texture of Australian nationhood, the concepts of civic and ethnic nationalism are helpful. Ethnic nationalisms put a premium on blood kinship as the primary tie of community, and assume an organic connection between culture and biological ancestry. Civic nationalisms, on the other hand, emphasise shared rights, responsibilities and values as the foundations of national cohesion. However, as the prominent British scholar Anthony Smith argues, the distinction between them — while analytically useful — is never absolute. No nationalism is purely one or the other; all are compounded of both civic and ethnic elements, though in varying degrees and proportions that typically change over time.[4] Australian nationalism at the beginning of the twentieth century was strongly ethnic in orientation, flaunted in its celebration of whiteness as the key criterion of national membership. Over the course of the century, the ethnic elements were diluted by a stronger stress on civic attributes, promoting a more open conception of Australian nationhood. However, the door was never more than partially ajar.

The legacy this book traces is an ambiguous one. Over the middle decades of the twentieth century, Aboriginal people were incrementally, though incompletely, incorporated into the national community. Inclusion was always conditional, and the dominant group — settler Australians — set the terms of inclusion. Although settler Australians have in the past baulked at opening their hearts and minds to the full inclusion of Aboriginal people in the Australian nation, I hope the light this book sheds on the tentative steps of the past will encourage a greater openness in the future.

Notes on Terminology

Throughout this book, I use terms such as 'half-caste', 'full-blood', 'mixed-blood' and 'part-Aboriginal'. Although these terms, and the distinctions they impute, are today widely regarded with distaste — even repugnance — this was not the case in the period under discussion. Then, words such as 'half-caste' and 'full-blood' were used by, among others, Aboriginal people as terms of self-designation. Moreover, they were terms that made distinctions which were meaningful and consequential in the context of their times. Hence, they cannot be avoided in historical works seeking to understand the world of people in the past. In the following chapters, I use these words without quotation marks, except in quotation or, as in the first sentence of this paragraph, where the words themselves rather than their referents are under consideration. The same principle applies to my use of other, heavily value-laden words such as 'progress', 'advancement', 'primitive' and 'civilised'. The absence of quotation marks in no way indicates endorsement of the hierarchies they impute.

The word 'Aboriginal' is less problematic, but not entirely free of complications. In the period under consideration, it was commonly used to refer to all the Indigenous inhabitants of Australia — that is, it was inclusive of Torres Strait Islanders. Sometimes, specification of the latter group was added, as in the case of the Federal Council for Aboriginal Advancement (FCAA), founded in 1958, which changed its name to the Federal Council for the Advancement of Aborigines and Torres Strait Islanders (FCAATSI) in 1964. The combination term, 'Aboriginal and Torres Strait Islander', was more prevalent in Queensland than elsewhere, and its level of usage rose somewhat towards the end of the period covered by this book. However, it was not standard usage at the time. Following contemporary convention, I often use the word 'Aboriginal' to encompass all Indigenous Australians, but vary this usage as seems appropriate.

Abbreviations and Acronyms

AAAS	Australasian Association for the Advancement of Science
AAF	Aboriginal-Australian Fellowship
AAF records	Records of the Aboriginal-Australian Fellowship, Mitchell Library, ms. 4057
AAL	Australian Aborigines' League
AALSA	Aborigines Advancement League of South Australia
ABC	Australian Broadcasting Commission
ABM	Australian Board of Missions
ACC	Australian Council of Churches
AFASA	Aborigines' Friends' Association of South Australia
AIATSIS	Australian Institute of Aboriginal and Torres Strait Islander Studies
ANZAAS	Australian and New Zealand Association for the Advancement of Science
APA	Aborigines Progressive Association
ARPNC	AR Pilling newspaper clippings, AIATSIS, ms. 3511
AWB	Aborigines Welfare Board of New South Wales
Bonner papers	Papers of Neville Bonner, National Library of Australia, ms. 7903
Bryant papers	Papers of Gordon Bryant, National Library of Australia, ms. 8256
CARV	Council for Aboriginal Rights, Victoria
Christophers papers	Papers of Barry Christophers, National Library of Australia, ms. 7992

Abbreviations and Acronyms

Cleland collection	JB Cleland Collection, South Australian Museum Anthropology Archives, AA60, Acc. 238
CPD	*Commonwealth Parliamentary Debates*
CPP	*Commonwealth Parliamentary Papers*
Duguid papers	Papers of Charles Duguid, National Library of Australia, ms. 5068
Elkin papers	Archives of Professor AP Elkin, University of Sydney Archives, P130
FCAA	Federal Council for Aboriginal Advancement
FCAATSI	Federal Council for the Advancement of Aborigines and Torres Strait Islanders
FCAATSI records	Records of the Federal Council for the Advancement of Aborigines and Torres Strait Islanders, Mitchell Library, ms. 2999
Hasluck papers	Papers of Sir Paul Hasluck, National Library of Australia, ms. 5274
NAA	National Archives of Australia
NADOC	National Aborigines Day Observance Committee
NADOC records	Records of the National Aborigines' Day Observance Committee, National Library of Australia, ms. 3677
NLA	National Library of Australia
NMC	National Missionary Council of Australia
NT	Northern Territory
NTCAR	Northern Territory Council for Aboriginal Rights
PM	Prime Minister
QPP	*Queensland Parliamentary Papers*
SAMAA	South Australian Museum Anthropology Archives
Simpson papers	Papers of Colin Simpson, National Library of Australia, ms. 5253
SMH	*Sydney Morning Herald*
Street papers	Paper of Lady Jessie Street, National Library of Australia, ms. 2683
VAAL	Victorian Aborigines Advancement League
VAG	Victorian Aboriginal Group

Prologue

The Crimson Thread of Whiteness

In the ten years of debate that preceded the federation of the Australian colonies, the Federation Fathers gave no thought to how Aboriginal people might be included in the nation-to-be. Nor did they give any thought to how Aboriginal people might be excluded. Indigenous Australians barely registered in their planning for the new nation. The only significant exception came at the beginning of the federation debates, not from an Australian but from a New Zealand delegate, Captain William Russell. (At this time, New Zealand was a potential member of an Australasian nation-state that might also have included Fiji and other Pacific islands.) Russell pointed to the Australians' failure to address the status and rights of the Indigenous people as a serious flaw in the proceedings and a substantial point of difference between the countries on either side of the Tasman Sea.[1] However, this trans-Tasman warning fell on deaf Australian ears, and New Zealand's withdrawal from the federation debates soon afterwards spared the Federation Fathers further reminders of their remissness in Aboriginal affairs.

While the federation debates and referenda lurched towards their ultimate goal, anthropologists Baldwin Spencer and Frank Gillen were conducting research among the Aboriginal people of central Australia. In 1899 they published a book, *The native tribes of central Australia*, which became a classic of Australian anthropology; it was followed by numerous other works, written jointly or individually. In line with contemporary evolutionary theory, their studies were premised on the assumption that 'the Australian aborigines are the most primitive or backward race' on Earth.[2] Relics of the Stone Age, they were doomed, and little more could be done other than make their 'path to final extinction...as pleasant as possible'.[3] Spencer and Gillen's investigations revealed new intricacies in

Aboriginal cultures, influencing the theories of European intellectuals such as Emile Durkheim and Sigmund Freud. Yet they also entrenched the twin assumptions that Aboriginal people were peculiarly primitive, and that their grasp upon life was remarkably tenuous. These assumptions pervaded popular as much as scientific perspectives.

Although attitudes toward Aboriginal people were negative, they were not necessarily malicious. Insofar as turn-of-the-twentieth-century white Australians thought about Aboriginal people at all — and this seems to have been seldom — their attitude was more commonly apathy than malevolence, since Aboriginal people were not usually perceived as a threat. Lyn Spillman observes that while Aboriginal people 'were occasionally seen as an "other" to a national identity built around racism and progress, they were not a threatening other'.[4] There were local concerns about Aboriginal people: they were unsanitary or unsightly in the view of townspeople living near fringe camps; they were drunk or disruptive in the view of the guardians of public decency; they still posed a physical danger to white intruders out on the far fringes of the frontier in the Centre, Kimberley and Arnhem Land. But none of these added up to a threat to Australia's national existence. In his influential 1893 forecast of looming global racial conflict, *National life and character,* Victorian member of parliament Charles Pearson very seldom mentioned Aboriginal people, and then only to dismiss them as an 'evanescent race', in contrast to the dynamic, virile, enduring and therefore dangerous Asian.[5]

Despite being dismissed as weak and ineffectual, and despite inattention to them in the federation debates, the Constitution that consummated the federation process referred twice to Aboriginal people. Both references were exclusionary. Section 51(xxvi) empowered the federal parliament to make laws with respect to the 'people of any race, other than the aboriginal race in any State for whom it is deemed necessary to make special laws'. Section 127 stated that, 'In reckoning the numbers of the people of the Commonwealth, or of a State or other part of the Commonwealth, aboriginal natives shall not be counted.' The records of the federation conferences and conventions give little indication of why these clauses were included in the Constitution, though several commentators have proffered explanations.

Robert Garran, who officiated at the federation conferences of the late 1890s and later became one of the most respected authorities on the Australian Constitution, claimed that the reference to 'the aboriginal race' in section 51(xxvi) was a mere afterthought. He recalled that 'throughout the debate I don't think a word was said about the aborigines. It simply did not occur to anybody that Federal power over them was needed.' He explained that the targets of the provision were 'introduced races, like the Kanakas', and the reference to Aboriginal people was inserted because the 'federating colonies were very jealous of their powers, and assigned nothing to the Federal Parliament unless they thought it very definitely a matter of federal concern'.[6] Garran's explanation seems plausible insofar as Aboriginal people — unlike Asians and Pacific Islanders — were not considered a threat to the Australian nation, and therefore did not warrant the federal parliament having powers to make 'special laws' in regard to them. However, it seems inadequate to explain why, when Aboriginal people were usually completely ignored in the constitution-making process, this sub-section should refer specifically to them. After all, no other race or ethnic group was specified anywhere in the Constitution.

But perhaps the 'aboriginal race' of section 51(xxvi) did not originally refer exclusively to Indigenous Australians. The clause that eventually became section 51(xxvi) first appeared in the constitutional draft of 1891, at which time New Zealand was a prospective member of the federation. Hugh Mahon, a member of the first Commonwealth parliament, noted that this section possibly 'originated in a desire to preserve the rights of the New Zealand Legislature in respect to the Maoris'. At this time, Maori enjoyed far more extensive civil rights than did Aboriginal people in any Australian colony, and non-indigenous New Zealanders already boasted of the superiority of their race-relations record over that of their trans-Tasman neighbours. After New Zealand withdrew from the federation process, the clause limiting Commonwealth powers over the 'aboriginal race' may have been retained because of the federal leaders' lack of interest in Aboriginal affairs. As Mahon explained, in a reversal of Garran's claim: 'It is not clear that the States were unduly desirous of retaining control of the natives. The position is probably due to the reluctance of the Federalists to assume a burden rather than to the determination of the States to preserve a right.'[7] Despite their differences, Mahon's and Garran's explanations share one notable theme: for the federal leaders, Aboriginal people were of little consequence.

The motives behind section 127, which appeared in a 'Miscellaneous' chapter near the end of the Constitution, are equally uncertain. Its primary purpose probably concerned financial apportionments between the states and the Commonwealth, which were to be made on a per capita basis. Excluding 'aboriginal natives' from the count implied that they were insignificant for the purposes of public expenditure. This section also meant that 'aboriginal natives' would not be counted for the purpose of determining the number of parliamentary seats to be allocated to each state, but it did not debar them from exercising the franchise.[8] Like section 51(xxvi), section 127 rested on an assumption that Aboriginal people counted for little. Neither section formally excluded them from the legal rights and entitlements of Australian citizenship, but both implied that Aboriginal people were outside the community of the Australian nation.

One reason why Aboriginal people were shut out of the national community was that, as an irredeemably primitive race, they were deemed incapable of exercising the rights of citizenship or appreciating its responsibilities. Moreover, they were considered a fleeting problem. Some contemporary commentators lamented their projected extinction; some celebrated the prospect; most simply accepted it as the outcome of inexorable forces of nature over which human beings were ultimately powerless. At the time of Federation, it seemed to settler Australians that the Aboriginal race literally had no future. A forward-looking nation foresaw an Australia devoid of Aboriginal people.[9]

The other reason behind the national exclusion of Aboriginal people lay in the ideas of ethnic nationalism, the paramount expression of which was the white Australia policy. Projected outwards, the white Australia policy was directed primarily against Asians, but it was more than merely the sub-text of a restrictive immigration program. Whiteness was a treasured quality of early twentieth-century settler Australians, an emblem of their status as a civilised race and their place in the world at the forefront of progress. Whiteness was also a badge of Britishness, and it was Britishness that underpinned Australia's nationhood, providing the heritage, history and culture that made Australia heir to a glorious past and embedded it in deep time. In 1890, Henry Parkes invoked the 'crimson thread of kinship' to affirm the ethnic solidarity of white Australians, both with each other and with their British parent. His metaphor became a slogan of the federation movement. Britishness, conceived as a combination of biological ancestry and cultural heritage, provided the ethnic foundations of Australian nationalism.[10] Its outward manifestation — whiteness — put Aboriginal people beyond the pale of the nation.

In the federation era, Aboriginal people and the white Australia policy were seldom discussed together. In one of the few instances in which they were, Attorney-General and future Prime Minister Alfred Deakin declared in 1901 that:

> In another century the probability is that Australia will be a White Continent with not a black or even dark skin among its inhabitants. The Aboriginal race has died out in the South and is dying fast in the North and West even where most gently treated. Other races are to be excluded by legislation if they are tinted to any degree. The yellow, the brown, and the copper-coloured are to be forbidden to land anywhere.[11]

Deakin's assumptions were widely shared: active measures had to be taken to safeguard white Australia against coloured aliens, but not against the coloured indigenes, since they were expiring independently of government action or inaction. The white Australia ideal faced little threat from a dying race.

Early twentieth-century Australians maintained that nationhood, equality and democracy could flourish only in a society whose members were drawn from a common stock, the outward sign of which was similarity of complexion.[12] Yet Aboriginal exclusion from political participation in the new nation was not a foregone conclusion at the time of Federation, as demonstrated by the passage through parliament of the first item of legislation to specify the rights of the Australian citizen, the *Commonwealth Franchise Act 1902*.

As originally introduced by Senator Richard O'Connor, government leader in the Senate, the franchise Bill guaranteed a uniform adult franchise with no exclusions on racial or gender grounds. Parliament devoted far more debating time to the Bill's enfranchisement of women than to its awarding the vote to Aboriginal people, but the latter did affront some members. Western Australian Senator Matheson protested that it would be 'repugnant and atrocious' to enfranchise 'an aboriginal man, or aboriginal lubra or gin — a horrible, degraded, dirty creature'. He proposed an amendment excluding the 'native races' of Australia, Asia, Africa and the Pacific from the franchise.[13]

Defending the Bill in its original form, Senator O'Connor proclaimed his devotion to the white Australia policy, but protested that Matheson's

Prologue

amendment represented 'a monstrous and a savage application of this principle of a white Australia'. It was entirely appropriate, O'Connor argued, to prohibit the entry of coloured races into the nation, but improper to curtail the rights of coloured persons already legitimately resident here. He pointed out that in four states (New South Wales, Victoria, South Australia and Tasmania), Aboriginal people already possessed the state franchise on the same basis as white people; in the other two (Queensland and Western Australia), they held a restricted right to vote according to a property qualification. To deprive these people of the federal vote would be to apply the white Australia doctrine 'with a savagery which is quite unworthy of the beginnings of this federation'.[14]

In the ensuing debate, some senators argued that Aboriginal enfranchisement should be considered separately from that of 'coloured aliens'. South Australian Senator McGregor said that he would 'be very sorry if we took away a right from a declining race like the aborigines, but with respect to Chinese, Japanese, Africans, and other aliens, who are much more dangerous than the aborigines, I should be quite willing to take some step'.[15] A majority of senators seem to have agreed with McGregor's assessment of Aboriginal people as 'a harmless race', as against the menacing Asian and African, for they passed the Bill in a form enfranchising Aboriginal people but disfranchising Asians, Africans and Pacific Islanders.

The Bill then proceeded to the House of Representatives, where much the same arguments were rehashed. Here, however, a majority of members were in favour of reinstating the exclusion of Aboriginal people, primarily on the grounds that the Aboriginal vote would be manipulated. Most Aboriginal people, several members claimed, lived in the vast pastoral lands of northern and central Australia where they were employed under conditions of servitude. They were too ignorant and unintelligent to appreciate the significance of voting, and so firmly under the control of their white bosses that they would do his bidding and vote *en masse* as the station owners directed. Implicitly, these members agreed with Senator McGregor's assessment of Aboriginal people as in themselves 'harmless', but considered them potentially harmful because of their manipulability. No one expressed a fear that Aboriginal people, acting independently, might exercise the franchise in ways hostile to white interests, as if they could not credit them with sufficient intelligence and initiative to do so. It was not the agency of Aboriginal people they feared, but its lack: their supposed weakness, ineffectualness and propensity to be manipulated by others.[16]

When the Bill returned from the House to the Senate with the clause excluding Aboriginal people reinstated, the arguments for and against exclusion were recycled yet again. By this time, however, Senator O'Connor conceded that the government was prepared to accept the exclusion, because it was 'not worth while, for the sake of this particular provision, to stand out for our own way, and so run the risk of losing the Bill'.[17] The government was willing to sacrifice the principle of racial equality in the franchise to preserve the principle of gender equality. After all, as O'Connor explained several times, racial equality in the franchise would affect few voters, and that few would diminish over time as coloured aliens were denied entry and Aboriginal people continued to die out. The senators eventually passed the *Commonwealth Franchise Act 1902* with the stipulation that, 'No aboriginal native of Australia, Asia, Africa or the Islands of the Pacific except New Zealand shall be entitled to have his name placed on an Electoral Roll unless so entitled under section forty-one of the Constitution.' The right to vote would be circumscribed by what Senator O'Connor had only a few weeks before disparaged as 'a monstrous and a savage application of [the] principle of a white Australia'.

One reason many senators agreed to pass the amended franchise Bill is that they believed section 41 of the Constitution guaranteed the federal vote to Aboriginal people in those states where they already possessed the franchise.[18] Section 41 provided that:

> No adult person who has or acquires a right to vote at elections for the more numerous House of the Parliament of a State shall, while the right continues, be prevented by any law of the Commonwealth from voting at elections for either House of the Parliament of the Commonwealth.

This provision had been inserted to ensure that women in South Australia (the only colony to have enfranchised women at this stage of the Constitution's drafting) would qualify for the federal vote. It also might appear to protect an Aboriginal right to the federal vote in those states that enfranchised Indigenous people.

However, Robert Garran and fellow lawyer John Quick propounded a different interpretation, insisting that a right under section 41 must have been acquired by an individual prior to the passage of the 1902 *Franchise Act*. Thus only those Aboriginal persons who were on the electoral rolls of New South Wales, Victoria, South Australia and Tasmania in 1902 possessed the Commonwealth franchise under this section. For all others, including later generations of Aboriginal people, the provision was inapplicable. It was an extraordinarily narrow construal of section 41. However, it prevailed throughout the first half of the twentieth century, despite a 1924 ruling in the case of an Indian, Mitta Bullosh, which interpreted section 41 as a guarantee of prospective, rather than merely retrospective, voting rights. In the *Bullosh* case, the Commonwealth failed to press a High Court challenge because of pressure from Britain, concerned about the status of its Indian subjects throughout the empire.[19] Lacking supporters as influential as the British Secretary of State for the Colonies, Aboriginal people continued to have their voting entitlements under section 41 curtailed.

The *Franchise Act 1902* set the precedent for future legislation. Acts such as the *Invalid and Old-Age Pensions Act 1908* and the *Maternity Allowance Act 1912* included similar clauses excluding 'aboriginal natives of Australia, Asia, Africa and the islands of the Pacific' (usually excepting New Zealand) from rights and entitlements enjoyed by other Australians. John Chesterman and Brian Galligan observe that, once in place, 'the exclusionary regime developed an administrative logic of its own in which the category of "aboriginal native" was developed by generations of ministers and bureaucrats'.[20] A fast-growing thicket of legislation and interpretation progressively excluded Aboriginal people from the political nation.

The states, meanwhile, developed their own regimes in Aboriginal affairs. Before Federation, each colony had its own Aboriginal laws and administrations, and the differences between them deepened in the decades thereafter. State policies in the early twentieth century were inconsistent, vacillating between protection, segregation and absorption. While Queensland, for example, adopted an increasingly rigorous segregation policy, New South Wales and Victoria pursued a course of partial absorption, interlaced with contradictory elements of segregation and protection. Some public figures recommended that the chaos of state Aboriginal laws and administrations be replaced by a unified system of Commonwealth control since, as Hugh Mahon put it, responsibility for the native people 'is one of the inevitable appendages of nationhood'.[21] The Commonwealth's acquisition of responsibility for the Northern Territory in 1911, and thereby its entry into Aboriginal administration, raised hopes that this might be a step towards federal control of Aboriginal affairs.[22] It was not. Divided responsibility continued, as did the *de facto* national policy in Aboriginal affairs: neglect.

Aboriginal exclusion from the rights and entitlements of citizenship was complicated by the ambiguity of the word 'aboriginal'. In the early twentieth century, the legal category 'aboriginal native of Australia' was much narrower than that encompassed by today's 'Aboriginal'. Following Attorney-General Deakin's 1901 determination that half-castes were not 'aboriginal natives' within the meaning of section 127 of the Constitution, the rule followed for determining a person's eligibility for the Commonwealth franchise and social welfare payments was that those who were preponderantly of Aboriginal descent were 'aboriginal natives', while those of 50 per cent or less Aboriginal ancestry were not. Thus a person who was literally half-caste was not an 'aboriginal native' for Commonwealth legal purposes and was, in theory, entitled to the rights and benefits of the white citizen. For many, this was negated by a further proviso that those persons of any degree of Aboriginal ancestry who lived on state reserves or received state welfare benefits were ineligible for Commonwealth welfare payments.[23] In this, as in most respects, the federal authorities shrugged aside responsibility for Aboriginal people on to the states.

Deakin's 50 per cent ruling was a mere legal convenience drawing boundaries around the category 'aboriginal native'. It meant little in practice, since each state had its own definition of 'aboriginal' and 'half-caste', usually inconsistent with each other and with the Commonwealth determination. Nonetheless, Deakin's ruling carried the implication that quantum of white ancestry determined whether an individual was included within the community of Australian citizens. The fact that Deakin set the quantum at 50 per cent indicates that appearance and colour were not to him the sole criteria; persons of 50 per cent Aboriginal ancestry are overtly Aboriginal in complexion and physical features. Yet the notion that the 'crimson thread of kinship' could draw persons of Aboriginal descent across the racial divide into white Australia had a long, albeit contested, career. Some administrators in the interwar years took the notion much further than Deakin's determination of convenience, as we shall see in Chapter 1.

Chapter 1

Preserving the National Complexion

After the First World War, Australians began to notice a new trend among the Aboriginal population. Within their own enclaves, people of mixed descent were reproducing faster than white Australians. Remarking on this trend, demographer Jens Lyng observed in 1927 that 'the idea of the White Australia ideal eventually being shattered from within cannot be dismissed as altogether absurd'.[1] Lyng's wording was guarded, and there is no evidence to suggest that the Australian public was alarmed by half-caste reproduction rates or fearful that it posed a threat to the national ideal. Some administrators of Aboriginal affairs were alarmed and fearful, however — or at least their statements on the issue were alarmist and fear-provoking. Two administrators in particular — Western Australia's Chief Protector of Aborigines (later Commissioner of Native Affairs), AO Neville, and the Northern Territory's Chief Protector of Aborigines, Cecil Cook — elevated the 'half-caste menace' to their highest priority.

Neville's and Cook's solution to the half-caste problem was biological absorption, colloquially called 'breeding out the colour'. This entailed directing persons of mixed descent into marital unions with white people, so that after several generations of interbreeding all outward signs of Aboriginal ancestry would disappear. It held an incongruent array of aims and means. Absorption promised to resolve the supposed problems resulting from racial intermixture by encouraging still more intermixing. It aimed to uphold the ideal of white Australia but flew in the face of popular notions of white Australia as a doctrine of racial purity. While racist in many ways, absorption simultaneously defied prevalent racist assumptions of hybrid inferiority. It parallelled eugenicism in certain respects, but also clashed with eugenic principles. It was inspired partly by humanitarian welfarism, but evinced profound disdain for the subjects of its welfare interventions.

Despite these myriad inspirations and aspirations, absorption's primary objective was accurately stated in its colloquial designation. It aimed to 'breed out the colour' — to physically transform persons of Aboriginal ancestry into white Australians and thereby bleach out the as yet small coloured stain in the national fabric. Half-castes must become white since whiteness was the essential qualification for national membership. Breeding the colour out of persons of Aboriginal descent was equally a program of breeding them into the community of the nation. This chapter argues that biological absorption in the interwar years should be understood in the context of a strongly ethnic conception of Australian nationhood, whereby myths of blood kinship provided the core of national cohesion. It also argues that while absorption was a variant of assimilation, it was in crucial respects different to the social assimilation which some critics were beginning to advocate in the 1930s, and which came to the fore after the Second World War.

Managing miscegenation

Ideas of biological absorption long predated the 1930s, though earlier observers tended to assume that the merging of half-caste into white would occur 'naturally', without any need for state intervention. The first jurisdiction to attempt to accelerate the process was Victoria, with an 1886 Act that sought to keep full-bloods on reserves where they could conveniently expire while pushing their mixed-descent progeny into the wider community. This legislation was initiated not by the colonial government but by the Board for the Protection of Aborigines, which sought to reduce its financial commitments and to stymie the Coranderrk Aboriginal community's increasing assertiveness against the Board's authority.[2] Later absorptionist programs, too, were typically instigated not by parliaments but by bodies charged with the administration of Aboriginal affairs.

In the early twentieth century, state intervention in Aboriginal lives intensified. Among the interventions, fair-complexioned children of mixed descent were commonly taken from their families and raised in institutions or foster homes to facilitate their absorption into the white population.[3] Yet these absorptionist practices were unsystematic, their potential impact confounded by the simultaneously pursued policy of segregation. It was, after all, the high reproduction rate in segregated, more or less closed, mixed-descent communities that gave rise to the contemporary 'half-caste problem'.

The distinctiveness of 1930s absorptionist policies lay in their attempted systematisation. Instead of merely removing fair-complexioned, mixed-descent children from their families as they happened to appear, officials would actively intervene to promote the reproduction of increasingly fair-skinned individuals. The reproductive futures of mixed-descent people would be regulated, with each successive generation becoming progressively more European in ancestry until ultimately all outward signs of Aboriginal descent were 'bred out' (see Plate 1). This required both the promotion of interbreeding between white and part-Aboriginal Australians, and the curtailment of unions between full- and part-Aboriginal people, these restrictions extending across several generations. It is this attribute of trans-generational reproductive management that distinguishes interwar programs of 'breeding out the colour' from earlier haphazard attempts at 'merging'. It must be noted at the outset, however, that while these breeding programs were clearly set out on paper and partially put into operation, nowhere were they comprehensively implemented.

In the interwar years, intensifying state intrusions into Aboriginal lives were not always motivated by absorptionist aims. In Queensland, state intervention was arguably more intense than in any other jurisdiction, but Queensland did not pursue a policy of 'breeding out the colour'.[4] Western Australia did, and that state's *Native Administration Act 1936* gave Commissioner Neville greater powers over a wider range of persons of Aboriginal descent than hitherto, including legal guardianship of their children, limitations on those with whom they could legally associate and control over their choice of marital partner.[5] 'Breeding out the colour' was nowhere prescribed as the objective of the Act, but it provided the mechanisms deployed by Neville to that end.

Since no government ever enshrined biological absorption in legislation, its status as policy has been disputed.[6] The word 'policy' may be open to several interpretations, but if it is taken to refer to a set of objectives and a course of action endorsed and pursued by those charged with authority within an area of governance, biological absorption was surely official policy in Western Australia and the Northern Territory for most of the 1930s. However, it was a policy initiated not by parliament or any minister, but rather by senior members of the bureaucracy. That the initiative in policy-making should be so delegated is indicative of the slight importance attached to Aboriginal affairs. It is likely, too, that politicians deliberately distanced themselves from this policy initiative, for whenever proposals to breed out the colour were aired publicly, they provoked a chorus of condemnation.[7]

Even within the bureaucracy, misgivings were expressed. Sometimes these were on pragmatic grounds, as when JA Carrodus, Acting Administrator of the Northern Territory in 1934, stated that while the 'effort to breed out colour' was 'commendable', it would never be accomplished. 'It will be found,' Carrodus averred, 'that half-castes will prefer to marry half-castes', and Aboriginal administrations would better be served by facing squarely the fact of 'a large natural increase in the half-caste population from the mating of half-caste with half-caste'.[8] Sometimes ethical concerns were raised, as when HC Brown, Secretary of the Department of the Interior, pointed out the impropriety of state intervention in so private a matter as choice of marital partner.[9]

Such misgivings notwithstanding, the inordinate powers vested in the senior administrators of Aboriginal affairs allowed Neville and Cook to pursue their ambitions with little overt official hindrance. The impediments came from elsewhere. Government parsimony was a far greater restraint than deliberate obstruction, with neither Neville nor Cook being granted anywhere near adequate funds to achieve their grand ambitions.[10] Missionary opinion on absorption was divided but predominantly hostile, with the Australian National Missionary Conference of 1937 proclaiming its opposition.[11] Neville represented Christian missions as the single greatest impediment to his plans; he complained that missionaries 'allow the half-castes under their control to marry anybody'.[12] To Neville, it was axiomatic that half-castes should have no such freedom of choice of marital partner. However, while he could prohibit 'undesirable' marriages, he could not compel 'desirable' ones, and half-caste women displayed no overwhelming desire to marry white men (or vice versa). In the eleven years of Cook's Chief Protectorship, fewer than fifty such marriages were celebrated. Neville's plans met with no more success.[13] Gender sensitivities posed insuperable problems since the only interracial unions considered potentially acceptable were between half-caste women and white men. Sexual intercourse between half-caste men and white women was so repugnant as to be almost unthinkable, leaving only half the half-caste population eligible for participation in absorptionist programs.

Despite these serious — arguably insurmountable — difficulties, Western Australia and the Northern Territory persisted with the policy for roughly a decade. In other states too, absorption was an element of Aboriginal policy, though pursued less relentlessly than in these two jurisdictions. Whatever its other outcomes, it produced a bitter harvest of broken families of the kind revealed in the 1997 *Bringing them home* report.[14]

Yet absorption also manifested humanitarian intentions. It was an austere and arrogant humanitarianism, but exponents of 'breeding out the colour' were committed to the welfare of those they sought to whiten. Neville insisted that 'our coloured people must be helped in spite of themselves'.[15] By 'help' he meant not merely the provision of economic, educational and vocational facilities, but eradication of the perceived root cause of their ostracism and disadvantage: the colour that set them apart from the national community. Whiteness, in this conception, was the greatest boon that could be conferred upon a people, both for their individual well-being and for the sake of the nation as a whole. The same combination of humanitarian solicitude with white Australian arrogance is apparent in Cook's assertion that, for their own welfare, it was 'absolutely essential that [the half-caste] should be given an opportunity of evolving, more or less into a white man'.[16] In Cook's view, there could be no smoother pathway to social advancement than the one that led to whiteness. Equally, there could be no other route to national membership.

While Neville considered half-castes worthy of help, he was convinced that full-bloods were beyond assistance. At the 1937 Conference of Commonwealth and State Aboriginal Authorities, he explained that full-bloods constituted a 'problem…which will eventually solve itself [since] no matter what we do, they will die out'. By this, he did not mean that they would leave no descendants, merely none of full descent. This was the pertinence of JA Carrodus's statement that, 'Ultimately, if history is repeated, the full-bloods will become half-castes.'[17] It was on this supposition that the more ardent advocates of 'breeding out the colour' envisaged the process eventually subsuming the entire Aboriginal race.

No advocate was more ardent than Neville. At the 1937 conference — which marks the peak of official endorsement of absorption — he posed a rhetorical question that encapsulated the zenith of absorptionist fervour: 'Are we going to have a population of 1,000,000 blacks in the Commonwealth, or are we going to merge them into our white community and eventually forget that there ever were any aborigines in

Australia?'[18] It was an extreme expression, and perhaps not meant to be taken literally. Neville wrote several books and many articles on Aboriginal issues, which were surely a way of memorialising rather than 'forgetting' them. Yet his rhetoric calls to mind Ernest Renan's remark about nationhood being founded as much on selective forgetting as it is on remembrance of the past.[19] At the 1937 conference, Cecil Cook also raised the scaremongering scenario of 'a large black population' in the Northern Territory, rapidly reproducing and threatening to 'swamp the white'. Although more circumspect than Neville, Cook also proffered absorption as the only viable prophylactic.[20] Other officials at the 1937 conference were broadly in agreement, although there were differences of opinion about how far the state could go in pursuit of this end.

The only significant discordant voice at the 1937 conference was Queensland's Chief Protector, JW Bleakley. He maintained that 'the half-breed…cannot happily be absorbed into the white race' and that while a minority of 'crossbreeds' could take their 'place in the white community', the vast majority would be 'more happily absorbed by their mother's people in circumstances where they can be given vocational and domestic training to take their part in the development of a self-contained native community'. Bleakley's regime in Queensland represented the acme of authoritarian paternalism towards Aboriginal people. Yet he insisted that 'we have no right to attempt to destroy their national life. Like ourselves, they are entitled to retain their racial entity and racial pride.'[21] Bleakley sought to protect and control Aboriginal people as an ethnic minority, whose membership included most (though not all) persons of mixed descent. Proponents of 'breeding out the colour', on the other hand, aimed at preventing the perpetuation of such a minority.

Above all else, 'breeding out the colour' sought to maintain 'an All White Australia'.[22] The nation was to be white not merely in a metaphorical sense, but physically, tangibly, epidermically white. As a Western Australian advocate of absorption, Dr Cyril Bryan, stated, 'the continued infiltration of white blood will finally stamp out the black colour, which, when all is said and done, is what we object to'.[23] At least some absorptionists, including Cook, were astute enough to acknowledge that 'colour' in itself was trivial, assuming significance only through specific sociocultural circumstances.[24] This in no way diminished his commitment to changing the colour rather than the circumstances, for the sociocultural context in which whiteness assumed such significance was Australian nationhood itself.

The white Australia imperative was particularly overt in one line of argument pursued by Cook. On several occasions, he drew attention to 'the very grave problem' of interbreeding between half-castes and 'alien coloured races' — that is, Asians.[25] The 'multiplication of multicolour humanity by the mating of Halfcastes with alien coloured blood shall be reduced to a minimum,' he declared.[26] The most effective way of doing this was to ensure that half-caste women were safely married to white men. Cook was quite candid about this, stating that part-Aboriginal women 'must be married to men substantially of European origin' in order to control 'the propagation of the hybrid [of] alien coloured' ancestry.[27] Advertising the virtues of his policy, he explained that the 'success achieved by encouraging the marriage of half-castes to whites has curtailed the birth rate of hybrids of coloured alien paternity'.[28] In this rendition, reproductive control was directed primarily at stifling an Asian infusion into the nation, and half-castes were merely the conduits through whom Asian blood could flow. Cook's arguments highlight the fact that his and other absorptionist strategies were directed against colour — any colour other than white — rather than against Aboriginality *per se*.

Colour — or its absence — was vital because a nationalism that emphasises ethnicity necessarily puts a premium on shared descent. What matters for ethnic cohesion is not the veracity of the claimed common descent but its plausibility, so the binding power of myth can cohere the group. Absorption strove for this plausibility. If all Australians were white, they could be attributed a shared origin, history and descent. A coloured minority could not be attributed these shared characteristics, since their discordant origins and descent would be on permanent public display. To be brought within the fold of the mythic community of descent, their colour had to be 'bred out'. If nationhood was to be conceived in potently ethnic terms, the incorporation of new members must depend on their shedding all attributes — biological as well as cultural — that could set them apart as an alternative ethnic community. On these assumptions, absorptionists sought to maintain the ethnic constitution that had been founded at Federation. Their program entailed the sacrifice of racial purity, but that was an inevitable cost of including a racial minority in an ethnically oriented nation.

However, many — probably most — Australians regarded racial purity as the central and sacrosanct principle of white Australia. The contemporary Labor Party's objectives included the cultivation of 'an Australian sentiment based on the maintenance of racial purity'.[29] From the other side of party politics, Emily Curtis, Secretary of the Women's Section of the United Country Party, used the same idea to attack the 'monstrous innovation' of biological absorption. In response to alleged attempts to surreptitiously transfer several mixed-descent girls from central Australia to Melbourne, she informed the federal government of her organisation's resolutions:

> That, it is greatly to be deplored that the Federal Government is so far lost to the knowledge of our deep rooted sentiments and pride of race, as to attempt to infuse a strain of aboriginal blood into our coming generations.
>
> That, the Women's Organisations of Australia be urged, that, for the race heritage that we hold in trust for the generations to come, for the sanctity of our age old traditions, and for the protection of our growing boys, to combat with all their power this insidious attempt to mingle with the community, women of illegitimate birth, tainted with aboriginal blood, the offspring of men of the lowest human type, many of whom are Asiatics and other foreign nationalities.[30]

This was the most persistent theme in the many complaints against 'breeding out the colour': far from safeguarding white Australia, absorption would irreparably corrupt it, polluting the national bloodstream with the dregs of inferior races.

Hiding heredity

Although absorption attracted little public support, it was endorsed by some sectors of the scientific community. According to one prominent theory, the Aboriginal and Caucasian races were closely related.[31] In 1925 the Adelaide anthropologist Herbert Basedow suggested that because of this racial affinity, their mixed progeny could rapidly be whitened through successive accessions of white 'blood', without danger of Aboriginal characteristics reasserting themselves in later generations.[32] His suggestion was elaborated by other scientists, notably those on the Board for Anthropological Research at the University of Adelaide, whose chairman,

JB Cleland, became Australia's leading scientific advocate of biological absorption. The Board's efforts to scientifically appraise the feasibility of absorption culminated in the Harvard–Adelaide Universities Expedition of 1938–39, conducted by the Adelaide ethnologist Norman Tindale and the Harvard physical anthropologist JB Birdsell. On the basis of their detailed genealogical research, plus the assertion that 'the Australian aboriginal is recognised as being a forerunner of the Caucasian race', they concluded that absorption was both possible and desirable.[33]

However, theories of race-relatedness did not lead inexorably to the conclusion that 'colour' should be 'bred out'. Like all scientific ideas, the race-relatedness theory was polyvalent. Humanitarian activists frequently used it to assert Aboriginal claims on the Australian nation and garner white sympathy for their plight. On the opening page of her 1930 book, *The Australian Aboriginal as a human being*, Christian philanthropist Mary Bennett stated that, 'Like us they belong to the Caucasian stock.'[34] She was an uncompromising opponent of absorption. Moreover, the theory of Aboriginal–Caucasian relatedness commanded no scientific unanimity. Australia's only professor of anthropology, AP Elkin at the University of Sydney, rejected it along with proposals to 'breed out the colour'.

While both Neville and Cook invoked the race-relatedness theory to validate their programs, that theory provided no legitimation for the actual procedures by which they pursued their goal: child removal, controlled marriages and ever-extending interventions in the lives of persons of mixed descent. Insofar as the scientific proponents of absorption suggested any practical measures, they were often at odds with official practice. Among other things, Tindale recommended the relaxation of administrative controls, by which means absorption could proceed 'naturally' — as he observed it already had in some places.[35] His reasoning may have been founded on the mistaken assumption that the efforts of mixed-descent persons 'to establish themselves as elements in the general Australian population' equated with a desire to metamorphose into white people. But his recommendations ran counter to the intense state interventionism pursued by administrators of the day. Legitimation of those interventions derived from other sources: partly from the fact that high levels of state intervention had been an accepted — even valued — component of Australian social life since Federation;[36] more immediately from the assumption that Aboriginal people could be treated as an inert mass, to be moulded into whatever shape — or colour — white officialdom decreed.

There was a still greater discrepancy between the scientific and bureaucratic exponents of absorption. Whereas bureaucrats like Neville saw the process culminating in the disappearance of the entire Aboriginal race, Cleland, Tindale and other scientific advocates of absorption envisaged a continuing future for a distinct Aboriginal people. These scientists urged the creation of vast, inviolable reserves in central and northern Australia, where full-bloods who still pursued their ancestral ways could continue to do so. The reserves they advocated would be hermetically sealed off from the outside world, shielding the primitive tribes from the deadly touch of civilisation and allowing them to maintain their traditional mode of life — supposedly the only mode of life these peculiarly backward people were capable of following.[37] Had they been implemented, these segregationist schemes would have kept the 'uncontaminated full-bloods' outside the national community, in enclaves in which their presumed primitivity could be preserved in perpetuity. While their proposals manifested a low opinion of Aboriginal capacities for adaptation, these scientists were as dedicated to the perpetuation of Aboriginality as to the effacement of evidence of mixed-race ancestry.

As well as validating the biological absorption of mixed-bloods, Tindale's 'Survey of the Half-caste Problem' included a lengthy section urging the preservation of the inhabitants of the Western Desert as 'an unmodified and virile people' by their total isolation from the outside world. This necessitated a vast expansion of the existing Central Aboriginal Reserve, more rigorous policing of its boundaries, prohibition on the entry of all whites including missionaries and miners (though scientists were allowed a special dispensation) and the removal of all the contaminants of civilisation. His aim was to allow 'the present fullbloods of the Western Desert [to] continue to live unmolested within their country as nomads'.[38] Reserves could serve contrary purposes, however. Neville regarded the same Central Aboriginal Reserve as a place on which the remnant full-blood population would inevitably die out.[39] While Tindale and Neville agreed that half-castes should be submerged into white Australia, they disagreed on how this submergence should be achieved, on whether full-blood people had a future and on the destiny of Aboriginality itself.

Because absorption was a program of reproductive management, many scholars unhesitatingly label it 'eugenic'.[40] Yet the mainstream Australian eugenicist movement of the 1930s reviled 'breeding out the colour' in the strongest terms. Immediately after the 1937 Aboriginal Welfare

Conference, the eugenicist journal *Health and Physical Culture* published a stinging attack, proclaiming that the consequences of absorption could only be profoundly dysgenic, the creation of 'a class of low white trash'.[41] This was continuous with a long history of Australian eugenicist hostility toward Aboriginal–white intermixing, going back to the movement's nineteenth-century pioneer, Dr Alan Carroll.[42] There were certain parallels between eugenics and absorption, but there were also serious points of discord.[43] Here, I shall focus on the latter to tease out the rationales behind 'breeding out the colour'.

In one of the few studies critically appraising absorption's eugenicist credentials, Tony Austin identifies its endorsement of miscegenation as the major point of disagreement.[44] However, hostility to miscegenation was not ubiquitous among eugenicists. Promoting race-mixture was a minority taste among eugenicists in the English-speaking world, but even in the heartland of racist eugenics, the United States, some conceded the beneficial results of miscegenation.[45] Moreover, Nancy Stepan has shown that 'constructive miscegenation' was a prominent part of Latin American eugenicism.[46] On the face of it, this Latin American eugenicism seems closely allied with Australian absorptionism, for it too sought 'progressive whitening' through reproductive management. Yet on closer inspection the similarities fade. Latin American eugenicists sought to achieve white ascendancy in a predominantly mestizo population, whereas Australian absorptionists were trying to hide the small dark stain of a tiny half-caste minority. Latin American 'constructive miscegenation' had much more ambitious goals than Australian absorption, for while the former encouraged a change of complexion as one aspect of a larger process of hereditary improvement, the latter had whitening as its sole goal.

Therein lay absorption's major dissonance with eugenics. Absorption promised little by way of genetic enhancement of the Australian population. 'Breeding out the colour' sought to homogenise the nation's complexion, not to improve its gene pool. Although absorption implied the eventual diffusion of Aboriginal genes throughout the entire Australian populace, no one attempted to legitimise absorption on the grounds that this would bring biological benefit to the majority population. Rarely — very rarely — a few absorptionists were bold enough to suggest some positive racial results from the blend. Cecil Cook, in one of his more enthusiastic paeans to absorption, rounded off the list of its virtues with the claim that:

the aboriginal inheritance brings to the hybrid definite qualities of value — intelligence, stamina, resource, high resistance to the influence of tropical environment and the character of pigmentation which even in high dilution will serve to reduce the at present high incidence of Skin Cancer in the blonde European.[47]

However, this comes at the end of a long passage in which other benefits of absorption — saving white Australia, ensuring equal citizenship for all its inhabitants and promoting the progress of the Northern Territory — were given priority. Similarly, Tindale suggested that 'the introduction of a low percentage of a primitive Australian strain may provide just that extra range of variation necessary for the ultimate selection and development of a white stock adjusted to the tropical parts of Australia'.[48] Again, this was a mere fragment in a larger argument, which laid stress on other imperatives for absorption. Cook and Tindale sought to reassure white Australians that the mixing they advocated would have no detrimental effects on the white race. However, their scant suggestions that racial benefit might follow seem to have been mere rhetorical embellishments of arguments whose foundations lay elsewhere.

Nor did absorptionists argue that continual accessions of white 'blood' would improve the physical, moral and mental constitution of mixed-descent people in any respect save one — it would make them whiter. Absorption sought not to make fitter people, but rather to make people better fit in. Even the theory of Aboriginal–Caucasian race-relatedness, which held some potential for eugenicist advocacy, was very seldom used to assert the intrinsically eugenic qualities of the Aboriginal–white 'cross'. Persistently, however, it was invoked to validate the claim that Australians of mixed descent would not 'throw back' to the Aboriginal side of their ancestry, as was alleged to occur in Negro–white 'crosses'. Cleland's statement is typical for its fixation on complexion and its implication that the Aboriginal hereditary constitution was puny, unable to assert itself against stronger white genes:

> The physical characteristics of the Australian aboriginal are not dominant and there are not throw-backs to the original type when individuals with native blood marry whites. An octoroon is almost indistinguishable from a pure-blooded white person.[49]

Cleland's point, shared by other absorptionists, was that Aboriginal ancestry could be hidden. With no risk of embarrassing atavisms — such as black babies suddenly popping up in white families — Aboriginal genes could safely be diffused throughout the entire white Australian population. Provided those genes lacked physically observable manifestations — as long as genotype was not manifest in phenotype — all was well. This assumption, which was axiomatic to the absorptionist position, is difficult to reconcile with eugenicism. It is, however, entirely compatible with an ethnic nationalism that sought to incorporate a minority by maintaining a myth of shared ancestry.

Opponents

Much public opposition to absorption, as already noted, was on nakedly racist grounds, as a violation of white Australia. Humanitarians opposed it for quite different reasons. William Morley, secretary of the Association for the Protection of Native Races, condemned the 1937 conference for its 'vague talk about absorption which means progressive extinction'.[50] Singling out Neville for particular censure, Morley maintained that the 'absolute extinction of the native race appears to be the objective of the Commissioner'.[51] The accusation of deliberate 'extinction', even 'extermination', was reiterated by other campaigners for the Aboriginal cause.[52] What was needed, in their view, was Aboriginal uplift — advancement into civilisation — not programs of controlled breeding.

Aboriginal activists, who appeared on the Australian political scene in the interwar years, also opposed absorption. In June 1937, William Cooper, Secretary of the Victorian-based Australian Aborigines' League, informed Thomas Paterson, Commonwealth Minister for the Interior, that it was 'most decidedly wrong' to imagine that 'the dark man admits the superiority of the White and desires incorporation in that race'.[53] Two years later, he told Paterson's successor, Jack McEwen, that Neville's 'policy of absorption of aborigines into the white population is as unfavourably viewed by us as by the white organisations'. Neville, he asserted, 'is regarded by us and most aboriginal emancipatory organisations as the greatest enemy of our race'.[54]

The statements on absorption by another Aboriginal activist group, the New South Wales-based Aborigines Progressive Association, were more ambiguous. In 1937, Association leaders Jack Patten and Bill Ferguson stated that:

> Professor Archie Watson, of Adelaide University, has explained to you [the presumed white reader] that Aborigines can be absorbed

into the white race within three generations, without any fear of
a 'throw-back'. This proves that the Australian Aboriginal is somewhat similar in blood to yourselves, as regards inter-marriage and
inter-breeding. We ask you to study this question, and to change
your whole attitude towards us, to a more enlightened one.[55]

Some historians have read this as an endorsement of 'breeding out the colour'.[56] I read no such endorsement into the passage. Patten and Ferguson, like many contemporary humanitarians, were simply affirming the race-relatedness of Aboriginal and white Australians, thereby attempting to promote white sympathy for their cause. Their wording was injudicious, but they did not support programs of managed miscegenation.

Patten and Ferguson were themselves of mixed descent, or half-castes — a term they used in self-designation. Unsurprisingly, they affirmed not only that race-mixing had no deleterious consequences, but also that half-castes were the equals of white Australians. To that extent, they legitimised miscegenation. But legitimising miscegenation must be distinguished from attempts to channel miscegenation to a predetermined end — in the case of Neville's and Cook's absorptionist schemes, the end of eradicating Aboriginality. None of these Aboriginal activists endorsed that goal. As we shall see in Chapter 3, the Aboriginal activists of the 1930s sought social, economic and political inclusion in the Australian nation, but that did not extend to their biological digestion by the dominant race.

Continuities and discontinuities

Some historians claim that the assimilation policies pursued by Australian governments after the Second World War were a continuation of the pre-war policy of biological absorption.[57] That there were continuities is indisputable, but in this final section of the chapter I argue that the discontinuities were greater. Both prewar absorption and postwar assimilation sought Aboriginal inclusion in the Australian nation. However, the former proceeded through biological reproduction, focusing on the eradication of colour. The latter proceeded through sociocultural change, focusing on the inculcation of Western norms and values. Several historians have alluded to this policy shift, from one predicated on blood and breeding to another founded upon culture and 'way of life'.[58] I suggest here (and shall elaborate on this in later chapters) that the change from a biological to a sociocultural model entailed more than merely a change in the mode of assimilation; it entailed a shift in how the Australian nation was imagined, from a stress on ethnic qualities to an emphasis on civic attributes.

The moment chosen by some historians as the official beginning of a national assimilation policy is the 1937 Conference of Commonwealth and State Aboriginal authorities.[59] That conference's 'Destiny of the Race' resolution stated that 'the destiny of the natives of aboriginal origin, but not of the full blood, lies in their ultimate absorption by the people of the Commonwealth, and that it therefore recommends that all efforts be directed to that end'.[60] Political scientist Scott Bennett claims that in 1937 'assimilation' was formally adopted as policy 'by all governments' and 'supported by all major parties'.[61] There are two substantive problems with this claim. One is that the 1937 conference was completely dissociated from party politics, and its link with state and federal governments was indirect. Except for the Victorian MLA HS Bailey (who appeared in his capacity as chairman of that state's Board for the Protection of Aborigines), none of the delegates to the 1937 conference was a politician or member of parliament. They were senior bureaucrats in Aboriginal affairs, plus a scientist (Cleland). Their resolutions were mere recommendations, and there is no evidence that any government paid them heed. In those jurisdictions where absorption was already policy (such as Western Australia), it continued to be so after 1937; in those where it was not (such as Queensland), no moves toward absorption were made after 1937.

The other problem with Bennett's claim is terminological. Not only did the key resolution of the 1937 conference fail to refer to 'assimilation', that word is not recorded anywhere in the thirty-six pages of conference proceedings. The proceedings make twelve references to 'absorption', eighteen to 'absorb(ed)', seven to 'merge(d)' and four to 'assimilate(d)'. It seems strange to attribute the formal adoption of a policy to a document which nowhere uses that policy term. Years later, the anthropologist AP Elkin, who claimed responsibility for New South Wales becoming the first Australian jurisdiction to adopt a policy designated 'assimilation' in 1940, stated that he deliberately chose the word to distinguish his policy from that recommended by the 1937 conference. According to Elkin:

> The goal of welfare and progress came to be summed up in the word 'assimilation'. A Conference of Commonwealth and State Aboriginal Authorities held in Canberra in April 1937, did not mention this concept, but saw the solution of the Aboriginal

problem in the absorption through marriage of mixed bloods into the general community.'

He maintained that 'assimilation', in his and broader New South Wales usage around 1940, 'had no reference to miscegenation or absorption and loss of racial identity. It meant that Aborigines should be similar to other members of the Australian community, with regard to all the privileges and responsibilities of citizenship.'[62] In fact, the terminological distinction was not as clear as Elkin intimated: 'assimilation' was sometimes used in the sense of biological absorption in the 1930s, although it was not the usual word for that process. However, this does not negate Elkin's substantive point: that when he and others seeking change in Aboriginal policy cast around for a term to express the desired changes, they chose a word other than that endorsed by the 1937 conference.

Rather than regarding the 1937 conference as the beginning of a formal policy of assimilation, it would be more apt to see it as the high-water mark of official endorsement of biological absorption. From that point, the tide rapidly ebbed. With the interruption of the war, no further conferences of Commonwealth and state Aboriginal authorities were held until 1948. At that conference, the issue which had dominated its 1937 predecessor — the need for reproductive management to suppress 'colour' — did not rate a mention. Nor was this issue raised in subsequent Commonwealth–state conferences held in 1951, 1952 and thereafter. Instead, the emphasis in these postwar conferences was squarely on the Aboriginal attainment of citizenship, which was understood by delegates as requiring change in Aboriginal sociocultural attributes, not in their complexions. Many at these later conferences expressed the commonplace view that half-castes were more 'ready' for citizenship than full-bloods, but no one suggested that rising half-caste numbers constituted a problem, or that 'breeding out colour' might provide a resolution to the difficulties under consideration. Instead, there was a clear understanding that all Aboriginal people, regardless of caste or complexion, should ultimately become equal citizens of the Australian nation.[63] Whereas the 1937 conference discussions were framed by an assumption that half-castes comprised the only significant problem group, since full-bloods were destined to extinction, the postwar conference delegates presumed that full-bloods came equally within their projections for the future.

This is not to suggest that ideas of biological absorption vanished after the 1930s. Well after mid-century, some Australians expressed a hope that interbreeding could provide a solution to the Aboriginal problem.[64] Others feared the same prospect.[65] Many Australians, having no more than a fleeting interest in Aboriginal affairs, may have entertained vague ideas about assimilation resulting in a gradual loss of physically distinctive Aboriginal features.[66] Some government officials charged with implementing policy in the postwar period may have thought along similar lines.[67] Such continuities indicate the incompleteness of the displacement of biological absorption by concepts of sociocultural assimilation, a process discussed at length in CD Rowley's pioneering studies of Aboriginal policy published in the early 1970s.[68] They do not contradict the fact that a fundamental change had occurred.

Sociocultural assimilation policies held features in common with biological absorption: both presumed the rightness of state interventions in Aboriginal lives, and both were concerned with building national cohesion. But sociocultural assimilation figured the nation differently, for it presaged black citizens. Banal as this might seem at the beginning of the twenty-first century, in the mid-twentieth it challenged commonly held notions of Australian nationhood. If Australian citizens could be black, no longer would the nation be bound by the crimson thread of kinship; no longer could a common complexion denote membership of the national community. Sociocultural assimilation did not entail the abandonment of all ethnic components of nationhood, but it did entail a shift of emphasis toward the civic attributes. While biological absorption sought to maintain the outward marker of shared descent as the keystone of national cohesion, sociocultural assimilation put a premium on civic qualities as the basis of national unity.

Postwar policies of assimilation were rooted not in ideas of biological absorption but in a constellation of other concepts concerning race, progress and national inclusion. These were the ideas advanced by humanitarian reformers, scientists, feminists and political activists (including Aboriginal activists), emphasising the adaptability of human cultures and the responsibility of the powerful for the under-privileged and marginalised. Once taken into the domain of the state, much of the idealism was squeezed out of these ideas, but it is to them we should look for the foundations of the more optimistic approaches to the national inclusion of Aboriginal people pursued after the Second World War. These ideas are the topic of the next chapter.

Chapter 2

Primitive Possibilities

In 1929, Katherine Susannah Pritchard published *Coonardoo*, a novel with a theme of sexual attraction between a white man and an Aboriginal women that bears comparison with the proposals of Neville and Cook.[1] The differences are striking, however. Neville and Cook sought to channel white men's lust into unions with fair-complexioned part-Aboriginal women. Pritchard wrote about love. The mere fact that she attributed love, along with the full range of other human emotions, to an Aboriginal woman was itself a major achievement. Neville and Cook regarded part-Aboriginal women primarily as breeding stock in the service of white Australia. Pritchard explored a human tragedy resulting from white Australians' hypersensitivity to colour. *Coonardoo* won *The Bulletin*'s literary prize for 1928, although it was controversial when first published since its subject matter touched a raw nerve in many white Australians. Perhaps the fact that it was a woman who dared broach the subject of interracial love and sexuality added to its contentiousness.

Xavier Herbert's 1938 novel, *Capricornia*, was replete with interracial sex and — insofar as such a savagely cynical work could deal with this theme — even interracial love.[2] This dented neither its critical acclaim nor its wider popularity. It won the Sesquicentennial Prize for Literature in 1938. Set in a thinly veiled Northern Territory, in which the arrival of white people is rendered as 'the coming of the dingoes', the novel mercilessly lampoons Territory officialdom, including Cecil Cook (Dr Aintee in the novel). The popularity of *Capricornia* doubtless owed something to its vernacular style, spinning yarns laced with hyperbole and satire. Nonetheless, its subject matter was white Australians' perfidy in their dealings with Aboriginal people, and the novel's success suggests a significant level of popular interest in this theme. Like *Coonardoo, Capricornia* broke new ground in Australian fiction for its critique of Aboriginal–European relations.

Interest in Aboriginal issues extended far beyond fiction. Australian antiquarians in the interwar years sought to encourage in settler Australians a stronger attachment to place and a deeper appreciation of the continent's history through attentiveness to Australia's Aboriginal heritage.[3] Their interest was typically driven by fascination with the exotic; it focused on what was regarded as the authentic culture of primitive full-bloods, and was infused with nostalgia for a disappearing race. Their concern was more to incorporate a remembrance of the Aboriginal past into Australian history than to integrate living Aboriginal people into the national community. Yet their interest was one among many manifestations of the growth of a sympathetic popular attitude towards Aboriginality in the interwar years.

Yet while nostalgic interest in Aboriginal antiquity was growing, the plight of real Aboriginal people could not be ignored. In 1926 the Forrest River massacre in the Kimberley provoked an outcry from humanitarian groups, who forced the Western Australian government to hold a Royal Commission into the killings.[4] Two years later, there was a louder outcry against a series of massacres — probably involving around seventy Aboriginal deaths — carried out by police-led parties in the vicinity of Coniston in central Australia. Again an official inquiry was held, though as in the Forrest River massacre the police were exonerated.[5] The humanitarians flexed their muscle again in 1933 in response to plans to send a 'punitive expedition' against a Yolngu group in Arnhem Land whose members had allegedly killed several Japanese and white men, including a police officer. Although their success was compromised by the fact that one of the accused Yolngu, Takiara, disappeared during the course of proceedings (probably he was killed by local police officers), the humanitarians did stop the 'punitive expedition', showing that they now had sufficient influence to rein in the more brutal attempts at subjugation.[6] These events not only stirred the public conscience; they provided vivid reminders of bloody means by which white people had wrested control over the continent. Many Australians at the time may have conceded the necessity of such actions in a conveniently distant past, but for growing numbers — especially in the cities — they were unacceptable in a modern age of democracy and the League of Nations.

Neither the extent of the humanitarians' influence nor the amount of publicity given to Aboriginal affairs should be exaggerated. Except at times of spectacular injustice, such as the massacres and threatened punitive expedition just mentioned, Aboriginal affairs were not the stuff of everyday newspaper reportage in the 1920s and 1930s. Nonetheless, there was an expansion of public interest in Aboriginal people and cultures, and a growing optimism about their prospects for survival. This chapter examines the changing views of Aboriginal people and Aboriginality in the interwar years, as expressed by anthropologists, artists, writers, humanitarian reformers and feminists, revealing their increasingly positive — though still ambivalent — assessments of Aboriginal abilities and attributes.

Reappraising the primitive

Throughout the West after the First World War, artists and intellectuals expressed disenchantment with the civilisation that had inflicted the horrors of mechanised warfare upon the planet. Many turned for inspiration to primitive societies and cultures, seeking alternatives to the materialism, alienation and anomie of the West. No longer merely the zero-point of human progress, primitivity came to be evaluated positively for its spirituality, sociality and environmental sensitivity. This intellectual shift was less pronounced in Australia than in Europe, but the changing postwar mood did exert an influence here.

Anthropology occupied an ambivalent position in this reappraisal of the primitive.[7] On the one hand, its practitioners presented it as a discipline that could assist the colonial venture by uncovering the internal dynamics of native societies, thereby promoting their effective governance. British social anthropologists — generally functionalist in theoretical orientation — pushed this practical application of their discipline hard. On the other hand, anthropological techniques of participant observation revealed hitherto unsuspected depths in indigenous cultures; and functionalism itself, by accentuating the harmonious integration of individuals and groups, tended to impute those virtues to the societies under scrutiny. Thus anthropologists were among the most prominent purveyors of the worth of indigenous life-ways, while at the same time they promoted colonial intrusions that inevitably changed those ways of life.

When Australia's first department of anthropology was founded in 1925 at the University of Sydney, a leading British functionalist, AR Radcliffe-Brown, was appointed to the chair. Radcliffe-Brown vigorously promoted the practical relevance of anthropology, especially to native administration in Papua and New Guinea, though he suggested that its usefulness in Aboriginal administration was limited.[8] His successor after 1933, AP Elkin, was even more committed to the practical applicability of his discipline and, unlike Radcliffe-Brown, he was determined to direct anthropology to the benefit of Aboriginal people. Among Elkin's goals was to awaken Australians to the value and virtues of Aboriginal societies and cultures. A decade of writing in this vein culminated in his first major book aimed at a general readership, *The Australian Aborigines: How to understand them*, published in 1938. It was premised on the assumption that if white Australians came to appreciate the richness of Aboriginal cultures and the complexity of their social systems, they would be more ready to accept Aboriginal people as fellow Australians.[9]

Among Elkin's innovations, he insisted that traditional Aboriginal spiritual beliefs and rites were genuinely religious, not mere superstition and idolatry as they had long been regarded. Indeed, he was the first Australian intellectual to consistently designate Aboriginal beliefs as 'religious'. Against Mary Bennett's accusation in 1934 that he had encouraged 'sorcery' at Mount Margaret Mission, Elkin asserted that the specified ritual practices were 'religious through and through'.[10] Elkin was not only an anthropologist but also an Anglican priest, firmly committed to the right — or duty — of Christian missionaries to propagate the faith. However, he insisted that this must not be at the expense of Aboriginal religiosity, which he believed provided the foundations on which the 'higher faith' of Christianity could be built. In an often-repeated metaphor, he depicted Christian conversion as a process of Aboriginal people 'building up a "New Testament" on *their own* "Old Testament"'.[11] His metaphor presumed the supremacy of Christian revelation, but by equating traditional Aboriginal religious beliefs with the Old Testament, it was also an affirmation of respect.

In the secular as in the religious sphere, Elkin argued that Aboriginal progress must come incrementally, building upon existing traditions. This demanded a respectful appreciation of those traditions, valuing them for both their intrinsic worth and their utility as the foundations of social progress. He cautioned that he did not wish to 'give the impression that [Aboriginal] life is all good, noble and attractive'.[12] Yet running through many of his writings, especially those from the early 1930s, is a tone of disenchantment with modernity and its ills of individualism and anomie, and a corresponding regard for the reciprocity of traditional Aboriginal social arrangements. Although never suggesting the superiority of primitive over civilised ways, and always maintaining the desirability of progress from the former to the latter, he intimated that primitive peoples possessed something that civilised people had lost: an integrated sociality based on shared religiosity.[13] The need of civilised people to remedy that loss was a prominent theme of his social advocacy in the 1930s. He urged it again in a series of lectures delivered in 1940 when, for the second time in Elkin's life, the civilised world was tearing itself apart in total war. Civilisation surely could learn from those who did not practise such barbarities.[14]

While Elkin maintained that the only viable future for Aboriginal people lay in their advancement into civilisation, some anthropologists argued to the contrary. The Melbourne anatomist and anthropologist Frederic Wood Jones, for example, maintained that Aboriginal people could survive only in their primitive state. He wrote glowingly of the 'extraordinarily complicated, but highly efficient, social code for the regulation of the moral and physical welfare of his communities', but his adulation was confined to the uncorrupted primitive. It was 'as a stone-age hunter', Wood Jones declared, 'that we must always regard him'. Aboriginal individuals were intelligent and their culture was admirable, but as a race they were 'absolutely unfitted to cope with the demands of our civilization'.[15] Convinced of both the worth of primitive Aboriginality and the incapacity of the people to exist other than as primitives, Wood Jones advocated the segregation of tribal full-bloods on vast reserves, where they could maintain their traditional economy, culture and social order unchanged.

As noted in the previous chapter, scientists on the Board for Anthropological Research at the University of Adelaide, including JB Cleland and Norman Tindale, shared Wood Jones' enthusiasm for segregation, as did his protégé, Donald Thomson.[16] Aboriginal people, in their view, were entitled to the protection of the Australian state. Indeed, it was only by the Australian state erecting a protective wall around them that they stood any chance of survival. However, attempts to engineer their entry into the nation could spell only their doom. For tribal people, they claimed, the rights, duties, expectations and benefits of citizenship were worse than useless — they were poisonous. Reserves rigorously excluding the modern world offered the only means of ensuring Aboriginal survival. While these arguments were consistent with the entrenched image of Aboriginal people as irredeemably primitive, they were conjoined with a new, more positive, appraisal of primitivity itself.

Cleland was particularly effusive on the harmonious coexistence of Aboriginal people with nature. The Aborigine, he claimed, made 'little impression on his surroundings', as against the 'devastation' wrought by Europeans, and in the arid regions Aboriginal people made 'a much better use of this country than we ever can'.[17] Tindale also asserted the ecological desirability of traditional land-use practices, and maintained that the hunting and gathering mode of subsistence of the Western Desert tribes secured 'a far more effective occupation of the country' than white people could ever manage.[18] Their arguments manifested both a changing environmental sensibility and a new appreciation of primitive Aboriginality. More than that, they represented the beginning of the confluence of those strands into an image of Aboriginal people as exemplary stewards of Australian nature.

In the interwar years, settler Australians increasingly turned to the Aboriginal heritage as a source of emblems of national distinctiveness. In 1934, Robert Turner and Milton Boyce published *Australian Aboriginal signs and symbols for the use of boy scouts*, the stated purpose of which was 'to assist Troops to have real Australian totems, signs and symbols' and to dispense with 'imported signs' as much as possible. They provided numerous illustrations, with explanatory glosses, of Aboriginal signs, designs and words that could be incorporated into the scouting repertoire to lend it an authentic Australian flavour. Their booklet might be deprecated as an instance of cultural appropriation for white Australian nationalist purposes, but Turner and Boyce strove to convey a respectful attitude towards Aboriginal cultures, almost always specifying the provenance of Aboriginal words, symbols and artworks in terms of their tribal origins or geographical location rather than simply presenting them as generically Aboriginal.[19]

Turner and Boyce's publisher was the ardent Australian nationalist, PR ('Inky') Stephensen, who in 1935/36 wrote a pugnacious cultural critique, *The foundations of culture in Australia*. 'Culture in Australia,' he asserted, 'begins not from the Aborigines, who have been suppressed and exterminated, but from British culture, brought hither by Englishmen, Irishmen and Scotsmen throughout the Nineteenth Century.' This disclaimer notwithstanding, Stephensen's passionate commitment to building a distinctively Australian national culture led him to endorse Aboriginal models:

> The Aborigines, our admirable predecessors in sovereignty over the territory of Australia Felix, had their Bora ceremonies, their Initiation Corroborees; during which the seniors took the young men away into a sacred place, knocked out with a sacred stone a tooth from each candidate for knowledge...and then told them, with awe-inspiring circumstance, the holy secrets of the tribe. We White Australians should consider the advisability of doing something of the same kind.
>
> Just as the sacred traditions and legends of an Aboriginal tribe provide that tribe with a collective soul and a continuity, *so written history and literature provide a civilised nation with a national soul and coherence.* The recitation of national lore provides the foundation of a national survival-idea...This is the true meaning of culture in any Place — preservation of tribal or national experience in a memorable form; in holy scriptures, in churinga, in *literature*; because of the coherence-value, the discipline-value, the survival-value of that experience and lore.[20]

Stephensen did not suggest that white Australians should acquire their 'national lore' from the country's Aboriginal heritage, but he did suggest that they might learn from Aboriginal people's intuitive sense of community.

For its pungency and fervent nationalism, Stephensen's *Foundations of culture* struck a chord with many of Australia's intelligentsia. More deeply struck than most was the young Adelaide poet Rex Ingamells, who was inspired to write his own manifesto, *Conditional culture*, after reading the first instalment of Stephensen's tract. While Stephensen extolled the 'Spirit of the Place', Ingamells rushed into fanatical devotion to 'environmental values'. More stridently than Stephensen, Ingamells sought 'to free Australian art from whatever alien influences trammel it', insisting that a 'fundamental break...with the spirit of English culture, is the prerequisite for the development of an Australian culture'. To foster this break, he enlisted the aid of Aboriginal culture, 'a culture which was closely bound in every way with their environment'. The 'culture of the aborigines', he averred, 'must be of primary importance to the proper evolution of our culture', and 'to ensure imaginative truth our writers and painters must become hard-working students of aboriginal culture'.[21] Ingamells' own status as a hard-working student of Aboriginal culture is open to question, since his knowledge of the subject was entirely second-hand. Even his

Aboriginalist aspirations were not entirely new, many of his ideas having been anticipated by the poet Mary Gilmore.[22]

In the year he published *Conditional culture*, Ingamells founded the Jindyworobak literary movement. Taken from James Devaney's 1929 collection of stories, *The vanished tribes*, the word 'Jindyworobak' purportedly meant 'to annex, to join'. Although Ingamells later confessed to choosing the name not only for its meaning but also 'because of its Aboriginality…and its outlandishness to fashionable literary taste',[23] the purported meaning of the word invites comment. At its most superficial, the 'joining' meaning of 'Jindyworobak' referred to joining together words from English and Aboriginal languages — a lexical grab for Australian authenticity that produced some absurd jumblings of Aboriginal-sounding words.[24] At another level, Ingamells' ambition was to join Indigenous traditions to the culture imported by Europeans. Above all, he aspired to join settler Australians to Australian lands, spiritualising their ties with the national territory. Australians would come to truly belong to this land, he argued, if they were open to the 'spirit' of Aboriginal culture. Much of that culture, he claimed, was already 'dead' and 'forever lost to our appreciation', but enough remained to permit the 'assimilation of much of the spirit of it'. Assimilating Aboriginal culture was not a matter of mimicry but a creative process of interpretation and modification: 'From Aboriginal art and song we must learn much of our new technique; from Aboriginal legend, sublimated through our thought, we must achieve something of a pristine outlook on life.'[25]

While Ingamells urged the joining of Western and Aboriginal traditions into a national Australian culture, he held out little hope that Aboriginal people might be joined into the national community. The Jindyworobak aim was to incorporate Aboriginalia into Australian nationalism, not Aboriginal people into the Australian nation. In a romantic rendition of the doomed race idea, Ingamells suggested that Aboriginal people had lost their primitive vitality and gained nothing:

> One by one the tribes have vanished from their hunting grounds. No longer do the tribes go out in the dark before the dawn to stalk the kangaroos; no longer do they fish, with their spears or nets, in the rivers or billabongs or at the edge of the sea. They no longer hold their sacred corroborees under the twisted fire-reflecting branches of massive gum trees or among the stunted mallee. The

blacks that remain are a degenerate, puppet people, mere parodies of what their race once was.[26]

The Aboriginal people were beyond salvation, but their cultural legacy could help redeem the nation that now laid claim to their lands.

Humphrey McQueen argues that for Ingamells 'the attractiveness of Aboriginal culture lay in his supposing that it was cut off from its living roots in human experience and was thus available for appropriation by European Australians who could cannibalise it'.[27] Ann McGrath's assessment is less harsh, pointing out that 'the Jindyworobaks represented a brave step towards achieving a cultural convergence' between settler and Aboriginal Australians.[28] Both assessments are accurate. The Jindyworobak agenda was an instance of cultural appropriation, but appropriation inevitably entails appreciation of that which is appropriated. Ingamells supposed that Aboriginal culture was 'cut off from its living roots' because he, like most of his contemporaries, assumed Aboriginal people to be on the brink of extinction. Unlike most, however, he did not assume that their cultural heritage should vanish with them. His level of cultural appreciation may have been naive, but his writings were expressions of respect — even veneration — for a cultural heritage that had long been belittled and disdained.

The covers of some Jindyworobak anthologies were designed by the modernist artist Margaret Preston, whose Aboriginalist efforts predated those of Ingamells by over a decade. In 1925 she published an article urging the creation of a national Australian art that drew nourishment from Aboriginal sources. Identifying Australianness with Aboriginality, she wrote:

> In wishing to rid myself of the mannerisms of a country other than my own I have gone to the art of a people who have never seen or known anything different from themselves, and were accustomed always to use the same symbols to express themselves. These are the Australian aboriginals, and it is only from the art of such people in any land that a national art can spring.[29]

From around this time, Preston began incorporating Aboriginal motifs in her works, but she wanted the influence of Aboriginal art to extend well beyond the art galleries, into the everyday visual environment of ordinary Australians. Aboriginal decorative motifs, she urged, should be integrated into Australian homes and cafes, fabrics and ceramics, for their intrinsic aesthetic merit as well as their explicit Australianness. It was not until the 1950s that Aboriginal artistic design was widely popularised in this manner, and then often in ways lacking Preston's high aesthetic standards.[30] Nonetheless, in the 1920s and 1930s Preston pioneered a new sensibility toward the Indigenous artistic heritage (see Plate 2).

Preston was not the first white Australian to appreciate Aboriginal art, but hitherto that appreciation had primarily been ethnographic, as the productions of a primitive people. One of Preston's innovations was to appreciate Aboriginal cultural productions as art rather than as artefacts. That is to say, she shifted focus from the anthropological significance and traditional meanings of Aboriginal artworks to their aesthetic qualities. Yet her project was not purely aesthetic, for her other innovation was to imbue Aboriginal artworks (or, perhaps more accurately, elements of Aboriginal aesthetics) with new social significance and meaning as expressions of Australian nationhood. As art historian Ian McLean explains, Preston was not only 'the first modernist to take up the cause of aboriginal art', but also 'the first artist to find in Aboriginal art the source for a distinctive Australian identity'.[31]

Refiguring the federation

Around the time Preston was developing her ideas on Aboriginal aesthetics, Colonel JC Genders, founder of the Aborigines' Protection League of South Australia, put forward one of the most innovative pro-posals for Aboriginal advancement to date. He advocated the creation of an Aboriginal state within the Commonwealth, which would

> ultimately [be] managed by a native tribunal as far as possible according to their own laws and customs but prohibiting cannibalism and cruel rites…Provision to be made that ultimately the Government may be conducted by aborigines, and that it would be possible at some future time that the Administrator himself could be a native.

Genders cast his argument in terms of white Australians' moral obligation to care for a dispossessed people who were 'fast dying out' through cruelty, oppression and neglect. He was also alert to the pragmatic argument that an Aboriginal state would be 'of immense help in developing our empty Northern Estate particularly in the more torrid zones'.[32]

Genders' proposal was innovative on three counts. First, he insisted that the competence and intelligence of Aboriginal people must be recognised. Too often, he complained, even well-meaning philanthropists treated the Aborigine as 'a brainless, helpless child, incompetent to own any land or work out his own destiny'.[33] At a 1929 conference of missionaries and others interested in Aboriginal welfare, he admonished his fellow delegates: 'it is time we recognised that we cannot take over an intelligent people and tell them how to run their own business'.[34] Genders conceded that for some time Aboriginal people would require the advice and assistance of whites, but these should be offered in a manner befitting intelligent adults, not pressed as demands upon incompetent minors.

Second, Genders assessed Aboriginal culture as flexible and adaptable rather than fixed and brittle, inevitably shattering on impact with the West. He insisted that 'we are wrong in seeking to impose our civilisation on the native and to substitute our mind and our methods for those he has acquired over countless ages. Progress, not necessarily on our lines, must come from within, not without.'[35] The Aborigine, he maintained, must be given 'a chance to work out his destiny on his own lines'.[36] These gestures toward cultural relativism were diluted by his avowal that some customs ('cannibalism and cruel rites') must be proscribed. Yet he clearly envisaged Aboriginal people progressing into civilisation by renovating, rather than abandoning, their Indigenous culture.

Third, Genders reconceptualised the Australian federation. In his proposal, federalism would provide a framework for maintaining and managing ethnic and cultural diversity. Australia would become a multi-ethnic state. He anticipated Aboriginal people initially exercising only limited powers within their own jurisdiction, but over time the Aboriginal state (eventually states) would come to possess the same share of sovereignty as the already established states of the Australian federation.[37]

Genders' proposals offer a window on to contemporary thinking about nations, national minorities and indigenous peoples, so it is worth considering the inspirations behind those proposals. One inspiration was New Zealand. Genders frequently referred to Maori precedents — recommending, for example, that the Model Aboriginal State 'have representation in the Federal Parliament on the lines (in a modified form at first) of the Maoris in New Zealand'.[38] He and fellow League members often exaggerated the freedoms enjoyed by the Maori, but they were in a long line of Australian reformers who looked across the Tasman for exemplars of better policies and practices in indigenous affairs.

Genders seems to have been influenced by the ideas of self-determination that American President Woodrow Wilson had put firmly on the international agenda after the First World War. At its fullest, self-determination referred to the right of a nation to its own sovereign state. However, the postwar treaty-makers and the League of Nations knew that if this right were universally applied, established states and the international order would disintegrate. In a weaker sense, self-determination referred to the right of national and ethnic minorities who were resident in states dominated by another nationality (such as Hungarians in Romania and Czechoslovakia) to maintain their national existence and ethnic cultures. Self-determination thus connected with ideas of minority rights that were written into the treaties imposed on many Eastern and Central European states.[39] Genders' proposals did not correspond exactly with the European minorities' rights treaties, but like those treaties they sought a workable compromise between minority rights to autonomy and the reality of an international order built around sovereign states.

The mandate system set up after the First World War was also an influence on Genders' thinking. Under the mandate system, the former colonies of Germany and large parts of the former Ottoman Empire passed into the trusteeship of the victorious powers, who were supposed to administer them with a view to their eventual independence. Australia acquired a mandate over New Guinea in 1920. Its administration of this territory may not have lived up to the high ideals of the League of Nations, according to which Australia held New Guinea as a 'sacred trust' to be administered for the benefit and progress of its native inhabitants. But the ideal of administering colonies with a view to their future self-government, and the idea that white people could not continue forever to lord it over natives, were in the air. Genders breathed this atmosphere. He claimed that the terms of the mandate over New Guinea entailed 'the preservation of native laws and customs and the participation of the natives, to an increasing extent, in the Government of the Territory', implying that similar provisions should apply to Aboriginal Australians.[40]

Genders' Aboriginal state idea had some parallels with the Austro-Marxist ideal of autonomous nations nesting within a multi-national state. In the late nineteenth and early twentieth centuries, Austro-Marxists such as Otto Bauer had urged the reformation of the Habsburg Empire into a federation of states, one for each of its national groups (Germans, Hungarians, Czechs and so forth), each exercising autonomy under an overarching federal authority. Thereby, it was hoped, cultural and linguistic diversity would be reconciled with equality and democracy.[41] Lenin picked up these Austro-Marxist ideas, and in attenuated form they influenced the federal structure of the Soviet Union. Despite the commonalities, it is questionable whether Genders was influenced by Austro-Marxism. He was a conservative gentleman, unlikely to have dabbled in revolutionary doctrines. Moreover, the Austro-Marxist proposal concerned recognised nations, and Genders did not recognise Aboriginal people as such. He looked forward to the development of an Aboriginal 'sense of nationhood', but that was an achievement for the future rather than a present reality.[42]

Genders' proposal attracted some influential supporters. Members of his Aborigines' Protection League included the anthropologist and state MLA Dr Herbert Basedow, the feminist Constance Ternent Cook, the classicist Professor Darnley Naylor, the Commonwealth minister P McMahon Glynn and the Aboriginal spokesman and inventor David Unaipon.[43] The 1926 petition for the creation of a Model Aboriginal State gathered 7000 signatures and had the support of the leading Adelaide newspaper, *The Advertiser*. Genders' proposal also had some powerful detractors. In a 1928 report to the Commonwealth government, Queensland Chief Protector of Aborigines JW Bleakley argued that an Aboriginal state was 'impracticable' since the people were divided into closed, inward-looking tribes, and had 'no conception of democracy' and no appreciation of the responsibilities entailed by modern forms of government.[44] The detractors won the day. No Model Aboriginal State was established.

Soon after Genders' Aboriginal state movement petered out, the Communist Party of Australia took up the separate state idea. Its 1931 fourteen-point program for Aboriginal rights included the 'handing over to the aborigines of large tracts of watered and fertile country, with towns, seaports, railways, roads, etc., to become one or more independent aboriginal states or republics'. Despite their near-contemporaneity, the Communists had not borrowed the idea of an Aboriginal state from Genders. They were following Comintern policy, which prescribed that national minorities had a right to self-determination. In this instance, the Aboriginal state idea had descended, via Lenin's model of 'autonomous' republics within the Soviet Union, from the Austro-Marxist ideal of a multinational federation. The Communist Party's program went further than Genders', advocating an Aboriginal state with full sovereign powers, including the capacity 'to make treaties with foreign powers, including Australia, establish their own army, governments, industries, and in every way be independent of imperialism'.[45]

Genders drew support from some prestigious members of the Adelaide establishment. The Communist Party lacked that advantage. But whether championed by respectable figures such as Colonel Genders and his Protection League or by radical groups like the Communist Party, the idea of an Aboriginal state got nowhere in the interwar years. It was unacceptable to those in authority because it credited Aboriginal people with more intelligence and initiative than they were prepared to acknowledge, and because it entailed a fundamental change in the character of the Australian federation. The federation envisaged by Genders was one that sanctioned cultural and ethnic diversity within an overarching political unity. The federation that had been established in 1901 was founded on the contrary principle of ethnic homogeneity as the basis of national existence.

Humanitarians and activists

The Aborigines' Protection League was only one of many Aboriginal welfare groups active in the interwar years. Driven by a combination of domestic factors (such as revulsion against the massacres instanced at the beginning of this chapter) and international trends (including the ideals of benevolent colonialism promoted by the League of Nations), established organisations such as the Association for the Protection of Native Races and the Aborigines' Friends' Association were revitalised, and several new groups founded, including the Victorian Aboriginal Group. Other organisations with more wide-ranging concerns, such as the Australian Federation of Women Voters and the Women's Non-Party Association of South Australia, began to take a close interest in Aboriginal affairs. The interwar years also saw the foundation of several political groups with exclusively Aboriginal memberships. Consideration of the latter will be deferred to the next chapter, while this section focuses on the white humanitarian and feminist organisations who campaigned on behalf of Aboriginal people.

While there were differences of aims and means among these organisations, they shared a conviction that the Australian nation had a moral responsibility for the well-being of Australia's Indigenous people. In line with this, they advocated federal control of Aboriginal affairs.[46] Above all, moral responsibility meant ensuring the survival of the race. Without that, all other efforts would come to nought, and for white Australians at the time Aboriginal survival seemed far from assured. Preserving the race had long been connected with protectionism, and this continued to be the case in the interwar years. Protectionism slid easily into paternalism and maternalism, and sometimes further into authoritarianism. For as long as the sheer physical survival of Aboriginal people remained in question, it was difficult for humanitarian reformers to avoid these concomitants of protectionism. Even the names of the humanitarian organisations carried the legacy of protectionism. One of the most influential was the Association for the Protection of Native Races, whose journal — which began publication in December 1935 — was entitled *The Aborigines' Protector*.

Yet these interwar humanitarian bodies understood that protection, as hitherto practised, was inadequate to the task of meliorating race relations in Australia. AP Elkin's early critique of protectionism is illustrative. In a 1931 address to the Association for the Protection of Native Races, he criticised the 'negative' protectionist policies of the past and urged a 'positive policy' of social advancement for the future. White Australians, Elkin averred, were 'morally bound to aid the development of the primitive race'. This was a 'responsibility of a civilized nation', which could best be fulfilled by reforming Aboriginal governance along the lines recommended by the League of Nations for colonised peoples. He did not shy away from authoritarian prescriptions, advising that in northern Australia the senior official in charge of Aboriginal affairs 'should be clothed with strong administrative powers, and be as free from control by a distant Parliament or bureaucracy as, say, the Lieut-Governor of Papua'.[47] Elkin's 1931 policy statement made no mention of Aboriginal citizenship, instead focusing squarely on white Australians' responsibilities toward them. At this time, his priority was to save the Aboriginal people from extinction — and he had some doubts about whether this was feasible. Only in the second half of the 1930s, when he had come to feel reasonably assured of the prospects for Aboriginal survival, did Elkin begin to make recommendations for Aboriginal rights and equality, and even then strong elements of protectionism still infused his advocacy.

The key concept in the interwar humanitarian discourse was not rights but responsibility. In particular, it was a discourse emphasising the responsibility of the dominant (and, in the humanitarians' view, advanced) race for the well-being of the disadvantaged (and, in the humanitarians' view, backward) race. Reformers did not totally ignore Aboriginal rights, but they gave responsibilities greater weight. Their priorities were in accord with those of the League of Nations, which endorsed the need of primitive peoples for guardianship and tutelage as they made the difficult transition into the modern world. They were also in line with the views of prominent Aboriginal spokespeople. David Unaipon, amateur inventor and member of the Aborigines' Friends' Association, insisted that it was 'the duty of the white man to stand by the aborigine, to guide him and to help him until he can help himself in this new world which has grown up around him'.[48] According to the humanitarians, Aboriginal people could ultimately become modern; they were not irredeemably primitive but, with appropriate guidance and assistance, could become participants in the modern world. In the 1930s, this was a new and challenging notion.

Interwar feminist campaigners also emphasised responsibilities, particularly their responsibility to ensure the proper treatment of Aboriginal women and to protect them from the sexual depredations of men, both white and Aboriginal.[49] In her evocatively titled study of these feminist campaigners, *Loving protection*, Fiona Paisley stresses their call for the moral reformation of the Australian nation, to 'build a new era in race relations in Australia, and thereby bring the nation to maturity and fulfil its potential in the modern age'. Paisley notes that they were 'a group of predominantly middle-class liberal women with strong ties to Britain [who] sought to make sense of Australia's claim to be a modern nation within the British Commonwealth'. Her account suggests that these interwar feminists saw their interventions in Aboriginal affairs very much in terms of bringing the wayward race relations of Australia back to true British ideals of justice and respect for humanity. This was their self-appointed duty, to be carried out not in dialogue with Aboriginal people but on their behalf.[50]

Consistent with their emphasis on the moral realignment of Aboriginal governance, the humanitarian and feminist groups were more interested in bringing Aboriginal people under the auspices of the national government than in their becoming members of the national community. Yet by the latter part of the 1930s, citizenship began to assume a place in their agendas. With a growing appreciation of the limits of protectionism came a nascent recognition of the need for Aboriginal people to exercise some control over their own affairs. Typically, they recommended that only 'civilised aborigines should have the rights and privileges of citizens', as Helen Baillie, founder of the Victorian Aboriginal Group, put it in 1935.[51] Or, as the group recommended two years later, 'full citizenship rights should be granted to aboriginals who can pass an education test'.[52]

As the next chapter shows, citizenship was much higher on the agenda of contemporary Aboriginal activists, though they shared the white humanitarians' views on its cultural prerequisites. These Aboriginal activists deserve greater credit than they have generally been given for pushing citizenship to the forefront of Aboriginal affairs. In the interwar reformers' writings, I can find few instances before about 1935 where they explicitly called for Aboriginal citizenship. It was Aboriginal activists who first made this call loudly, and their demand was pushed into prominence by the publicity given their Day of Mourning protest at the beginning of 1938. Only belatedly — essentially in the second half of the 1930s — did white reformers take up the demand for Aboriginal citizenship with any enthusiasm.

Despite their tardiness in adopting citizenship as an objective, the interwar humanitarians and feminists did promote the public profile of Aboriginal affairs and did put governments on notice that they must make a more sustained effort to advance Aboriginal well-being. Their labours were not altogether barren: their greatest achievement at a governmental level came in the form of a Commonwealth policy declaration in early 1939. This declaration, the subject of the next section, was broadly in line with reforms advocated by the humanitarian lobby, and equally infused with moderation and restraint.

A new deal

In February 1939, Commonwealth Minister for the Interior Jack McEwen issued a policy statement dubbed the 'New Deal for Aborigines'. For the first time, an Australian government specified 'citizenship' as the 'final objective' of Aboriginal policy, although as Commonwealth policy its application was limited to the Northern Territory. Citizenship would not simply be granted to Aboriginal people; it would be awarded only after their transformation 'from their traditional nomadic inclinations to a settled life'. This would be a slow process, the New Deal warned, since 'to transform people from a nomadic tribal state to take their place in a civilised community will certainly take not only many years, but many generations'.[53] In the meantime, Aboriginal people in the Territory would continue to be governed by an apparatus in which they had little involvement and less influence. Arguably, by shifting the primary aspiration of Aboriginal governance from protection to advancement, the New Deal intensified administrative intrusions into Aboriginal lives.

Elkin had a major hand in drafting the New Deal. Following recommendations he had made throughout the 1930s, the New Deal remodelled Aboriginal administration in the Territory along the lines of that in New Guinea. Aboriginal administration in the Northern Territory was to be reformed according to the precepts of enlightened colonialism propounded by the League of Nations. As if to underline the point, when McEwen toured the Northern Territory in 1938 in preparation for his policy innovation, he was accompanied by EWP Chinnery, Director of Native Affairs and District Services in the Mandated Territory of New Guinea. Chinnery was Elkin's first preference for the position of director of the new Native Affairs Branch, and the first incumbent.[54] Aboriginal administration in the Northern Territory was essentially to be colonial administration.

Cecil Cook thought otherwise. He argued that circumstances in the Northern Territory were crucially different to those in genuinely colonial situations such as Papua and New Guinea. In the latter, natives comprised the vast majority of the population and their sociocultural order remained strong — neither of which, he claimed, was the case in the Northern Territory. The Administrator of the Northern Territory, CLA Abbott, agreed.[55] Elkin acknowledged that 'there is some slight difference in the problem, for the peoples of Papua and New Guinea are settled horticulturalists, while the Australians are nomadic food-gatherers', but he considered it inappropriate to place 'too much emphasis' on this distinction.[56] Getting closer to the central issue, he later pointed out that:

> The difficulties are especially great in a country like Australia, where the native people and the invading immigrant population, and also their mixed offspring, live continually in close contact. The problem is different in a dependency like Papua, where the local white population is small, the culture-contact almost solely of a limited economic and missionary nature, and the administrative policy is only slightly hampered by local or distant white opinion. In Australia, however, the contact could be described as 'totalitarian', with disastrous results to the aboriginal population.[57]

Even this side-stepped the most fundamental difference. New Guinea, under the benevolent colonial policy of the mandate system, was (in theory) being prepared for eventual sovereign statehood. The Northern Territory was part of the national state of Australia, and even the most benevolent form of governance did not anticipate eventual independence for either the Territory or its Aboriginal inhabitants.

The administrative machinery of the New Deal was set up, with Chinnery as Director, in 1939. One of his first tasks was to translate policy objectives into concrete strategies. Since 1936, persons classified as half-castes had been eligible for exemption from the provisions of the Aboriginals Ordinance, and Chinnery sought to widen the scope of exemptions to encompass full-bloods as well. In April 1939, he came up with a list of four 'qualities which should be held by any aboriginal requiring the privileges of a European', none of which made any reference to degree of white ancestry but all of which were culturally prescriptive. The first of Chinnery's qualities was very general, stating that exempted persons 'should be capable of exercising the privileges and of fulfilling the obligations of citizenship'. The second specified that the Aboriginal person 'be of proved good character, vouched for by a reputable and responsible European'; the third stipulated that the 'aboriginal should be capable of earning his own living…in the manner of a European'; and the fourth that 'he should have the capacity for education', though literacy was not demanded. Chinnery acknowledged that it was 'difficult to set down the precise standards' required of each individual, suggesting that some were 'obviously' entitled to full citizenship while there were 'others less outstanding who would also make useful citizens if given the full privileges'.[58]

Under the New Deal, the Commonwealth began reforming its administration of Aboriginal affairs in the Territory, in line with its policy objective of all Aboriginal people ultimately qualifying for citizenship. Six months after its proclamation, war broke out and Aboriginal affairs were relegated to their usual low priority. Wartime demands impeded implementation of the New Deal and inhibited policy innovation in the states as well. Yet in the longer term, the repercussions of the Second World War promoted the tenor of the New Deal, and the postwar national and international environment pushed this tendency further.

Commenting on the New Deal thirty years later, CD Rowley observed that in the context of its times it was 'epoch-making', since 'it formulated a long-term objective for policy that was other than some kind of social engineering for the disappearance of the race into the white majority, taking the emphasis off miscegenation…The objective was a positive one, envisaging a common citizenship, without postulating genetic changes'. For this, and for the fact that it covered all Aboriginal people regardless of caste, Rowley stated that the New Deal 'might fairly be regarded as the foundation of the assimilation policy' that was implemented after the Second World War.[59] It could equally fairly be regarded as a manifestation of the limited reassessment of the possibility of including Aboriginal people in the national community that had taken place over the course of the 1930s.

Chapter 3

Aboriginal Activists Demand Acceptance

Contemporary Aboriginal activists applauded the New Deal. William Cooper, Secretary of the Australian Aborigines' League, called it 'the Aboriginal Magna Carta' and urged Prime Minister Menzies to implement it without delay, the emergency of war notwithstanding.[1] Cooper was so impressed with McEwen's policy innovation that when, in 1939, Menzies began selection of a new Cabinet, he wrote to the prime minister requesting that McEwen's policy momentum be maintained: 'Will you please select a minister for the Interior who will continue to maintain his administration with the desire to fully help the natives into full British Culture?'[2]

The Aborigines Progressive Association concurred. At its January 1940 meeting, the Association resolved that 'the major portion of Mr McEwen's...policy be proceeded with'. Its only significant disagreement was with the New Deal's proposal to establish a 'native constabulary', because 'wherever this has been carried out, the system has proved most harmful to the aboriginal'.[3] Neither the Association nor the League was dismayed by the New Deal's provisos on Aboriginal citizenship. Both organisations, in fact, prescribed the same prerequisites to Aboriginal people acquiring the rights and status of citizenship.

There were some differences between the Aborigines' League and the Progressive Association. The former, Victorian-based body adopted a more nationwide perspective, whereas the Association focused more closely, though not exclusively, on issues in its home state of New South Wales. The League was sympathetic toward missionaries; its founder, William Cooper, was himself a mission-educated Christian. The Association tended to be anti-missionary; its leaders, Jack Patten and Bill Ferguson, had been schooled, respectively, in the rough and tumble of the professional boxing circuit and the even greater rough and tumble of organising for the Australian Workers Union and the Australian Labor Party in rural New South Wales. The disagreements, however, were superficial. Both organisations were dedicated to securing citizenship for Aboriginal people. They sometimes worked collaboratively on this, most notably in staging the Day of Mourning on 26 January 1938, the largest Aboriginal protest action Australia had yet witnessed (see Plate 3).

The Day of Mourning was a riposte to the official celebration of 150 years of white occupancy of Australia. More specifically, it was a protest against Aboriginal exclusion from the nation founded upon that occupancy. For the occasion, Patten and Ferguson published the manifesto *Aborigines claim citizen rights!*, which includes the demand for Aboriginal inclusion in the Australian nation quoted at the beginning of this book. Beyond the 'citizen rights' of their title, Patten and Ferguson demanded the respect and esteem due to fellow citizens: 'We ask you to be proud of the Australian Aboriginal, and to take his hand in friendship.' They invoked Aboriginal war service as Anzacs; they pleaded for an end to the 'insult' of 'comic cartoons and misrepresentation'; and they asked 'to be accepted into the Australian community on a basis of equal opportunity'. Asserting their commonality with other Australians, they explained that 'Aborigines are interested not only in boomerangs and gum leaves and corroborees! The overwhelming majority of us are able and willing to earn our living by honest toil, and to take our place in the community, side by side with yourselves.'[4]

Commonality and community with other Australians were prominent themes in the writings of the Aboriginal activists of the 1930s, but at the same time they insisted on recognition of their Aboriginality. They demanded respect and esteem not only as Australians but also as Aboriginal people; they cherished an Aboriginal identity and sought an expansion of that identity. Indeed, they were early exponents of pan-Aboriginality, seeking to foster a solidarity that was not only continent wide but also transcended 'the white man's discrimination between the half-caste and the full blood'.[5] In their view, this Aboriginal identity complemented, rather than conflicted with, their commitment to inclusion in the Australian nation. This chapter explores these activists' simultaneous quests for national inclusion and Aboriginal identity.

The Aborigines' League and Progressive Association were not the only Aboriginal political organisations to emerge in the interwar years.

They were preceded by at least two others. The first was the Australian Aboriginal Progressive Association (AAPA), founded in 1924 by Frederick Maynard, an Aboriginal man from the Hunter Valley. (Despite the similar names, this body was quite distinct from the Aborigines Progressive Association of Patten and Ferguson, which was founded in 1937.) Drawing inspiration from Marcus Garvey's Universal Negro Improvement and Conservation Association, the AAPA adopted a more militant stance than the later Aborigines' League and Progressive Association.[6] On the other side of the continent, in 1926, William Harris founded the Native Union of Western Australia, a more moderate lobby group devoted to advancing the interests of mixed-descent people in the south of that state.[7] While these predecessor organisations were important, this chapter focuses on the Aborigines' League and the Progressive Association, which had a higher public profile due particularly to the publicity given to their Day of Mourning protest.

Conditional citizenship

While the Aboriginal activists of the 1930s demanded citizen rights, neither the Progressive Association nor the Aborigines' League sought immediate, unconditional citizenship for all Aboriginal people. Both bodies consistently stipulated the attainment of civilisation as the essential prere-quisite. After years of letter writing to ministers and government officials, William Cooper summed up his organisation's aspirations in a letter to Prime Minister Menzies: 'The whole of this correspondence and our other representations would be fully met if you were to pass amending legislation granting *full rights to aborigines who have attained civilised status*.'[8] Like their non-Indigenous contemporaries, these Indigenous campaigners considered citizen rights contingent upon their bearers acquiring the competencies that would enable them to act effectively as members of a modern national community.

Both the Association and the League asserted that the Aboriginal future lay in modernity. As Ferguson and Patten explained: 'We have no desire to go back to primitive conditions of the Stone Age. We ask you to teach our people to live in the Modern Age, as modern citizens.'[9] Cooper expressed similar sentiments by locating Aborigines within a universal trajectory of human progress:

> We do not want our people to remain primitive, uncultured and a prey to all comers. Why should we remain in the near Stone

Age? The British were once as we are now. The conquering power of Rome, whatever else it did, lifted the British to culture and civilisation. We want that same uplift.[10]

Australian governments, he claimed, had deliberately sought 'to keep the Aboriginal down and not allow them to rise to the full standard of European culture'. This was not a mere oversight, but the result of a 'definite will' to retard Aboriginal advancement. Only by implementing 'an official policy of uplift' would it be possible 'to stop the rot and save the race'. History, Cooper declared, was on the Aboriginal side because: 'Whether the white man likes it or not, every native is headed for the culture of the white man.'[11] It may be difficult today to appreciate this as an instance of Aboriginal assertiveness. Recent interpretations generally maintain that white Australians forced 'the culture of the white man' down unwilling Aboriginal throats. But Cooper's statement *was* an instance of Aboriginal assertiveness, demanding that Aboriginal people be fitted with the cultural competencies that would enable them to take their rightful place as members of the Australian nation.

According to Cooper, the 'question of the uplift of the whole aboriginal population to full European culture depends on the capabilities of the race to assimilate that culture'.[12] He had no doubt that Aboriginal people possessed both the capability and the desire to do so, and it was on this basis that he pressed his demand for Aboriginal citizenship. Cooper argued that since Aboriginal people had hitherto acquired civilisation 'merely by picking it up', much better results could be expected from 'an ordered plan of uplift'.[13] On several occasions, he submitted to the Commonwealth government detailed proposals for 'the progressive elevation' of all Aboriginal people 'from one class to an higher one till the whole race is fully civilised and cultured'. He and the majority of Aboriginal people in southern Australia were already 'fully civilised and cultured', and hence eligible for immediate citizenship; the presently uncivilised elsewhere would qualify after tuition.[14]

In earlier studies, I characterised the agendas of the Progressive Association and the Aborigines' League as 'assimilationist'.[15] Some historians dispute the label on the grounds that these activists envisaged 'an ongoing state of (Aboriginal) difference'.[16] Such objections assume a highly restrictive conception of assimilation, equating it with the total erasure of Indigenous distinctiveness. As this book shows, the meanings of assimilation were far more open than that. The Aboriginal activists' program was assimilationist because it proposed that only by conformity to dominant cultural norms would a minority group qualify for membership of the majority nation. That they had other agendas, including the maintenance of Aboriginal identity and solidarity, qualifies but does not negate their assimilationism.

These activists were well aware that mere quiescent conformity to national norms by Aboriginal individuals would do little to promote their acceptance as a people. Collective action was required to demonstrate Aboriginal people's dutifulness as citizens and their ability to contribute to the well-being of the nation. I shall exemplify this aspect of their advocacy through an exposition of one line of argument pursued by William Cooper: his promotion of Aboriginal involvement in the development of northern Australia.

Virile, capable and black

In the 1930s, Australians fretted over their 'empty north' as both an invitation to invasion and a moral affront to a nation that prided itself on its pioneering spirit. Developing the north was a national ambition imbued with the nationalist myths of white Australia. Beyond pragmatic considerations of economic productivity and military preparedness, northern development called for collective action to remedy the deficiency — even disgrace — of vast lands lying empty and unused. Northern development was a civic enterprise, but it was deeply embedded in the ethnic nationalism characteristic of Australia at the time. Development was to be by and for the white race, a primary purpose being to close off the country to non-whites. If the teeming millions of Asia were to be stopped from laying claim to Australian lands, those lands had to have white millions of their own, both to validate the moral claim to country and to provide the personnel necessary for defence. In most interwar proposals for northern development, Aboriginal people did not feature at all — or if they did, it was as no more than colourful background and convenient labour. William Cooper sought to change that.

In 1939 he asked the Minister for the Interior, Jack McEwen: 'Why has it never occurred to the white minds to link the Aboriginal problem of the North and the Centre with the problem of the empty spaces[?]' He was arguing against proposals for sequestering Aboriginal people in reserves where they could maintain their primitive lifestyles. This, Cooper complained, was both unethical and impractical: unethical because it denied Aboriginal people the right to advancement in civilisation, amounting to their 'compulsory retardation' and preservation as mere 'zoological specimens'; impractical because it denied the reality of global needs for land. If land were reserved for primitive economic use, he asked: 'Is there any power on earth which could hold such land in the face of an increasingly land hungry world?' There was a viable alternative. According to Cooper, 'the Aboriginal has proved his worth in every sphere of primary industry', so 'White Australia should face the problem of the Aboriginal as much in self-interest as the Aboriginal interest, and self-interest demands that the one problem shall solve the other'. This, he acknowledged, was 'a new angle on the subject' of northern development, and therefore demanded a new slogan, 'The Aboriginal as asset and not a liability'.[17]

Affirming Indigenous people's status as a national asset, Cooper informed McEwen's predecessor, Thomas Paterson, that:

> In the aboriginal you have all the manpower required for the development of Australia's unsettled parts if they are given due training, direction and leadership and, might I add, inspiration, and its peopling by a population not merely European in culture but British in sentiment and loyalty would be a bulwark of defence.[18]

Cooper's statement resonates with his conviction that the Aboriginal destiny lay in Indigenous people adopting European culture and British loyalties. It resonates, too, with orthodox concerns about defence. Where it departed from conventional renditions of the northern development narrative was in proposing a central role for Aboriginal people. Northern development, according to Cooper, was a desirable project since it was one in which both white and black could share, thus promoting his vision of an Australian nation in which both races would possess equal entitlements and duties under a common citizenship. As a civic enterprise, he realised, northern development could work to Aboriginal people's advantage, but only if it were cut free from its moorings in ethnic white Australian nationalism.

One of the weakest points in the white Australia–northern development nexus derived from lingering doubts about the viability of the white race in the tropics. Since the early twentieth century, the doctrine that white people were inherently unfit for residence in tropical lands had been eroded by the combined forces of medical research and white Australia enthusiasm. But in the 1930s, misgivings remained. As late as 1937, a board of inquiry into the industries of the Northern Territory reported that although white men could live and work without ill-effect in the tropics, for white women 'it is different'.[19] If white women could not acclimatise to the tropics, how could the white race propagate itself there, and how could the north be peopled prolifically?

Cooper exploited the weak point of acclimatisation to the full. Referring to northern Australia, he wrote:

> The problem of those parts is climatic. It is unsuited to white labor, and particularly to white women. But it is all the natives have ever known and from it, for milleniums, they have won their livelihood. In it they became and remained a virile race, and they would be that now but for the intrusion of the white, with the consequent devitalisation that ensued.[20]

Involvement in northern development would revitalise a people left dispirited and destitute by the European invasion. In another letter to the Minister for the Interior, Cooper reinforced his assertion of Aboriginal acclimatisation and virility, drawing attention to their implications for defence. For Aboriginal people, he stated, 'the out back presents no climatic problem', so involving them in developmental projects 'will produce a virile, capable people, who will prove an efficient bulwark for the defence of your country and theirs'.[21] Creating a virile and capable people resonated perfectly with the orthodox northern development ideal — except that these people were to be virile, capable and black.

Northern development programs, according to Cooper, were misguided for their obsession with Europeans as the only permissible people to populate the land: 'We claim that it is not British stock that is wanted for the Territory, certainly not Southern European but Aboriginal, British Australian aborigines.'[22] With a stronger insinuation against southern Europeans and a stronger appeal to contemporary preoccupations with defence, he informed McEwen in February 1938:

> We believe and contend that aborigines, not southern Europeans, are those who should develop the outback. We can do it, under white guidance, better than any others for the climate has no terrors for those who have never known a more favourable one. We claim that the peopling of Australia's unsettled areas with

civilised aborigines is the best way to close Australia's back door for the aboriginal is loyal and efficient.[23]

The 'development of the North and Centre by Colored Australians' was preferable to 'the proposed immigration of Nordic peoples and Southern Europeans', Cooper argued, since the 'aboriginal is most loyal to the person of the King and His administration' and already imbued with 'British sentiment'.[24]

Drawing together the threads of his arguments on northern development, Cooper declared:

> We claim that, given a trial, we are capable of producing a yeomanry that can open up and develop the outback better than anyone else. We are acclimatised, and as our now primitive people become civilised, they lose the aboriginal culture and outlook taking on the psychology of the white man. The aboriginal is loyal to the Throne and person of His Majesty. The development of Australia by civilised aborigines is therefore sound in that it provides a bulwark for the defence of your land and ours.[25]

Cooper accepted the loss of traditional Aboriginal culture (though not the loss of a distinct Aboriginal identity) as a concomitant of becoming civilised.

By involving Aboriginal people in northern development, Cooper reasoned, they would learn modern ways, including techniques for the productive use of land. This was the pedagogical aspect of Aboriginal involvement in northern development. 'Who,' he asked, 'could better deal with the great problem of the Northern territory than an educated race of Aborigines?'[26] Cooper conceded an initial need for 'white guidance' in helping Aboriginal people develop the north. However, he placed greater emphasis on the need for educated Aboriginal people to assist in the advancement of their uncivilised compatriots:

> We suggest that the proper method of dealing with the primitive people would be to send educated and cultured Aborigines to their own uncivilized people. These men, of the same blood, would understand their people and would be able to suggest to the government means whereby the hardships and sufferings of these people could be alleviated.[27]

He did not suggest that Aboriginal people from southern Australia should emigrate *en masse* to the north; their role was not to make up the numbers but rather to provide education and training.

Nor did Cooper, in this context, refer to a spiritual affinity between Aboriginal people and their lands. Aboriginal people should develop the north not because they were spiritually bonded to those lands, but because they were good farmers. Cooper himself came from Cumeroogunga on the Murray River, which — like many Aboriginal missions and reserves in southern Australia — had a history of successful agricultural enterprise until their productive land was reallocated to white settlers in the late nineteenth and early twentieth centuries.[28] Drawing on this background, he affirmed that 'we have proved our aptitude for primary industry, so proving that it is not merely visionary when we talk of an aboriginal race, civilised, industrialised and bearing his share of responsibility for his country'.[29] The 'we' in this statement applied immediately to people like himself, already familiar with agricultural techniques, but Cooper was clearly extending the term to cover all Aboriginal people. If some were not yet skilled in farming, under appropriate — preferably Aboriginal — guidance, they soon would be.

While Cooper valued northern development for potentially modernising the Aboriginal people who lived there, his arguments went well beyond such instrumental considerations. Northern development was a great national drama, and Aboriginal participation in it would secure their position as members of the nation. Aboriginal people, he complained, 'have never had the opportunity to prove that we can make good citizens and be useful to the country under white men's rule'. Northern development offered just such an opportunity. Cooper's arguments on this score meshed with his pleas for Aboriginal people to prove themselves worthy and self-reliant, as against the stultifying, initiative-crushing burden of protectionist administration. 'The State,' he complained, 'has no useful work for us to do, and no educational move has been made to incorporate our people in national industry.'[30] Northern development held enormous promise for Aboriginal people to make themselves useful for the sake of their individual self-respect, their collective advancement and the benefit of the nation.

Cooper's attempts to insert Aboriginal people into the reigning narratives of Australian nationhood entailed no denial of Aboriginal solidarity and identity, but rather the enhancement of these qualities. As an advocate of an incipient pan-Aboriginality, he spoke confidently on behalf of Aboriginal people far distant from his own homeland, such as those in northern Australia with whom he had very little, if any, personal acquaintance. He envisaged northern development being undertaken not by an ensemble of individuals who happened to be Aboriginal, but by Aboriginal people as a collectivity. Northern development simultaneously offered a showcase for Aboriginal abilities and an opportunity to foster greater pride and sense of community among Aboriginal people themselves. Yet, while Cooper espoused the maintenance (or creation) of an Aboriginal identity, he envisioned that identity nesting within a sense of belonging and commitment to the Australian nation.

Cooper's pleas for Aboriginal inclusion in the Australian nation emphasised Indigenous people's Britishness. 'We need hardly impress on you,' he told Thomas Paterson in 1937,

> that the natural tendency of the aboriginal is to lose his native culture and assume the culture of those associated with his uplift. We claim that the civilised aboriginal is a black Britisher, having adopted the psychology and outlook of the people who displaced him. The aborigines are intensely loyal to the Throne and Person of Their Sovereign Lord. In many cases it might be affirmed that they are 'more British than the British'.[31]

The Britishness invoked by Cooper was not the ethnic Britishness of white Australian nationalists; rather, it referred to a configuration of values, attitudes, demeanour and institutions — civic attributes capable, at least in theory, of adoption by any people, anywhere. Consequently, Cooper could declare without any sense of contradiction: 'We ask [for] the right to be fully British. In claiming this we protest with all our might against the discrimination between the full blood and the half caste. All are aboriginals and prefer to be so'.[32] As Britishers and as Aboriginal people, Indigenous Australians were entitled to membership of the nation.

Cooper demanded that Aboriginal people be enabled 'to take our place beside the white race in full equality and responsibility'. The final word warrants comment. Australian scholars have only recently regained attentiveness to the responsibilities of citizenship, after decades of focusing narrowly on rights. Yet Cooper's writings (like those of his contemporaries, Indigenous and non-Indigenous alike) were suffused with the assumption that rights were bonded to responsibilities.[33] As citizens,

Aboriginal people would possess rights; as citizens, they would also have duties and responsibilities to the national community. This was axiomatic to Cooper. Contributing to the development of the land was one such citizen responsibility, and according to Cooper Aboriginal people were exceptionally well fitted to meeting this responsibility in tropical parts of the country. Aboriginal involvement in northern development was an affirmation of their dutifulness as citizens, and consequently a validation of their membership of the nation. Not by equal rights alone, but also through shared duties and responsibilities, would an inclusive nationhood prevail.

Representation and rights

The paramount demand of Cooper and his fellow Aboriginal activists in the 1930s was Aboriginal inclusion in the Australian nation as rights- and responsibilities-bearing citizens. To secure that goal, they recognised that the ideal of legal equality had to be interpreted with sufficient flexibility to take account of Aboriginal people's special circumstances. Cooper argued that, as a disadvantaged minority, Aboriginal people should be entitled to special benefits, namely dedicated representation in the Commonwealth parliament and grants of land. Some historians, such as Bain Attwood, interpret these demands as part of a radical political agenda prefiguring more recent ideologies of distinctive Indigenous rights.[34] To an extent they were — and certainly they were confrontational claims to make in the 1930s. Yet they were confrontational more for the fact that they were made by Aboriginal people than for their intrinsic political content.

There was nothing extraordinary about liberal democracies making special benefits available to specified groups. Numerous precedents could be cited, and in fact were by Aboriginal activists. In Australia, women had access to benefits such as maternity allowances that were not accessible to men; the aged and infirm received pensions that were not available to the young and able-bodied; former military personnel had access to a raft of benefits inaccessible to those who had not served in the forces. These rested on the recognition of differences among the body of citizens, but they were not regarded as conflicting with a principle of equality. Indeed, they were intended to enhance equality and to reinforce the national allegiance of their beneficiaries. In similar fashion, the Aboriginal activists of the 1930s sought special entitlements to help secure a place for Aboriginal people in the Australian nation. The fact that they were unsuccessful, at a time when other groups in Australian society did have access to special entitlements, indicates not the radicalism of their claims but rather the dismissive attitude of governments and public to all things Aboriginal. The special entitlements to land and parliamentary representation sought by these activists were in fact moderate and restrained.

Cooper first advanced his demand for an Aboriginal parliamentary representative in a 1933 petition to King George V. From then until his death in 1941, it held a prominent place in his political program. It was intended, he explained, to give Aboriginal people 'a say in their own destiny', an entitlement that was 'in line with British policy'.[35] However, Cooper allowed that the parliamentary representative could be white. His 1933 petition requested that Aboriginal people be granted 'power to propose a member of parliament in the person of our own Blood, or White man known to have studied our needs and to be in Sympathy with our Race to represent us in the Federal Parliament'.[36] Cooper's clear preference was for the representative to be a 'person of our own Blood', and even if the alternative were pursued, the sympathetic white person would still be selected and elected by Aboriginal voters. But by allowing the alternative, he intimated that the parliamentary member's role was not so much to ensure a distinctive Aboriginal voice in the parliamentary forum as to guarantee a watchful eye over the legislative process.

Cooper was more explicit about the latter role in his exposition of the powers he envisaged for the parliamentary representative. He explained that: 'We only ask for a member with the same status as the Member for the White Population of the [Northern] Territory. We quote this separate representation as a precedent.'[37] The Member for the Northern Territory in the 1930s had no vote in the Commonwealth parliament; his role was to act as watchdog over legislation directly relevant to the Territory. Cooper knew this to be the case, explicitly stating that his proposed member of parliament 'would have no vote'. This he claimed as a virtue, arguing that the voteless representative 'would be the stronger for that fact' because he would be less likely embroiled in party politics and therefore more 'able to watch legislation on the floor of the House, able to speak for the native and to represent native interests'.[38] Although Attwood argues that 'a challenge to Australian sovereignty' was implicit in Cooper's call for parliamentary representation,[39] a demand for a voteless representative in the national parliament seems to fall well short of a challenge to the sovereignty of the state. Cooper had the much more modest ambition of ensuring that

Aboriginal interests were no longer neglected, as they had been ever since the creation of the Commonwealth.

He claimed that if a parliamentary representative were granted, 'the Aboriginal would only have what the Maori now has'.[40] In fact, it was much less than Maori already had. They were represented by four parliamentary members with full voting rights. Despite this precedent and the limited powers Cooper envisaged for the Aboriginal member, his call for parliamentary representation failed. The federal government gave its standard excuse for inactivity: under the Constitution, Aboriginal affairs were a state, not a Commonwealth responsibility, except in the Northern Territory.[41] Cooper's argument by analogy with Maori rights was given short shrift. JA Carrodus, Secretary of the Department of the Interior, stated baldly: 'What has been achieved for the Maoris in New Zealand cannot be done for the Australian aboriginals. The Maori is a much more highly developed native than the aborigine.'[42] So firmly was this hierarchy of natives embedded in white Australian imaginations that Maori people resident in Australia were eligible for many Australian citizenship rights that were denied Australia's own Indigenous people, including the right to vote in federal elections.

Cooper's envisaged parliamentary representation was a distinctive minority entitlement in the service of the more effective inclusion of that minority in the nation. Recognising that Aboriginal people were in certain respects different from other Australians, Cooper sought a means of ensuring that this did not result in their being permanently marginalised or their interests overlooked. His and the Progressive Association's demands for land carried a similar pertinence.

Both the League and the Association forcefully expressed their sense of grievance for unjust dispossession. 'You…took our land away from us by force' and in the process 'almost exterminated our people', Patten and Ferguson declaimed.[43] White Australians were morally obliged to make reparation for this evil, and one way of doing so was by returning some of the land stolen from Aboriginal people. However, Aboriginal people had obligations too, in particular an obligation to use lands returned to them in a modern, efficient manner. In their demands for land, the Aboriginal activists always specified that it would be utilised for modern agricultural or pastoral purposes. Cooper's proposals for Aboriginal involvement in northern development were premised on this assumption. For Aboriginal people across the continent, the League recommended that all lands granted to them 'should be fully developed by the most up-to-date methods under expert direction', and that 'trained and qualified aboriginals be allowed to settle on lands and to work them for their own profit, the ultimate design of all training in settlements being with this independency in mind'.[44] Land grants fitted into a broader vision of Aboriginal independence, but the envisaged independence was along the lines of the national ideal of the independent yeoman farmer.

The Progressive Association was equally prescriptive about land being put to modern agricultural usage with a view to creating independent Aboriginal farmers. It recommended that 'a special policy of land settlement for Aborigines should be put into operation whereby Aborigines who desire to settle on the land should be given the same encouragement as that given to Immigrants or Soldier Settlers, with expert tuition in agriculture, and financial assistance to enable such settlers to become ultimately self-supporting'.[45] On several other occasions, the Association drew parallels between the envisaged land grants for Aboriginal people and the immigrant and soldier-settler schemes, both of which aimed at populating the land with farming families, each cultivating its own small selection.[46]

Aboriginal demands for land in the 1930s were predicated on the special status of Aboriginal people (as the dispossessed original owners) and on their special needs (as an impoverished minority). Land grants were not intended as a means of perpetuating Aboriginal 'difference', but as a means of ensuring their more complete incorporation in the Australian community. Pragmatically, they were to provide Aboriginal people with economic security and material well-being equivalent to that of other Australians. Equally importantly, the specification that Aboriginal landholders would adopt modern methods of agriculture carried the message of the commonalities of settler and Indigenous Australians in their equal potential as productive contributors to the nation.

Citizen soldiers

In their *Citizen Rights* manifesto, Patten and Ferguson reproached white Australians: 'You had no race prejudice against us when you accepted half-castes and full-bloods for enlistment in the AIF [Australia Imperial Force]. We were good enough to fight as Anzacs. We earned equality then. Why do you deny it to us now?'[47] The First AIF may not have been as lacking in racial discrimination, as Patten and Ferguson suggested, but their substantive point was valid: military service earned citizenship — or rather, it should have done so.

3: Aboriginal Activists Demand Acceptance

In early 1938, William Cooper reminded the prime minister that 'at least a thousand Aborigines were among the first to enlist in the defence of the British Empires [sic] in the 1914–18 war…for which Empire they gave their lives'. But this, he bitterly recalled, was 'a thankless task for them, no thanks being given for the valuable services rendered'.[48] As the threat of another war loomed closer the following year, he recalled with more personal bitterness his experience of the First World War:

> I am the father of a soldier who gave his life for his King on the battlefield and thousands of colored men enlisted in the A.I.F. They will doubtless do so again though on their return last time, that is those who survived, were pushed back to the bush to resume the status of aboriginals…the aboriginal now has no status, no rights, no land and, though the native is more loyal to the person of the King and the throne than is the average white he has no country and nothing to fight for…We submit that to put us in the trenches, until we have something to fight for, is not right.

If Aboriginal men enlisted in the armed forces while they continued to be excluded from citizenship, they could be only mercenary-style soldiers akin to 'the native levies of European countries as, for instance, the Senegalese'.[49] Unless they were welcomed into the national community, Cooper maintained, Aboriginal men could not honourably discharge the duty of a citizen to fight in his country's defence.

Early in 1939, Cooper stated that 'the enlistment of natives should be preceded by the removal of all disabilities'.[50] War broke out in September that year. All discriminations had not been removed; Aboriginal people enlisted nonetheless. Claiming military service as grounds for citizenship, Bill Ferguson advised the New South Wales premier in March 1940 that the 'young men of our race are fighting with the armies of the British Empire for democracy, therefore we suggest that your Government must grant our people full democratic rights'.[51] The following year, in an appeal for Aboriginal citizenship broadcast by radio 2GB in Sydney, Aboriginal activist Pearl Gibbs referred several times to the past and present military service of Aboriginal people, including her own son, who as she spoke was 'somewhere on the high seas serving with the Australian Navy'.[52] By fighting and dying for Australia — by fulfilling the duties of the male citizen — Aboriginal soldiers surely earned citizenship for their people. A major difficulty in advancing this claim lay in ensuring recognition of the Aboriginal sacrifice.

Some Aboriginal spokesmen had attempted to deal with this difficulty before the outbreak of war. To ensure recognition of the Aboriginal contribution in the event of war, Jack Patten in 1938 proposed the formation of separate Aboriginal regiments within the Australian army. The Aborigines' League had earlier made a similar suggestion, that an 'Aboriginal citizen corp' be created.⁵³ After the outbreak of war, Ferguson wrote to Prime Minister Menzies:

> In times of National crisis, when the Mother Country is facing the world in a fight for freedom, it behoves every member of the community to join together in the common cause. It is this which urges me to write to you, on behalf of the Aborigines of Australia, requesting that instead of Aborigines enlisting in the AIF that we be allowed to form an Aboriginal Division.⁵⁴

An entire division was well beyond the resources of the Aboriginal population, but Ferguson's point was that distinct Aboriginal units would ensure public and political recognition of the Aboriginal contribution to the war effort. Without that recognition, he and other activists feared that the Aboriginal sacrifice would be ignored, as it had been after the First World War. Distinct Aboriginal units were advocated as a means of promoting a greater inclusiveness.

No such Indigenous military units were created. The closest approximation was the Torres Strait Defence Force, created in 1941. Like the formations advocated by Aboriginal activists, this was a segregated unit, but segregation had consequences other than that of ensuring recognition of military service. It allowed members of the Torres Strait Defence Force to be paid less than soldiers in the regular army, thus fomenting a sense of grievance among Islanders. Also formed were small, irregular Aboriginal units in the Northern Territory, who conducted reconnaissance and were to engage in guerilla action in the event of a Japanese landing. The most famous was Donald Thomson's Special Reconnaissance Unit in eastern Arnhem Land, formed in early 1942, although there were similar units on Bathurst and Melville Islands and on the Cox Peninsula. However, the men in these units were not formally enlisted in the army, received no pay, and the existence of the units was, as far as possible, kept secret until after the war.⁵⁵ They were a far cry from the type of unit Patten and Ferguson advocated to secure recognition of Aboriginal military service.

Not only did the authorities fail to create distinct Aboriginal units; they obstructed the enlistment of Aboriginal people into the regular armed forces. Enlistment was formally open only to persons 'substantially of European descent', a provision that was interpreted flexibly and inconsistently.[56] Especially as the Japanese threat loomed closer, military authorities became less fussy about the racial background of recruits — and many people of mixed ancestry were, in any case, substantially of European descent. Robert Hall estimates that by the end of the war, over three thousand Aboriginal and Torres Strait Islander people had enlisted in the armed forces.[57] Motives for enlistment were doubtless as varied for them as for white recruits, but the fact that so many did enlist despite official obstruction suggests a sense of commitment to the Australian nation.

The federal government's obstructions to Aboriginal enlistment indicate its reluctance to bring Aboriginal people into the national community. From a global perspective, military service has played a prominent role in nation-building, by disseminating the values, loyalties and symbols of the nation; at the same time, it has brought together people from throughout the national territory into units committed to advancing the national interest.[58] In the Second World War, the Australian military could have fulfilled such a role in the national incorporation of Aboriginal people, but the authorities inhibited it from doing so. Restrictions on Aboriginal enlistment may have derived partly from misgivings about the acceptability of black soldiers to their white comrades, particularly in the event of the former being raised to officer status. The long-standing reluctance of the federal government to get involved in Aboriginal affairs was probably also a factor. But it seems likely that the government and senior military authorities were apprehensive about Aboriginal enlistment for the very reason that activists encouraged it: Aboriginal military service might unleash irresistible demands for Aboriginal citizenship.

Governmental reluctance to grant Aboriginal citizenship provoked Cooper to call into question the sincerity of Australia's commitment to the democratic principles for which the war ostensibly was being fought. In August 1940, he wrote to Prime Minister Menzies:

> If Australia is sincere in her stand for democracy and her desire to free the peoples of other lands from the oppression of Hitlerism, her sincerity will be shown by the attitude she adopts towards her own exploited minority. Lip service to democracy and Christianity is not enough. 'By their fruits ye shall know them.'[59]

This was one of the last — possibly the very last — of Cooper's many letters to public figures. His disillusionment with the political process in which he had participated, and which he had sought to reform, is palpable. He died six months later.

At the end of the war, Cooper's cousin Shadrach James, who had collaborated with the older man in some of his campaigns, wrote two long letters to Prime Minister Chifley. In them, he set out a program for 'the amelioration of the condition of our people' along the lines the League had consistently enjoined: Aboriginal representation in the Commonwealth parliament; federal control of Aboriginal affairs; provision of education and training; uplift of uncivilised people, preferably by their educated compatriots; and citizen rights for all civilised Aboriginal people. James buttressed his arguments with frequent references to the Aboriginal sacrifice and comradeship with whites in wartime: 'our boys fought side by side with the white boys of Australia and some paid the supreme sacrifice'; 'they fought and died with their comrades'. Surely, he entreated, Aboriginal people had earned their citizenship and demonstrated their capacity to be productive and responsible members of the Australian community. In words that encapsulate the aspirations of the Aboriginal activists of the 1930s, James affirmed that: 'We are anxious to join you in the march to progress and to nationhood.'[60]

Chapter 4

Restricted Reconstruction

During the Second World War, Aboriginal activists were not alone in demanding the extension of citizen rights to Aboriginal people. In 1940, the impeccably conservative Returned Sailors', Soldiers' and Airmen's Imperial League of Australia (RSSAILA) urged Prime Minister Menzies to grant 'full citizen rights' to 'all aborigines who have served overseas in His Majesty's Forces'.[1] This was an assertion of its own members' interests, not a call for Aboriginal citizenship in general, but the RSSAILA clearly appreciated the moral claims on the nation won by military service. The even more conservative British Empire Union in Australia framed its plea for Aboriginal rights as an ethical and religious imperative. In a 1940 letter to Menzies, MF King, founder and editor of the Union's journal, *The Practical Patriot*, depicted the war as a global struggle of good against evil and warned that 'supernatural help from a righteous God cannot be expected by individuals or nations whose actions are inconsistent with righteousness'. Excluding Aboriginal people from the franchise and other citizen rights was unrighteous, he declared, and must be rectified by granting these rights to all 'educated aborigines'. Thereby, the nation would be reconciled with God and Australia would 'merit the help of the Great Father'.[2]

Such pleas fell on deaf ears. Wartime governments did little to extend the rights and status of Aboriginal people. As noted in the previous chapter, they even maintained restrictions on Aboriginal enlistment, partly to obstruct attempts to use military service as a lever in the struggle for Aboriginal citizenship. Yet many Aboriginal people did serve, and once in the forces the camaraderie of soldiering prevailed over distinctions of race. Military historian Robert Hall found that, especially among servicemen who interacted with Indigenous members of their units on a day-to-day basis, there was a remarkable level of acceptance and accommodation.[3]

Like all combatant nations, Australia mobilised its civilian population for total war. This extended to the Aboriginal population, especially in the Northern Territory where there was virtually no alternative labour supply and military labour demands were high due to its proximity to major theatres of battle. There, the military authorities found that by providing decent standards of pay, rations, housing and hygiene, they could rely on Aboriginal people as effective and efficient workers. The lesson was not lost on lobbyists for Aboriginal welfare, several of whom praised the army labour camps not only for their physical facilities but also for engaging Aboriginal people in meaningful, socially valued projects. The demands of war, they suggested, raised both the standard of living and the expectations of Aboriginal people.[4]

Robert Hall shows that the wartime roles of Aboriginal people, as both military personnel and civilian workers, induced more positive white Australian attitudes towards them. His study also suggests that the attitudinal shifts were somewhat shallow. At the end of the war, Elkin complained that the Australian authorities were still failing to acknowledge Aboriginal contributions to the war effort, and thereby their claims on the nation:

> One opportunity has already been missed, namely the sending of at least two of the Aboriginal returned soldiers to London with the other Australian soldiers to take part in the Victory celebrations. Why must we shut our eyes to the fact that Australia is the Aborigines' country, that they served in our war, and that they are citizens? Don't we want to admit in England that White Australia includes dark-skinned, in particular Aborigines of mixed-blood? To have included Aboriginal representatives in this contingent… would have increased the Aborigines' prestige and self-respect.

While Elkin insisted that Australians must accept Aboriginal people into the national community, he cautioned that acceptance 'does not mean that they will become just as we are…Rather, they will add another variation to our present varieties'.[5]

In December 1942, long before the end of the war or even assurance of victory, the federal Labor government set up a Department of Post War Reconstruction. Already, this government had extended its controls over banking, taxation, industry and development, and the new department flagged its intention to continue these interventions into peacetime. Aboriginal affairs did not come within the ambit of the Department of Post War Reconstruction and its director, HC Coombs, at this time showed only passing interest in Aboriginal welfare. When he did, in response to representations from Shadrach James, he supported James' proposals for Aboriginal citizenship. Coombs maintained that the Commonwealth government had 'a real moral responsibility' for Aboriginal people and recommended the creation of a Commonwealth Bureau of Aboriginal Affairs.[6] His recommendation was not acted upon, however, and Coombs seems not to have pursued the matter.

Although the Department of Post War Reconstruction made no innovations in Aboriginal affairs, shortly after the war the Australian nation changed in ways conducive to a greater inclusiveness of Aboriginal people. Advances in their legal status were slight, but the changes examined in this chapter provided the foundations for later, more substantial, moves toward Aboriginal inclusion. The chapter surveys, in turn, the changing international order under the auspices of the United Nations (UN); Australia's revised immigrant intake and growing misgivings about the white Australia policy; the citizenship advocacy of the anthropologist AP Elkin; and the increasing — albeit constrained — appreciation of Aboriginal people and Aboriginality in the immediate postwar years.

Postwar world order

Shortly after the defeat of Germany, the United Nations Organisation was created to ensure world peace and security. Australia was among the founding members and its Minister for External Affairs, HV Evatt, played a major role in drafting the UN Charter. He sat on several UN councils and committees, and between September 1948 and May 1949, he was president of its General Assembly. Far more ambitious in scope than its predecessor, the League of Nations, the United Nations assumed responsibility for, among other things, the promotion of human rights.

On 10 December 1948, the General Assembly of the United Nations (with Evatt presiding) formally adopted the Universal Declaration of Human Rights. This Declaration inaugurated a new era in which human rights — though far from universally observed — assumed unprecedented significance as the criteria by which the actions (or inaction) of states could be judged. The Declaration specified, more explicitly than any previous document, that freedoms and rights were matters of international rather than purely domestic concern. The rights it protected were individual, with the Declaration making no reference to group rights of any kind. In the early drafting stage of the Declaration, a minority rights clause had been introduced, but it was progressively watered down and ultimately rejected, apparently on the grounds propounded by Eleanor Roosevelt, that 'the best solution of the problem of minorities was to encourage respect for human rights'.[7] The Declaration discountenanced discrimination on the basis of race, sex, language and religion.

In the aftermath of the Holocaust, race carried exceptional significance. The United Nations Educational, Scientific, and Cultural Organization (UNESCO) launched a coordinated campaign against racism, issuing its first 'Statement on race' in July 1950 after extensive consultation among anthropologists, sociologists, biologists and geneticists. This statement proclaimed that for 'all practical social purposes "race" is not so much a biological phenomenon as a social myth', and that in view of the suffering inflicted in its name it would be best 'to drop the term "race" altogether and speak of ethnic groups'. UNESCO issued additional statements on race in 1951, 1964 and 1967, as well as numerous other publications explaining why doctrines of racial inequality lacked scientific foundation. They stressed the oneness of the human species and the superficiality of the differences among the world's peoples. Early UNESCO statements on race offered no guidance on how people or governments should deal with the facts of cultural differences other than, implicitly, to pay them little heed; UNESCO's aim, after all, was to combat racism of the kind that had inspired the murder of millions of Jews, Roma and other European minorities. Not until the fourth (1967) statement was there explicit recognition of the need to encourage ethnic groups to preserve their own 'cultural values'.[8] Other UNESCO publications dealt with the issue of cultural diversity much earlier, but its 1950, 1951 and 1964 statements on race could be taken to mean that human diversity was inconsequential.

Shortly after the war, the European overseas empires began to crumble. The United Nations did not initiate the process, but it did attempt to establish a framework within which decolonisation could proceed with a minimum of discord and bloodshed. A key concept was self-determination, interpreted by the United Nations as a right to sovereign statehood for people currently under foreign domination.[9] The UN stance on decolonisation and self-determination was formalised in its

1960 'Declaration on the granting of independence to colonial countries and peoples', which stated that: 'All peoples have the right to self-determination; by virtue of that right they freely determine their political status and freely pursue their economic, social and cultural development.' However, the declaration also affirmed that: 'Any attempt aimed at the partial or total disruption of the national unity and the territorial integrity of a country is incompatible with the purposes and principles of the Charter of the United Nations.'[10] In other words, self-determination must occur within already-established territorial boundaries, which in the case of colonies were the boundaries drawn by the colonising powers. Consequently, numerous ethnic and religious minorities who had been included in a colonial territory were now obliged, with the withdrawal of the colonial power, to become citizens of independent states dominated by other groups; such was the fate of the Ewe in Ghana, the Ibo in Nigeria and myriad others throughout Africa and Asia.

Unsurprisingly, the United Nations' enthusiasm for decolonisation and self-determination did not extend to the indigenous peoples of settler-colonial states such as Australia. Indeed, UN documents in the 1940s, 1950s and 1960s referred not to 'indigenous peoples' but to 'indigenous populations', to avoid the implication of a right to self-determination that attached to the term 'peoples'. The future envisioned by the United Nations for indigenous populations was very different from the one it upheld for colonised peoples. Until the late 1960s, the arm of the United Nations most concerned with indigenous populations, the International Labour Organisation (ILO), promoted policies of assimilation. Firmly committed to setting primitive peoples on the pathway of progress, the ILO regarded their incorporation into the national life-ways of their encompassing states as the appropriate means to attain this end.[11] Only via assimilation could indigenous peoples be raised to a standard of education, employment and material well-being commensurate with their survival in the modern world. According to human rights scholar Chris Tennant, 'the self-confident and enthusiastic project of the International Labour Organisation...in the 1940s, 1950s, and 1960s [was] to help indigenous peoples develop out of their miserable lives and into the modern world'.[12] The fact that the organisation pushing this line was a leading international champion of human rights and a vigorous opponent of racism might remind us of the instability of these concepts.

The fact that the ILO espoused assimilation and the elevation of primitive peoples into modernity does not, however, mean that it sanctioned any and every strategy aimed at those ends. Assimilation and progress were to be achieved by means compatible with other UN ideals concerning human rights and respect for human dignity. Reconciling these objectives and ideals was not always easy. International protocols on rights, propounded by different bodies for diverse purposes in varied contexts, were not always consonant with each other.[13] In expressing commitment to Aboriginal assimilation, postwar Australian governments were in accord with UN principles. However, the specific actions these governments took — or perhaps more often failed to take — were frequently inconsistent with UN precepts on human rights. In particular, as subsequent chapters show, even as Australian governments became increasingly vocal about their commitment to assimilation, they were remarkably sluggish in abolishing the discriminatory laws and practices that impeded its achievement and violated UN ideals.

Challenging white Australia

The Second World War impressed upon Australians the imperative to 'populate or perish'. Driven by revivified anxieties, Australian governments relinquished their earlier fixation on immigration from Britain and sought immigrants from further afield. The change was neither painless nor planned. In 1946, Labor Minister for Immigration Arthur Calwell expressed his 'hope that for every foreign migrant there will be 10 people from the United Kingdom'[14] — a formulation counterposing the 'foreign migrant' to the British migrant, which is nonsensical outside the composite British-Australian nationalism that had prevailed since Federation. He was forced to abandon this hope, and Australia turned not only to Northern but increasingly to Southern Europe for its immigrant intake. In the 1950s, for the first time, continental European immigrants outnumbered those from Britain.

Initially, however, there was no relaxation on the prohibition on Asian immigrants. So zealous was the Labor government in enforcing the white Australia policy that immediately after the war it tried to deport every Asian refugee who had come to Australia, including those who were British subjects, had spouses and children in Australia, and had served in the Allied forces against the Japanese. The white Australia policy held the approval of most Australians, but such heavy-handedness provoked both domestic disquiet and international condemnation. The Menzies government that came to power in 1949 moderated the hard-line stance of its Labor predecessor, allowing some 1700 Asian refugees and spouses of Australian military personnel to remain in Australia. This was partly a humanitarian gesture and partly an expedient to ensure the long-term viability of the racially restrictive immigration program by making its administration a little more flexible. It was not intended as a repudiation of the broad principle of excluding Asians and other 'coloured aliens'.[15] Nonetheless, admission of these Asian refugees as permanent residents represented, in Andrew Markus's words, 'the most significant challenge to the racially exclusive immigration policy since its implementation in 1901'.[16]

By the mid-1940s, some reformers were calling for a more thorough overhaul of Australia's immigration program. No one advocated an open-door policy or the mass immigration of Asians; reformers sought the relaxation, not abandonment, of immigration restrictions. However, some sectors of the Australian community clearly appreciated that the old order of blanket racial exclusions must be replaced by something more in tune with contemporary international standards.[17] The 'White Australia policy...must go!' proclaimed the Reverend Alan Walker in 1946, since it 'has heightened our intolerance and exaggerated our isolation'. Despite his condemnation of Australian 'racialism', however, Walker's tract made no mention of Aboriginal people.[18] For him, as for almost all commentators of the day, 'white Australia' referred to an immigration policy. Aboriginal affairs were important to many of the same commentators, but that belonged under a different heading.

In 1945, Elkin argued that 'rethinking the White Australia policy' was long overdue, since the policy had ossified into an emotionally charged dogma which Australians were unwilling to subject to rational inquiry. Unlike most contemporary commentators, Elkin did refer to Aboriginal people, assuring his readers that 'the Aborigines, both full-blood and mixed-blood, can attain the stature of full citizenship and make a valuable contribution to the development of Australia'.[19] He also suggested that successful inclusion of Aboriginal people in the national community depended on white Australians' willingness to accept coloured people more generally, including those from Asia.

Two years later, Elkin published another article asking 'Is white Australia doomed?' The 'slogan "White Australia",' he proclaimed, 'seems like an echo, as from a parrot shut in a cage back in the "1880s" — and it doesn't make sense.' He urged that whiteness be abandoned as a badge of nationhood and that the Australian nation imagine itself not as 'a defensive outpost of white culture in an Oriental world, but a co-operative unit in a world team...which will function only on a basis of equality and mutual respect and reciprocal economic and cultural relations'. He again raised the Aboriginal issue, recommending that:

> If we take all the necessary administrative methods for giving them a rightful place as citizens and a positive share in whatever development our north and centre are capable of, we will not only save them, but will gain prestige in the eyes of the world in general, and of the coloured people in particular. This is a great opportunity, let us seize it. The result may not be a 100 per cent white skin colour; but Australia is not all-white now. It will, however, be an Australia which has compensated the remnant of its original owners for the fate of the majority.[20]

In a May 1953 'Mission to the nation' program, broadcast over a net-work of sixty-two radio stations, the Reverend Alan Walker again attacked Australian 'racialism'. Unlike his 1946 tract, this broadcast spanned Aboriginal and immigrant issues. 'Australia's treatment of the aboriginal formed the darkest chapter of the nation's history', while the 'so-called White Australia Policy is...an offence to Asia'. Both areas demanded urgent reform — and both, Walker suggested, were connected.[21] Increasingly, commentators were coming to realise the mutually reinforcing character of racial attitudes in the domains of immigration and Aboriginal affairs.

By the time Walker made his 1953 broadcast, a trickle of Asian immigration was legally entering Australia. Markus estimates the number of Asian immigrants at 250 for each year of the 1950s, adding that precise numbers are unavailable since the government preferred to keep the matter hidden from view.[22] Asian immigration, it seems, was too controversial for governments to publicly acknowledge even the minuscule level it allowed.

There was no attempt to conceal the massive intake of continental European immigrants. Governments advertised the fact and embarked on propaganda campaigns to cultivate among resident Australians a welcoming attitude towards immigrants. With diversified immigration came cultural diversity. The governmental response was assimilation. Sometimes, immigrant assimilation was represented as a process of continental

Europeans becoming British in values and outlook. More usually, however, immigrants were entreated to adopt 'the Australian way of life', a new term of the postwar era that signalled a distinctively Australian national character.[23] By identifying the essence of Australianness in a 'way of life', it also signified a shift away from an ethnic towards a more civically orientated nationalism. The shift was hesitant and partial, but a 'way of life' — potentially capable of adoption by people of any ethnic background — offered a more open conception of Australian nationhood.

Postwar policy for immigrants had the same label as Aboriginal policy, and shared the same broad objective of national incorporation. Yet the practices of assimilation for the two groups differed greatly, to the extent that Tim Rowse characterises them as 'two parallel projects of nation-building'.[24] No one suggested that new arrivals from Greece should be declared wards of the state until they qualified for citizenship; no one suggested that Italian children might better assimilate by being removed from their families. Yet these practices were pursued in the name of Aboriginal assimilation. In part, the difference derived from the perceived magnitude of the cultural gulf between Aboriginal and white Australians, as against a much smaller cultural gap between the latter and European immigrants; in part, it was pragmatic — Australia could never advertise its desirability as a migrant destination if it treated migrants on arrival as it did its Indigenous people. Beyond those, the differences between Aboriginal and immigrant assimilation programs were symptomatic of the long-entrenched assumption of Aboriginal incompetence. Immigrants, it was assumed, needed encouragement to assimilate; Aboriginal people had to be coerced.

From the outset, there was a diversity of expectations on immigrant assimilation. Some hard-liners demanded total conformity to the Australian way of life, but many took a softer line. In 1951, Governor-General McKell explained that:

> By a wise handling of assimilation our migrants will not only conform to our standards of citizenship, but will add their own contribution. There will be give and take; assimilation will be a two-way process, demanding much of both the migrants and ourselves, and the result will be mutual enrichment. For the migrants are bringing to Australia not only the benefits of their knowledge and skills, but of their age-old cultures. The new and old should blend into a more varied community of people.[25]

The demographer WD Borrie observed in 1953 that there were 'many definitions of the term Assimilation, but essentially they add up to a process of immigrants and the local population merging together'. 'This does not,' he emphasised, 'necessarily mean that the two groups must be entirely alike, but rather that there should not exist between them differences which will prevent immigrants from participating in the economic, social and cultural life of their country of adoption on a basis of equality'. It was a process involving 'the gradual narrowing down of the differences between migrant and native groups', and this narrowing entailed changes in both immigrant and host societies and cultures. 'Nevertheless,' Borrie continued, 'the interaction between the immigrants and the indigenous population seldom results in complete uniformity of culture'.[26] As Chapter 6 shows, similarly open versions of Aboriginal assimilation were advocated, alongside others demanding the virtual obliteration of Aboriginality.

The European immigration program was intended to preserve the white Australia ideal, but due to its multi-ethnic makeup and greater emphasis on the individual suitability of the immigrant, it had the unintended consequence of undermining that ideal.[27] As the Director of Postwar Reconstruction, HC Coombs, later observed, the diverse European immigrant intake 'paved the way for the abandonment of the racist White Australia Policy'.[28] With more immigrants coming from continental Europe than from the traditional British source, white Australia could no longer be equated with British Australia. Change was slow, but the old equation had to give way in the face of hundreds of thousands of Italians, Greeks, Yugoslavs, Germans, Poles, Estonians and other Europeans. Effectively, the postwar immigration program hollowed out the ethnic core of white Australian nationalism. Without that core of Britishness, the white Australia ideal was flaccid and flabby, gradually deflating over the decades after the Second World War.

An anthropologist discovers citizenship

In 1944 Elkin published a 109-page tract, *Citizenship for the Aborigines*. It was very different to the 1931 policy statement that had first impelled him into public prominence. It expounded, in greater detail than any other work yet published, a set of objectives and strategies to ensure that Aboriginal people 'become an integral part of our own Australian life'. 'The aim,' Elkin declared, 'must be full citizenship, with all its rights, privileges and responsibilities — for *all* persons of Aboriginal descent'.[29]

Despite his italics, Elkin believed that not all Aboriginal people were yet ready to exercise those rights, privileges and responsibilities: different groups were at different stages along the pathway of progress. He divided the Aboriginal population into three broad groups: those in 'isolated regions', in 'marginal or frontier regions' and in 'thickly settled regions'. Most Aboriginal people in the thickly settled regions he considered eligible for immediate citizenship, while those in the isolated and marginal regions would have to undergo tuition before attaining that status.

Elkin listed ten 'general principles' that should guide Aboriginal policy. The first was that 'Group — or community — life is of fundamental importance to persons of Aboriginal descent'. This principle applied 'whether the region be isolated, marginal, or closely settled; whether the Aborigines be full-blood or mixed-blood and even of lighter caste'.[30] It was a principle Elkin never tired of reiterating throughout his innumerable publications, addresses, letters and appeals. From his anthropological perspective, all people needed a strong sense of collective belonging, but this was exceptionally important for Aboriginal people because for too long their social groups had been denigrated and despoiled, and because group membership provided the only secure vessel in which to navigate the hazards of social and cultural transformation. 'In the time of transition,' he had earlier written, 'let us safeguard for them their ties to the past, to the land, to one another, and to the "eternal dream-time"'.[31]

Another of Elkin's vital principles was cultural continuity. Sociocultural change was essential for Aboriginal survival and well-being, he maintained, but such change must come incrementally, articulating closely with established tradition, since 'preservation and progress depend on continuity with the past'.[32] Any attempt to sever ties with the past carried 'the almost certain risk of utter disintegration', which could be averted only 'if the change comes slowly, and, whatever be its source, is brought about from within, so that institutions may be evolved to express adequately the changed ideas'.[33] Persistently reiterating these themes, Elkin sounds at times like a latter-day Edmund Burke, venerating tradition and the collectivity as a community of destiny.[34] From this impeccably conservative perspective, Elkin insisted that Aboriginal advancement must come by building upon, not tearing down, the Indigenous cultural heritage.

In his 1944 book *Citizenship for the Aborigines*, Elkin gave eloquent expression to these precepts. 'Change and contact,' he proclaimed, 'must come':

> But it should be so organized or approached that the Aborigines will not lose their 'dreaming' without building in its place, probably on its foundation, another view of life and another sanction for behaviour, which will keep their personalities integrated (their souls healthy or 'saved') and which will prevent them from lapsing into a condition of moral apathy and 'lawlessness'. This process, being intellectual and emotional, individual and social, is not easy. It cannot be accomplished by a fiat: 'your old view is outmoded, here is a new one — a new philosophy, a new religion!' It must be worked out slowly by them as a group, and in the long run (certainly in the isolated and most of the marginal regions) it will be an Aboriginal version of the European view of life and religion.[35]

The frequent religious references are typical, since Elkin regarded religion as the social mortar that bound a community together. Religion, he explained, was 'a matter of cultural heritage...for what is at stake is not simply individual salvation, but national or tribal continuity'.[36]

Elkin expounded his ideas on progress and cultural preservation in a 1949 UNESCO book on human rights. It was a 'basic right of primitive man' to have access 'to world thought, science, technical achievement, literature and religion, to be used and built into their own changing culture as they find possible'. Another '*basic right of primitive man*', according to Elkin, was '*to be civilised according to the pattern which he will develop* — to each separate people its own pattern — but fitting into the general pattern of human values and rights on the world scale, with its economic and cultural relationships'.[37] In this chapter on human rights — indeed, throughout his writings on Aboriginal affairs — Elkin grappled with the tension between two divergent principles: on the one hand, a universal human right to progress in civilisation; on the other, the right of each group to maintain its cultural particularity. He conceived progress in essentially Enlightenment terms as the unfolding of a universal human potential for improvement. Within this overarching process, however, particular groups found their own way forward according to their own cultural scripts and predilections. Progress was a universal imperative, he believed, but the resilience of human cultures ensured that diversity would endure.

In his *Citizenship* book, Elkin asserted the duty of white Australians to help Aboriginal people into civilisation and citizenship. He also implored them to abandon the 'colour prejudice' and exclusionary practices that kept Aboriginal people outside the national community. White Australians, he urged, should drop their 'attitude of superiority and condescension', recognise Aboriginal people as in certain respects distinctive, but 'make no more of that fact than we do of the differences which exist between the various social and economic groups in the general community'.[38]

Citizenship for the Aborigines drew praise from Indigenous as well as non-Indigenous Australians. Shadrach James congratulated Elkin, affirming that his own views 'were very much the same' as Elkin's, and that 'there is only one way to solve the problem of the Aborigines, and that is by the methods set down in the book'. Nonetheless, James pointed out that the professor had neglected one vital strategy: that of educated Aboriginal people acting as the principal mediators in bringing civilisation to their people.[39] As much as activists like James esteemed the civilising mission, they were frustrated by white reformers' inattentiveness to their demand that Aboriginal people themselves be primary agents in the civilising process.

Bill Ferguson offered a more barbed compliment. Immediately after publication of the *Citizenship* book, the activist congratulated Elkin for being 'now in favour of Full Citizenship Rights to all Aborigines'. Evidently peeved, Elkin responded: 'I have never advocated anything other than full citizenship rights to all Aborigines.'[40] Perhaps he believed that in his earlier pleas for Aboriginal advancement and acceptance, he had effectively been advocating their citizenship. Or, more likely, he was merely trying to save face with Ferguson. In Elkin's published and unpublished writings, he almost never used the word 'citizenship' until around 1938; from then until 1944, he used the word sparingly — usually with specific reference to the Aboriginal people of New South Wales. Years later, he acknowledged that 'I didn't write re citizenship till 1944'.[41] From that time onward, 'citizenship' became one of the most commonly used words in his lexicon.

Elkin's use of the term 'assimilation' followed a similar trajectory. Although in the 1950s he became a leading exponent of assimilation, in the 1930s he almost never used the word. On several occasions in the 1950s and 1960s he recalled that

> those of us who were working in the 1930s for change of attitudes and policies in the Northern Territory and in the northern and central regions generally did not give a thought to assimilation

or integration. I certainly did not. My aim was to prevent the extinction of the full-bloods, which was said to be inevitable, and to ensure their social and economic progress, which was said to be impossible.[42]

Well into the 1940s, Elkin's usage of 'assimilation' was infrequent and restricted to specific contexts. In his 1944 *Citizenship* book, for example, he used the word only in relation to Aboriginal people in the 'thickly settled regions'. For those in the 'isolated' and 'marginal' regions, full citizenship was the goal; however, he did not refer to the means by which it would be attained as 'assimilation'.[43] Although the entire book was about the process Elkin would later call 'assimilation', the word appears only occasionally in its 109 pages. He was careful to specify that by 'assimilation' he meant inclusion in 'our economic and general social life. It does not mean advocacy of inter-marriage.'[44] However, he did not use 'assimilation' as a term of general applicability until the early 1950s, and then it was in response to broader usage of the word that had been initiated by others, notably the Commonwealth Minister for Territories, Paul Hasluck.[45]

In the 1940s, Elkin not only wrote about Aboriginal citizenship; he also got involved in campaigns to extend their civil rights, particularly their entitlement to the federal franchise. Campaigners advanced two major lines of argument.[46] One was for a more liberal interpretation of section 41 of the Constitution which, as noted in the prologue, was construed so as to enfranchise only those Aboriginal individuals who were on the state rolls in 1902. By the 1940s, few were still living. Since first learning of this restrictive interpretation of section 41, Elkin had questioned its validity, advising JA Carrodus, Secretary of the Department of the Interior, that in his opinion 'the Electoral Administration has been acting unconstitutionally' by constricting rights under section 41 in this manner.[47] The other line of argument for an expanded Aboriginal franchise was for the vote to be granted to all Aboriginal people judged to be educated or civilised.

Immediately after the war, the federal government expressed interest in the second option — that is, enfranchising all Aboriginal people who met a prescribed standard of literacy, numeracy and good character. Since Aboriginal affairs were a state responsibility, however, determination of who met these standards would have to be made in cooperation with state authorities. The two states that excluded full-bloods from the franchise (Queensland and Western Australia) refused to cooperate.[48] Consequently, the federal government defaulted to the line of least resistance, its

Commonwealth Electoral Act 1949 extending the Commonwealth franchise to all Aboriginal people entitled to vote at the state level. This would have been unnecessary had section 41 been interpreted more liberally from the outset, for the 1949 act merely brought Commonwealth voting entitlements into line with what was always a legally defensible interpretation of the Constitution. The Act also guaranteed the franchise, permanently and unconditionally, to all Aboriginal persons who had served or were serving in the military. Initially, this was to have been qualified by a proviso that debarred from the franchise those Aboriginal former servicemen whose discharge was due to misconduct. The proviso was dropped after representations from Elkin.[49]

Appreciating the Aboriginal

In November 1948, the Arrernte artist Albert Namatjira held his most successful exhibition so far, selling forty-six of his watercolours for a total of £1519.[50] His career as an artist had begun ten years earlier, and over the intervening years he had held major exhibitions in Melbourne, Adelaide, Sydney, Perth, Brisbane and Alice Springs; he had also been the subject of a book, *The Art of Albert Namatjira* (1944), and a film, *Namatjira the Painter* (1947). In the mid-twentieth century, no Aboriginal person had a public profile higher than Namatjira's. Reproductions of his watercolour renditions of his ancestral lands in central Australia hung in lounge-rooms around the nation. The suburban home-owners may not have understood Namatjira's spiritual affiliations to the lands he painted, but they did appreciate the beauty of the central Australian landscapes he depicted. Appreciation of these landscapes was itself quite new, having been pioneered as recently as the 1920s by the South Australian artist, Hans Heysen. From those beginnings, the arid centre came to occupy a prominent place in Australia's national iconography, and the desert began to be celebrated as an emblematic landscape of Australia.[51] Namatjira and other Arrernte artists, loosely grouped as the Hermannsburg school, were among the leading figures who cultivated an aesthetic appreciation of aridity and a nationalist attachment to the dry centre of the continent among mid-twentieth-century Australians (see Plate 4).

Namatjira's paintings were popularly celebrated not only for their aesthetic quality but also for showing the ability of an Aboriginal man to master Western artistic media. Some members of the contemporary cognoscenti were critical, even dismissive, of Namatjira's art for precisely that reason.

The director of the National Museum of Victoria, for example, regretted 'that an aborigine was producing a secondhand version of European art instead of developing his own native art'.[52] More recent studies demonstrate the fallacy of such assessments, showing that Namatjira's art was part of a series of complex engagements between himself and his Arrernte people on the one hand, and the Lutheran missionaries of Hermannsburg and the wider Australian society on the other.[53] During the artist's lifetime, commentators seem to have underestimated the extent to which Namatjira's art was embedded in his traditional Arrernte culture, but they were not completely blind to it. The linguist TGH Strehlow, one of Namatjira's strongest supporters, noted that his art was 'in close harmony with ancient Aranda mythological tales', and that his choice of scenes such as Mount Sonder, Mount Zeil and the Finke Gorge 'was undoubtedly based not merely on the natural beauty of these landscape features, but also on their mythological significance in the Western Aranda traditions'.[54] Strehlow found 'the same kind of distinctive Aranda feeling for balance, love of repetition and design, and sure sense of rhythm, that give such glorious vitality to their best verse' in the works of another Hermannsburg artist, Otto Pareroultja.[55]

Nonetheless, it was as an Aboriginal practitioner of a Western art form that Namatjira was praised (and deprecated). Strehlow, among others, celebrated his achievement for its impact on popular attitudes, noting that his success contained

> a grudging admission that a member of a race which had been regarded without scientific grounds for over one hundred and fifty years as genetically incapable of learning European techniques had unexpectedly acquired mastery of one of these techniques to such an amazing degree that his work had become virtually indistinguishable from that of a white artist. Albert Namatjira, in short, is one of those gifted aborigines who has destroyed the myth of the constitutional incapacity of the Australian native to learn and apply methods learnt from Europeans.[56]

Elkin, who opened Namatjira's successful 1945 exhibition, argued similarly that 'Namatjira's artistic success, so widely acclaimed, and so financially successful, should go far to establish sincere respect for the Aborigines, as human beings of like talents to our own, and to give them confidence in their efforts to become full citizens of Australia'. He ridiculed those critics who expected an Aboriginal artist to produce only primitive art, and lauded Namatjira for showing that Aboriginal people 'can do beautiful things in our way, a way which they can make their own'.[57]

In 1952, Mary Durack Miller claimed that Namatjira 'has probably done more, through his work, than any other individual to bring about a change of heart and attitude towards his people'. She sought to extend his achievement by publicising the artistic accomplishments of a group of Aboriginal children from Carrolup Native Settlement in Western Australia as a means of encouraging Aboriginal social acceptance more generally. Durack's efforts went hand in hand with an uncompromising assimilationism: 'The future of the aboriginal lies in assimilation into our society and in the opportunity to regain, in a different way, the happiness, well-being, and sense of *belonging to the land* that were lost to him after the coming of the white man.' In Durack's view, the Indigenous social and cultural order had completely collapsed, leaving no alternative to an assimilation so rigorous as to entail even the repudiation of Indigenous artistic styles.[58]

Durack dismissed the 'idealists who believed that the aborigines might well keep the best of their own culture, blending it with the best of ours'. Aboriginal culture was an integrated totality, she insisted, 'an intricate mosaic of meaning only in its entirety'; it could not be combined bit by bit with other cultures. Aboriginal people themselves realised this, she claimed:

> 'Black-fellow humbug!' the modern native remarks, with a disparaging gesture towards a rock-face resplendent with stylized godmen and culture heroes of the time long past that were to his ancestors the mainspring of life and religious inspiration. The modern aboriginal, in fact, regards the art of his forefathers rather as a snake regards its cast-off skin. He has grown out of it, and it is to him of no further use or interest.

Aboriginal artistic advancement, she argued, would not come as 'a *further development* of his own art or even a new and interesting culture fusion'. It was not the Aboriginal but the white artist, 'delighting in aboriginal design, often attracted also to the philosophy as reflected in the work, who effects the fusion of cultures'. She conceded that in the distant future some Aboriginal artist may be able to effect that cultural fusion, but not until 'he has come round full cycle to look upon the religious symbols of his past with the eyes of a white man'.⁵⁹ Aboriginal people, in Durack's view, were as yet unable to appreciate cultural traditions in the distanced, objectified manner of white people, and until they could their artistic expression was best confined to emulation. She considered Namatjira an excellent exponent of this.

Despite Durack's dismissal of traditional Aboriginal art, an increasing quantity of that art was being exhibited in galleries. In 1941, the David Jones Art Gallery in Sydney mounted an exhibition that included traditional Aboriginal artworks alongside works by Western artists influenced by Aboriginal design. This exhibition owed much to Margaret Preston, as did the inclusion of Aboriginal artworks in a collection of Australian art that toured the United States and Canada in 1941–42, the first time such works had been exhibited outside Australia as art rather than as ethnographic artefacts. Melbourne hosted a major exhibition of primitive art, including Aboriginal works, in 1943, while the David Jones Gallery exhibited a collection of Arnhem Land art, collected by Catherine and Ronald Berndt, in 1949.⁶⁰

Analysis of Aboriginal art in the 1940s was dominated by anthropologists, who tended to focus on its significance in the traditional sociocultural order, but art critics increasingly were drawn by its aesthetic appeal. So too was the wider Australian public, even if most preferred the easy accessibility of a Namatjira watercolour to the challenge of deciphering an ochre-on-bark depiction of the ancestral spirits of the Yolngu. By the 1940s, there was an increasing use of Aboriginal motifs in popular design and decoration. Observing this trend in 1943, the visiting British dance critic Arnold Haskell predicted that Aboriginal motifs 'will in the future occupy a larger place in Australian decorative art' as white Australians came to realise the worth of Aboriginal art as 'a part of their national heritage'. Aboriginal art, he noted, had already played 'a part in advancing Australian national consciousness', and he was confident that it would increasingly do so.⁶¹

In the 1940s, there were no Aboriginal writers analogous to the artists of the day, but there was a growing body of non-Indigenous authors who popularised an appreciation of Aboriginal people and cultures. Perhaps the most notable was Bill Harney, whose books recounted the trials and triumphs of Northern Territory Aboriginal people in their interactions with local whites. His exuberant yarns conveyed, in a popularly accessible manner, the worth of Indigenous cultures. His was not the distanced appreciation of writers like the Jindyworobak poets or artists like Margaret Preston, but the appreciation of a man who lived with Aboriginal people on intimate, everyday terms. Nor was it an intellectualised appreciation. Harney celebrated the rough camaraderie of bush life, the folkways of the pastoral frontier, its egalitarianism, mateship and lack of pretension, physical work and physical endurance. Effectively, his books promoted a bush-based version of Australian nationhood, expanded to include Aboriginal people and Aboriginality among its vital components.[62]

Among other writers who strove to convey a sympathetic appreciation of Aboriginal people was HE Thonemann, manager of Elsey station in the Northern Territory. In 1949 he published *Tell the white man: the life story of an Aboriginal lubra*, purportedly communicating the ideas and experiences of an Aboriginal woman, Buludja. Thonemann might be criticised for ventriloquising Buludja, but it was an early attempt to convey an Aboriginal perspective on interracial relations.[63] The previous year, Alan Marshall published an account of his travels in north Queensland, the Torres Strait and the Top End. Its title, *Ourselves writ strange*, advertised the message that Indigenous Australians were different from whites yet still part of a common humanity. According to the cover blurb, in the book 'we see our aborigines as they have never been depicted before, not as "our native problem", but as lovable individuals, kindly, intelligent members of the human race'. 'Any plans for the future of the blackfellow,' Marshall proclaimed, 'must be based on the fact that all human blood is the same… and that Racism is a myth superstition'.[64]

In 1951, Colin Simpson published *Adam in ochre*, an immensely popular work (it sold over 20,000 copies in hardcover) recounting his experiences in Arnhem Land, Kakadu, and Bathurst and Melville Islands. The entire book sought to convey an appreciative understanding of Aboriginal people, but in the final section, 'White delusion', Simpson directly rebutted commonly held stereotypes. The first was that Aboriginal people were dying out. Not so, Simpson stated: the demographic tide had turned and they were now increasing in numbers. Consequently, our 'attitude towards them must change'. The detail in which Simpson felt obliged to refute such ideas as the low intelligence and primitive mentality of Aboriginal people testifies to the extent to which these views still held credibility among the wider Australian populace. White Australians must come to appreciate Aboriginal people, he argued, since their future must be as fellow citizens. Much of their culture, too, would endure — though he noted that Australians were already displaying 'a rather ingenuous eagerness to borrow from [Aboriginal traditions] in order to build our own culture', and warned that the 'use of aboriginal theme and motif in our arts is successful in proportion to the understanding which goes with it'.[65]

By the immediate postwar years, even governments were showing some realisation of the need to appreciate the Aboriginal heritage. Following a resolution of the 1948 Conference of Commonwealth and State Aboriginal Authorities, the federal government developed an Aboriginal education system for the Northern Territory. Over the course of the 1950s, Aboriginal school enrolments in the Territory trebled, from 763 at the beginning of the decade to 2175 at its end.[66] Schools have long served the nationalist end of moulding youthful citizens-to-be into the desired national shape, and the Northern Territory Aboriginal schools of the 1950s were no exception. Yet, while the syllabus for these schools — devised in 1950 — sought to prepare Aboriginal children for living as part of the wider Australian community, it insisted that this 'can be achieved only by a constant and open recognition of the worth of native culture, by the deliberate process of creating a new outlook and approach to life through the skilful distillation of all the elements of the aboriginal way of life'. Teachers were instructed to cultivate in students an appreciation of the fact that 'there IS a place for aboriginals in Australian life', suggesting Doug Nicholls, Albert Namatjira and Harold Blair (an Aboriginal tenor) as appropriate role models.[67]

According to the 1950 syllabus, Social Studies deserved special attention as a subject that would prepare Aboriginal children 'for entry into the white man's world' and inculcate 'the new intellectual, emotional and moral attitude which is essential to the continued survival of the aborigines'. It also specified that through Social Studies the Aboriginal student should

> learn to respect his own cultural heritage and see the assumption of the new way of life as a necessary progression and not as the emergence from a shameful past...In his every approach, therefore, the teacher will draw out from the children the relevant essentials of their own way of life, praise these essentials, encourage the children to discuss them, hold up the merit of them for approval.

Covering such issues as the transition from hunting and gathering to pastoralism and farming, and the history of Australia from 'the Aborigines before the white men came' to the 'life of the Aborigines today', Social Studies taught the lesson of progress.⁶⁸ Yet it enjoined Aboriginal children not to abandon but rather to reinterpret their Aboriginality, and to appreciate the benefits of aligning it with the trajectory of Western sociocultural progress. Classroom practice in Territory schools in the 1950s may have often fallen short of the high ideals of the syllabus writer, but those in authority were clearly giving some thought to the question of how Aboriginal and Western heritages might be reconciled.

Chapter 5

To Live as We Do

In 1951, Paul Hasluck was appointed Commonwealth Minister for Territories, thereby acquiring responsibility for Aboriginal affairs in the Northern Territory. His credentials were impeccable and his appointment was applauded by advocates of Aboriginal advancement. In his earlier careers as a journalist and historian, he had appealed for improvement in the status of Aboriginal people in his home state of Western Australia.[1] In the mid-1940s, he had been a member of Australia's delegation to the United Nations, whose stance for human rights and against racial discrimination he strongly endorsed. As Minister for Territories, he approached his responsibilities for Aboriginal affairs with characteristic earnestness and energy. Although his formal responsibilities in this sphere were limited to the Northern Territory, he strove to bring state Aboriginal policies into line with those of the Commonwealth.

Shortly after his election to parliament, Hasluck delivered a speech seeking 'to arouse the Australian nation to some sense of its responsibility' for Aboriginal people. Most Aboriginal people already lived in 'close association' with Europeans, he said; the few who did not soon would, and among these 'already the tribal practices and beliefs which gave vitality to a primitive people are being sapped and are losing their force'. Therefore:

> the nation must move to a new era in which the social advancement rather than the crude protection of the natives should be the objective...Their future lies in association with us, and they must either associate with us on standards that will give them full opportunity to live worthily and happily or be reduced to the social status of pariahs and outcasts living without a firm place in the community.[2]

These themes would dominate his ministerial innovations in Aboriginal affairs.

This chapter explores Hasluck's ideas and reforms in Aboriginal affairs in the 1950s and early 1960s, which he advanced under the policy label 'assimilation'. Hasluck did not initiate assimilation, but he did develop the policy in influential ways and played a prominent role in popularising 'assimilation' as a key term in Indigenous affairs. Unusually among politicians, he carefully explained the principles and rationales behind his policy determinations. He was committed to a liberal political philosophy, and tried to apply it to Aboriginal governance. His was not the only version of assimilation on offer in the 1950s; each state had its own approach, and many non-governmental advocates of assimilation envisaged the process proceeding quite differently, as I shall explain in the next chapter. Nonetheless, Hasluck was among the most influential exponents of assimilation.

Hasluck's assimilation emphasised the civic dimensions of national belonging. Aboriginal people would become members of the Australian nation not through conformity to a common complexion, but through their adherence to the values and codes of conduct of other Australians and their enjoyment of equal rights and responsibilities. The ambition was clearly articulated in the definition of assimilation agreed upon by the 1961 Native Welfare Conference, whose primary draftsman was Hasluck:

> The policy of assimilation means...that all aborigines and part-aborigines are expected eventually to attain the same manner of living as other Australians and to live as members of a single Australian community enjoying the same rights and privileges, accepting the same responsibilities, observing the same customs and influenced by the same beliefs, hopes and loyalties as other Australians.[3]

Bonding equal rights and responsibilities to shared customs and beliefs, this definition exemplifies Will Kymlicka's and Anthony Smith's point that civically orientated nationalisms are seldom, if ever, culturally neutral. Conformity to a shared public culture is as intrinsic to civic models of nationhood as shared rights and responsibilities, and this public culture is typically determined by the nation's dominant ethnic group.[4] Civically oriented nationalisms differ from their ethnically oriented counterparts not by de-emphasising culture but by de-coupling it from ethnicity, making a shared public culture available to people from outside the circle of (imputed) common descent.

Smith's comments are worth elaborating. He maintains that 'civic nationalisms often demand, as the price for receiving citizenship and its benefits, the surrender of ethnic community and individuality, the privatization of ethnic religion and the marginalization of the ethnic culture and heritage of minorities within the borders of the national state'.[5] These were the demands levied upon Aboriginal people as the price of their citizenship. Against the claims of some historians, I argue that Hasluck's assimilation did not decree the eradication of all vestiges of Aboriginal identity and heritage; rather, it entailed their contraction into the private sphere and reduction to folkloric residues.

Stranded individuals

Within months of his ministerial appointment, Hasluck convened a Native Welfare Conference of Commonwealth and state officials. Indicative of the importance he attached to Aboriginal affairs, the delegates to the 1951 conference were not senior bureaucrats as had been the case at the 1937 and 1948 conferences, but ministers in charge of Aboriginal affairs. As in 1948, the 1951 conference focused on the political and social status of Aboriginal people, but it pushed citizenship to the foreground to a far greater extent than its predecessor. It issued a Statement on Citizenship Rights, which proclaimed that the 'Commonwealth and the States, having assimilation as the objective of native welfare measures, desire to see all persons born in Australia enjoying full citizenship'.[6] This conference, along with every other Native Welfare Conference held before 1961, was unable to offer a more precise definition of 'assimilation'.

Reporting on the conference to parliament in October 1951, Hasluck extolled the two 'abiding and treasured principles of our Australian life' on which his Aboriginal policy was founded. The first was 'the principle of equality of opportunity'; the second that 'there be no division into classes'. These two principles, he proclaimed,

> relate in part to the rights of the individual and in part to the general well-being of the community. On the one hand, we in Australia want to give the chance of a happy and useful life to all our people; on the other hand, we want to build a society in which there shall be no minorities or special classes and in which the benefits yielded by society shall be accessible to all. Such an Australian society will not be completed until its advantages cover, too, our aboriginal people.[7]

It was a fine rendition of the liberal ideal of nationhood, harmonising individual fulfilment with community cohesion.

Hasluck was a forthright exponent of liberal individualism. He later conceded that his Aboriginal policies had placed excessive faith in the malleability of the individual.[8] Even so, some scholars have overstated the extent to which his assimilation was driven by a doctrinaire individualism.[9] In fact, Hasluck was uneasy about the excesses of individualism in Australian culture, recalling in his autobiography that as far back as his student days he 'began to wonder whether individualism had gone too far' and to fear that 'individualism might be an element in disorder, disintegration and decay'.[10] His liberal individualism was counterbalanced by his commitment to the nation as the collectivity within which people could fulfil their personal potential.

On the difficulties of Aboriginal assimilation, Hasluck proclaimed that the 'behaviour of the individual, the response of the individual, the aspiration or effort of the individual, the heart and mind of the individual are at the core of our problem'. His point was not that Aboriginal people should be individualised, but that they already were. Therein lay the problem. Hasluck, like numerous commentators before him, assumed Aboriginal societies to be fragile, inevitably collapsing on contact with outsiders. The frailty of Aboriginal society had its benefits, he suggested, since the 'more it crumbles the more readily may its fragments be mingled with the rest of the people living in Australia'. But it also brought problems because 'the disappearance of aboriginal society leaves the aboriginal person with limited capacity to assert himself or to serve his own interests'. From the wreckage of Aboriginal society emerged the 'stranded individual', lacking the social and cultural wherewithal to realise his or her own best interests. These individuals had no viable prospect other than to 'enter the Australian society', and the state was duty bound to assist them.[11] The thrust of Hasluck's assimilation was to ensure that individuals did not remain 'stranded' but were resocialised into the community of the Australian nation.

Hasluck's assimilation was individualist insofar as he conceived it not so much as a process of social or cultural transformation, as one of individuals extricating themselves from the ruins of one society and relocating in another. He warned that the pathway of the 'stranded individual' from outcast to citizen was strewn with dangers, particularly the propensity of such persons to cluster together in enclaves of their own as refuge from a perplexing and inhospitable modern world. Such enclaves, Hasluck cautioned, 'have a tendency to harden and become less penetrable than the individual'. Consequently, 'the grouping together of aboriginal people may become one of the most serious obstacles to change'.[12] Hasluck expressed unease at the 'growth of race consciousness among the aboriginal people themselves', particularly those 'better-educated aborigines of the southern cities' who demanded 'their own aboriginal member of Parliament' and 'their own separate Christian church'. By 'withdrawing into racial groups', these people compromised their inclusion in the Australian nation and created 'yet another impediment to solving the problem of human relationships between white and black in Australia'.[13]

In deprecating what was, in effect, the emergence of pan-Aboriginal solidarities, Hasluck was not denying the human need for group membership. He was attempting to prescribe the groups to which Aboriginal people should offer their allegiance. He appreciated the inescapably social nature of human existence, and recognised that humans drew their sense of being from their membership of collectivities. The 'stranded individual' was a symptom of social pathology — not a desirable state — and the pathological condition could be remedied only by incorporating these individuals into another community. Hasluck appreciated, too, the essential role of emotion in securing commitment to a collectivity. 'It is not enough,' he contended,

> for an aboriginal person just to know that he will be better fed and better clothed in association with other Australians than he would be if he stayed in the bush. It is necessary for him to feel that he 'belongs' to something greater than himself, that he is accepted by and has his place among his fellows and that he can help in some way to shape society.[14]

A sense of collective belonging was essential, but in Hasluck's view that sense must be attached not to a tribe or a minority group but to the nation, the community appropriate to modernity.

To belong to the nation, and to feel that they belonged, Aboriginal people had to be inculcated with its values and aspirations, and conform to its established way of life. Hasluck put a premium on social homogeneity, insisting that to be part of the national community Aboriginal people must 'live as we do'.[15] This was assimilation with an emphasis on emulation. From their broken-down state, in Hasluck's scenario, Aboriginal people could do no more than emulate the established social norms of the nation. The possibility of innovative adaptation had vanished with the crumbling of their societies.

Philosophically, Hasluck followed the tradition of social liberalism that, descending from late nineteenth-century British theorists such as TH Green, had infused the political culture of Australia from the Federation era onward. In this tradition, the state stood not merely as a distant guarantor of individual rights, but as an agent intervening in social and economic affairs to enhance individual opportunity and the well-being of the citizenry.[16] Despite its merits, in Hasluck's hands this approach proved inadequate to resolving the problems of Australia's Indigenous minority. This may partly have been because of liberalism's assumption of the primacy of the individual and failure to appreciate the extent of people's embeddedness in their own social groups. More directly, it derived from Hasluck's assumption that many Aboriginal people were not merely individuals but (for the time being) extraordinarily incompetent individuals. Desocialised, deculturated and disorientated, they were capable of improvement only under the paternal guidance of the state. Hasluck's ideas on how state paternalism should be exercised resulted in the most remarkable piece of assimilationist legislation enacted in any Australian jurisdiction. Its genesis and implementation shed a revealing light on his vision of assimilation, so it is to that we now turn.

Avoiding 'Aborigines'

The Statement on Citizenship Rights issued by the 1951 Native Welfare Conference acknowledged that there were already 'many persons of aboriginal or part-aboriginal blood who are prepared for and capable of accepting the full responsibilities of citizenship', and anticipated their numbers increasing in coming years. It added that there were many others, 'particularly in the northern parts of Australia, who require the benefits of special legislation in order that their own interests may be safeguarded and in order that their advancement in civilization may be assisted'. This was conventional thinking at the time. The next part of the statement was not. Bearing the unmistakable imprint of Hasluck, it argued that legislative use of the term 'aboriginal' was fraught with intractable problems of definition, and could be taken to imply that Aboriginal people constituted 'a different class of citizen by their very nature'. Therefore, legislation should eschew the term 'aboriginal', and special provisions should apply not to 'aborigines' as a group but 'only to persons deemed to stand in need of…guardianship and tutelage', such provisions ceasing immediately they showed themselves capable of exercising the rights and responsibilities of citizenship. In the meantime, their legal designation should be 'wards of the state'.[17]

Immediately after the 1951 conference, Hasluck instructed his Northern Territory officers to draft new legislation in line with its recommendations — that is, making special provisions for Aboriginal advancement but without specifying 'aborigines' in legislation. What seemed a good idea in Canberra looked ludicrous in Darwin. Alternately bewildered and irritated by the minister's intransigence on the legislative non-specification of race, the Administrator penned numerous memos seeking clarification of ministerial intentions and insisting that, because 'many welfare measures must be peculiar to the needs of aborigines', it was impractical to avoid specifying this group in legislation.[18] Hasluck remained unmoved, insisting that 'a complete break from past approaches' was required.[19]

Eventually, the legislation took shape as the Northern Territory *Welfare Ordinance 1953*, coyly subtitled *An ordinance to provide for the care and assistance of certain persons*. It had some points of novelty, most of all in never using the word 'Aboriginal', although it was plainly an instrument of Aboriginal governance. In line with Hasluck's conception of citizenship, the Ordinance gave priority to education, vocational training and the 'social, economic and political advancement' of the 'certain persons' who came within its ambit, so that they and their descendants could 'take their place as members of the community of the Commonwealth'.[20] However, it did not mark the 'complete break' he had demanded.

For one thing, the provisions of the *Welfare Ordinance* generally followed those of the *Aboriginals Ordinance* that it replaced. For another, the *Welfare Ordinance* did not initiate a new direction in policy; it merely inscribed in legislation objectives which had been set down in the New Deal of 1939. The new ordinance provided for the declaration of Aboriginal people as 'wards of the state', but under earlier legislation they were already that, in fact if not in name. The new ordinance converted their *de facto* status as wards into their *de jure* designation, but the substantive rights of most remained unchanged. In the process, they were given a legal label reeking with derogatory and demeaning connotations. Moreover, the grounds on which an Aboriginal person could claim revocation of the status of ward were essentially those on which he or she could claim exemption from the earlier ordinance. Despite these major points of continuity, Hasluck preferred to emphasise the differences.

'Under the old system,' he told the 1952 Native Welfare Conference, 'it was assumed that every native came under restrictive legislation unless he applied for and was granted exemption from it. Under the new system it is assumed that every British subject has citizenship as a birthright.' This birthright came with the massive proviso that its entitlements could be 'withheld because a person stands in need of special care and assistance'.[21] However, to Hasluck's way of thinking the legislative revision rightly shifted the baseline in considerations of Aboriginal peoples' citizenship status, from presuming their non-citizenship (with provision for exemption into citizenship) to recognising their natal entitlement to citizenship (with provision for its suspension).

Hasluck and other senior officials were aware that, by virtue of the *Nationality and Citizenship Act 1948*, Aboriginal people were already citizens by birth, and to that extent citizenship was their birthright. They were equally aware that the enjoyment of rights depended not on the formal status of citizen but on the specific provisions of state and federal legislation. These points were raised during preparations for the 1951 Native Welfare Conference.[22] However, the legalistic implications of the *Nationality and Citizenship Act* were not major factors driving Hasluck's legislative reforms. The impetus came, above all, from his antipathy to racial — or any other — cleavages within the nation.

Hasluck's *Welfare Ordinance* still placed many Aboriginal people, as wards, outside the community of citizens. However, 'ward' was not a racial designation but a legal status applicable equally, in theory, to 'those of European race who need special care' as to Aboriginal people in similar need.[23] Moreover, it was a revocable legal status, capable of being 'removed as soon as the need for it disappears'.[24] Hasluck admitted that determining when that moment had arrived — when, that is, a person no longer stood in need of the guardianship of the state — was one of the more intractable problems of assimilation.[25] However, he contended that it was a lesser problem than those deriving from the legal recognition of race, which would abet deep divisions in the national community. The *Welfare Ordinance*'s eschewing of any reference to racial categories was meant to abate those divisions.

'Welfare', in Hasluck's usage, did not carry the welfare state connotations of 'cradle to the grave' provision of services by the state. To the contrary, he expressed serious misgivings about the extension of social security benefits to those people deemed not yet ready to use them wisely. Prefiguring more recent critiques of welfare dependency, he noted that in many cases 'the payment of social benefits to natives has, in fact, led to a decline in their living standards and has halted the advancement of their welfare in as much as they have accepted social benefit payments as a means of livelihood and have been content to live at the standard which such an income provides and give up wage-earning'.[26] To 'advance native welfare', Hasluck explained, 'we must also afford the people the means of sustaining the higher standards to which they are advancing', and this required attitudinal change and vocational opportunity. 'It is idle,' he continued, 'talking of citizenship for natives or their rights in the community unless you can also give them a chance of self-respect and self-support that comes from being able to do a job of work and do it well'.[27] Not as passive recipients of handouts, but only as active subscribers to the virtues of self-reliance and self-regulation, would Aboriginal people advance their own well-being.

Despite insisting on the non-recognition of race as a cardinal principle of legislation, Hasluck was forced to make two major concessions during the *Welfare Ordinance*'s difficult birth. The first was in late 1952, when it became apparent that the long delays in drafting the legislation would be followed by even longer delays in implementing it. As an interim measure, Administrator FJS Wise recommended that the *Aboriginals Ordinance* be amended to exclude all half-castes from its provisions. Senior Territory officials had long urged this, as had local members of the Australian Half-Caste Progressive Association, who demanded 'Complete exclusion from the Aboriginal and other Ordinances of all people of mixed blood and the granting of full Citizenship Rights'.[28] Wise claimed that most Territory half-castes lived in circumstances approximating European standards; they could be trusted to use their citizenship wisely and well; and in any case they were the only group agitating for citizenship.[29] He managed to convince his minister; the amended *Aboriginals Ordinance* was passed unanimously by the Legislative Council in January 1953; and the half-castes of the Northern Territory thereby acquired the legal status of other citizens. Hasluck insisted that this emancipation of mixed-bloods was strictly 'a temporary palliative during a transitional period and does not satisfy long-term policy on native welfare'.[30] Nonetheless, by agreeing to grant legal equality to the racially defined category 'half-castes', Hasluck compromised his own ideal that the state must eschew all legislative references to race.

His second concession was more debilitating. In January 1953, the *Welfare Ordinance* was introduced into the Northern Territory Legislative Council. Since the majority of its members were appointed by the federal government, the Council could normally be relied on to endorse legislation put before it. Not so for the *Welfare Ordinance*. Even the appointed members were outraged by what the Acting Crown Law Officer described as a denial of 'every principle of British justice'. They were outraged, too, that it permitted white people to be placed under the same proscriptions as black. The latter objection evidently carried most weight, since Legislative Council opposition was overcome at the June sitting by an amendment that restricted declarations of ward status to persons ineligible for enrolment under the Northern Territory Electoral Regulations. Those ineligible to enrol were Aboriginal. Thus amended, the Bill met little opposition in its passage through Council.[31] Again, Hasluck's cherished principle of racial non-specification was compromised, more fatally than before since the specification of race was merely displaced on to another item of legislation. Nonetheless, he accepted the amended legislation because he realised that the Legislative Council would pass it in no other form.

The problems of the Ordinance did not end there. For four years, its gazettal was delayed while the Welfare Branch compiled the necessary Register of Wards. Branch officers — most of whom were antagonistic to the Ordinance — seem to have deliberately dragged their feet. Meanwhile, Hasluck's assimilation program continued apace. New government settlements were established, older settlements and missions were revitalised, government expenditure on Aboriginal affairs escalated, and educational, vocational, housing and health services expanded. Although Hasluck complained that the long delay in implementing his pet legislation impeded his assimilation program, the record of expenditure and provision of services suggests otherwise. Welfare intervention in Aboriginal lives intensified, regardless of the non-gazettal of the *Welfare Ordinance*.

When the *Welfare Ordinance* was eventually gazetted in 1957, all but six of the estimated 15,700 full-bloods in the Northern Territory were registered as wards. While Hasluck had envisaged a majority of Aboriginal people being declared wards, he seems not to have imagined the majority being quite so massive as this. By 1959, his departmental office was complaining that, 'Too few aborigines are being declared not to be wards', and that in view of 'the way of living and working of many aborigines', Welfare Branch officers should be much more willing to strike their names from the Register of Wards.[32] A few years later, Hasluck expressed stronger reservations, advising Administrator Roger Nott that 'we should refrain from recommending the declaration of any person as a ward if it can possibly be avoided...We should regard the declaration of a person as a ward as the last resort if all other means of giving special care and assistance to that person are unsuitable'.[33] By this time, perhaps, criticisms of the Ordinance were beginning to bite.

Criticisms came from as far afield as the London-based Anti-Slavery and Aborigines Protection Society, as well as from such close quarters as the Labor member for Darwin, Dick Ward.[34] In 1958, the prosecution of Albert Namatjira (an Aboriginal citizen) for providing liquor to kinfolk (wards) provoked not only public protest but also a legal challenge to the constitutionality of the Ordinance. The challenge was unsuccessful, but in the course of proceedings both the Supreme Court of the Northern Territory and the High Court of Australia determined that the Ordinance was an item of legislation applicable solely to Aboriginal people.[35]

In 1959, Hasluck admitted that 'we made a mistake' in tying declarations of wards to the electoral regulations, and sought 'some other means of identifying the class of persons who cannot be declared wards'. Like his predecessors, Administrator JC Archer advised that the only effective way to do so was to specify race, as well as need, as criteria for declaration. Hasluck's departmental secretary, CR Lambert, agreed. Hasluck remained obdurate. It was 'fundamental to policy' that legislation be racially non-specific, and he was not prepared to accept any 'change of the principles on which the present Act is based'.[36] So sacrosanct was the principle of racial non-specification that no matter what problems it precipitated or protests it provoked, it must never be violated.

For all his intransigence on the wording of the Ordinance, Hasluck did not consider 'Aboriginal' a taboo word. To the end of his days, in innumerable public addresses, parliamentary speeches and published statements, he freely and frequently referred to 'Aborigines' and 'natives', 'full-bloods' and 'half-castes'. Assimilation propaganda booklets were published under Hasluck's ministerial authority bearing the word 'Aboriginal' in bold font on their covers and repeating it in almost every sentence. Hasluck sought to expunge 'Aboriginal' not from the lexicon but from the statute books. From the perspective of the state, he insisted, there were no races, merely citizens — all equal before the law — plus a residuum of persons who were temporarily incapable of exercising the freedoms of citizenship or appreciating its responsibilities. In legislation — and only in legislation — these persons were to be designated 'wards' rather than identified by race. Yet, as some of his critics pointed out at the time, by taking this approach Hasluck was compounding the very problems he sought to resolve.

In what was probably the first critique of the Ordinance, AP Elkin deplored the word 'ward'. In 1946, Elkin had insisted that governments must cease 'regarding adult Aborigines as wards of the State'.[37] Reviewing the *Welfare Ordinance* in early 1953, he was horrified to find wardship taking centre stage in the language of Aboriginal administration. 'The use of the term ward, though well meant, seems to add difficulties and remove none,' he protested, adding that the 'administrative declaration of persons (adults) to be wards is an abuse of justice'. Moreover, the term 'ward' perpetuated 'the old convenient fallacy' that Aboriginal people were a 'child race', irresponsible, impetuous and immature. Words, Elkin warned, 'are powerful creators of attitudes. The whole trend since 1930 has been to get away from the negative protective attitude; and although the Bill is designed to further that trend, the use of the term Ward for adults may well have the opposite effect.' He reminded the minister that 'Commonwealth action is before the eyes and the moral judgement of the United Nations and of the world…The implications of our words, as well as our actions, are watched'. Calling Aboriginal people 'wards' could only diminish Australia in the estimation of the world.[38]

More harshly, the Methodist missionary Arthur Ellemor condemned the Ordinance as 'a piece of hypocritical humbug'. Like Elkin, Ellemor raised the issue of international scrutiny of the legislation, suggesting that any impartial investigator seeking determination of the 'certain persons' of its subtitle could feel only 'amazement and disgust at the end of the quest'. Aboriginal people constituted 'a special racial group', not an ensemble of 'unmentionables', Ellemor insisted, adding that in the *Welfare Ordinance*,

> 'racial discrimination' (an unworthy thing) and 'racial distinction' (a realistic and necessary thing) have been confused. In the desire to avoid the former, we have fallen foul of the latter; and the result is that we do the Aborigines the doubtful honour of classing them as wards and grouping them with delinquents, lunatics and criminals.[39]

Hasluck was disarmingly frank in making exactly the analogies deplored by Elkin and Ellemor. On several occasions, he remarked that proceedings under the Ordinance would be 'analogous to the kind of action customary under the laws in respect of neglected children, the feeble-minded, or other persons who need special care'.[40] Incompetence had long been an assumed characteristic of Aboriginal people, and the language of wardship sustained that assumption. Hasluck himself had condemned earlier legislation for reducing Aboriginal people to the status of a 'born idiot'.[41] His own legislation did much the same, except that it assumed Aboriginal incompetence to be not inborn but rather a consequence of the social dislocation that had rendered them pathetically helpless in the modern world.

Although citizenship was the central aspiration of the *Welfare Ordinance*, it was not an instrument conferring citizenship upon Aboriginal people. It was premised on the assumption that the task was to make citizens rather than to grant citizenship. This assumption had informed Aboriginal administration in the Northern Territory since 1939, and more generally pervaded government programs of assimilation. Convinced that Aboriginal societies had been comprehensively disabled by their encounter with modernity, Hasluck could imagine their erstwhile members as no more than incapacitated individuals, appropriately designated 'wards of the state'. By his choice of a term redolent of incompetence and ineptitude, Hasluck subverted his ambition to inaugurate a new era of Aboriginal citizenship. He did, however, initiate the first government-sponsored campaign to promote the public acceptance of Aboriginal people.

Mobilising civil society

The 1952 Native Welfare Conference issued a statement acknowledging that

> some of the obstacles in the way of coloured Australians enjoying full citizenship are not legal but social barriers and that they will only enjoy the privileges of citizenship if they can live and work as accepted members of the community. To this extent the problem of assimilation is one of breaking down the colour barrier which has been erected by the white community.

This piece of understatement was followed by the observation that, 'Prejudice against a person because of his colour is not instinctive…but has been inculcated by environmental influences and it will undoubtedly take a considerable time to break down'. Consequently, 'an information campaign to combat colour prejudice should be sustained'.[42] The federal government made a start on this soon afterwards, though its information campaign remained desultory until 1957, when it began publication of a series of booklets, issued under Hasluck's authority, as part of the annual celebration of National Aborigines Day which began that year.

These booklets repeatedly reminded readers that assimilation was feasible (suggesting that many members of the public needed convincing) and continually enjoined them to accept Aboriginal people into their local communities (suggesting that such acceptance was often not forthcoming). The level of sophistication with which these appeals were made varied between booklets: some were dull, fact-stuffed tracts, while others — such as the 1961 booklet *One people* — were reasonably sophisticated in their use of anecdote, exposition and images (see Plate 5).[43] Overall, they could not be judged great triumphs of modern propaganda techniques, but they were the federal government's first foray into propaganda intended to sway mass opinion towards a more favourable view of Aboriginal people and greater involvement in Aboriginal affairs. Strangely, many historical studies overlook them (together with numerous other items of assimilationist propaganda produced at the time), claiming that assimilationist governments of this era made no effort to change public opinion about Aboriginal people.[44]

One of the few historians to pay heed to these booklets, Anna Haebich, dismisses them as mere 'spin' — self-congratulatory confections 'beam[ing] back to settler Australians a "beguiling" image of themselves living harmoniously with Aboriginal people in an assimilated White Australia'.[45] In fact, the consistent message of the booklets was that assimilation had not been attained, and to do so required white Australians to make a more energetic effort than they had to date. Haebich is right to point out that the federal government devoted far more resources to its contemporaneous campaign promoting public acceptance of immigrants than to its Aboriginal publicity. However, immigration was a federal responsibility, whereas Aboriginal affairs were not, and Hasluck's department was breaking new ground in launching a federally sponsored, nationwide Aboriginal awareness campaign. Haebich is also right to point out that the booklets simplified the issues and paid little attention to controversies and complications in Aboriginal affairs. But simplification is intrinsic to the genre of propaganda, and the booklets were not quite as inattentive to complexities as Haebich claims. She seems to interpret the booklets as attempts to gain mere public endorsement of government policies and practices, as if governments would secure the assimilation of Aboriginal people and desired merely the tick of approval from a supine public. In fact, the booklets sought far more than that. They endeavoured to mobilise civil society for the inclusion of Aboriginal people in the national community.

While the booklets (unsurprisingly) portrayed government achievements in Aboriginal affairs in the most positive possible light, they all stressed that governmental efforts were not enough, and that assimilation demanded concerted effort by all Australians. The 1963 booklet explained that 'while legislation and government action can assist assimilation, ultimately the success of the policy will depend on the attitude and work of the whole Australian community'.[46] *One people* noted that government action could achieve 'certain ends' such as legal reform and the provision of health and educational facilities, but,

> without co-operation in many ways by other Australians, both as individuals and groups, and ultimately co-operation in accepting aborigines and part-aborigines into the community with complete equality, these efforts can come to nought. It is a responsibility — indeed an obligation — for those who are able to do so to assist these people.[47]

The 1957 booklet, *Our Aborigines*, declared:

> Only members of the Australian community can make the newcomer to that community feel at home in it. The remarkable achievement of bodies such as the 'Good Neighbour Councils' in helping to assimilate the 'New Australians' from overseas might well be matched by communal and individual efforts to help the 'old Australians' to realize the best of our own life and the best of their own individual capacities.[48]

Good Neighbour Councils had been established in 1950 to promote the assimilation of immigrants. Through them, the interface between immigrant and host society was personalised, most Council activities being performed by civic-minded volunteers under the coordination, though not the direct control, of the Department of Immigration.[49] They relied on mobilising civil society, and the Aboriginal assimilation booklets urged a similar mobilisation on behalf of Aboriginal people. In this, as in other respects, the booklets bore the stamp of Hasluck.

5: To Live as We Do

According to Hasluck, the 'community itself is a much more potent element in social change than are governments', so social change always required the active involvement of civil society. However, he found the institutions of civil society to be sadly moribund in contemporary Australia. He declaimed: 'I deplore the expectation of the present-day Australian community that politicians should perform a series of miracles while the nation sleeps.' He was emphatically 'not one of those who share the current heresy that the politician, the social planner and the public servant can decide what is to happen in this world and it will happen'. The state could provide desirable conditions for Aboriginal assimilation, such as 'better housing, schooling, and creating an opportunity to earn a living, enjoy citizenship, and to participate in communal life', but these were merely 'opening the way' for civil society to fulfil its proper functions.[50]

For National Aborigines Day in 1958, Hasluck issued a press release advertising that year's propaganda booklet, *Assimilation of our Aborigines*, as well as a new film, *End of the walkabout*, conveying the same message. He also took the opportunity to rebuke the Australian public for its failure to respond adequately to Aboriginal people's needs. The purpose of the day, he declared, was to focus

> the attention of the Australian people on the complex task of native welfare. We want to show the need; tell what is being done to meet it; reveal some of the difficulties; and, above all, drive home to all the people of Australia that the task will never be completed without the sympathy and practical help of all Australians. This, too, is a field in which we want good neighbours to give a helping hand to the stranger in our gates. Although these people are truly the natives of Australia there are many of them who are strangers to comradeship and opportunity in their own land.

According to Hasluck, governments and missions were doing their best to improve the status and welfare of Aboriginal people, but the public was 'not doing enough to back them up'.[51]

In a July 1959 address, he forcefully asserted his view that it was 'not Governments but the community' that ultimately was responsible for ensuring the social acceptance of Aboriginal people. 'Are we neglecting our aborigines?' he asked his audience. 'Get out of the habit of firing that question at your government and leaving it to find an answer or take the blame. Shoot the question at yourself. Are *you* neglecting our aborigines?' Warming to his topic, he asked:

> Did you neglect to do anything on the Parents and Citizens Association to make sure that the little aboriginal boy or girl came to school, did well at school and that his parents, like other parents, were encouraging his progress? Did you neglect to see that the children joined the cubs or brownies or other organisation like other children?

'Did you fail to make a fuss if they were discriminated against?' he chided, before coming to his leading proposition: 'have you ever thought of forming a local group who will do for these old Australians what the Good Neighbour Councils have done for the "new Australians" by helping them to join the rest of the community?'[52] By insisting on community obligations, Hasluck was not attempting to dodge government responsibility. He was articulating the classical liberal principles of the limited sphere of government action and the need for civic-minded individuals to promote the public good through involvement in voluntary organisations.

Hasluck insisted that social — as against legal — equality cannot be 'conferred as a gift by governments',[53] and that 'even if the State decreed that black and white were equal, society could still treat them as unequal in a score of different ways'.[54] 'Society', therefore, had to be coaxed into fulfilling its obligations towards Aboriginal people. But 'society' in this formulation refers to white society. Aboriginal people would feel the hand of the state much more firmly — for example, by being treated as wards. There was a disjuncture in Hasluck's advocacy, on the one hand insisting that the civil institutions of white society must be mobilised by persuasion while on the other insisting that Aboriginal people stood in need of strict guidance, even coercion, by the state. Aboriginal people, he seems to have assumed, completely lacked the institutions of civil society. In fact, one of the assimilation propaganda booklets explicitly stated that 'there are no suitable aboriginal institutions that can easily be used as a basis for community growth'.[55] Although Hasluck lamented the weakness of civil society in white Australia, and the propensity of white Australians to expect everything of their governments, he believed that the rudiments of civil society were present and could be prodded into more vigorous action. Aboriginal people, on the other hand, were deemed to lack even the vestiges of civil society; there was nothing there to mobilise. This harks back to Hasluck's assumption that Aboriginal people constituted an ensemble of socially disabled individuals, lacking the wherewithal to act collectively for their own benefit and therefore dependent on an interventionist and paternalist state.

Attenuated identities

Assimilation, Hasluck claimed, 'does not mean the suppression of the aboriginal culture', but that the 'native people will grow into the society in which, by force of history they are bound to live'.[56] If Aboriginal culture was not to be suppressed but merely allowed to wither, would anything ultimately remain of that heritage? Did Hasluck allow the possibility of Aboriginal people assimilating into the Australian nation yet retaining an Aboriginal identity? Some of his statements tend toward a negative answer, while others gesture toward more positive outcomes. He suggested, for example, that through the process of assimilation 'the aboriginal people will carry a proud memory of their own ancient origin and that they will make their own contribution towards the shaping of distinctive Australian national characteristics'.[57]

In Hasluck's scenario of assimilation, the Aboriginal cultural heritage would not disappear, but rather would dissipate into folkloric remnants, and Aboriginal identity would not be erased but privatised, contracting to little more than an individual's sense of personal ancestry. 'The ancient pride can remain — and in fact may grow,' he suggested, looking forward to a 'future when a person whose great grandfather was an Australian aboriginal will be as proud of the fact as a Scot is rightly proud of his barbaric ancestry'.[58] Returning to the Scottish analogy in his 1988 retrospective, he remarked that assimilated Aborigines 'could recall and honour their own origins and traditions (in much the same way as Scotsmen wear kilts, play bagpipes, dance reels, celebrate ancient festivals and try to preserve Gaelic)'.[59] These, in Hasluck's view, were mere fragments of cultural exotica and superficial badges of ancestry, which individuals might value as part of an attenuated and privatised identity. That was beyond the concern of the state. Indeed, the assimilatory state could help perpetuate such an attenuated, privatised ethnic identity, as attested by the naming practices implemented in consequence of Hasluck's *Welfare Ordinance*.

Shortly after the *Welfare Ordinance* was passed, RK McCaffery, Acting Director of Native Affairs, explained the procedures to be followed in naming Aboriginal persons for the Register of Wards. McCaffery was well aware that Aboriginal individuals were already named. Indeed, he suggested that they had a surfeit of names: personal names, secret names, nicknames, totemic and Dreaming names, section or subsection names, local group or horde names, tribal or language group names, and some had European names as well; which of these were used depended upon social context. This was incompatible with the demands of the bureaucratic state, which required something 'in line with our European system of one or more Christian names and a family or surname'.[60] Among the Acting Director's duties was to ascribe the modern Western naming system to Aboriginal people.

McCaffery argued that some name should be selected, as a surname, from the ensemble of names an Aboriginal person already possessed. His preference was for the local group or horde name (which he considered closest to the Western concept of a surname); failing that, the totemic name or the subsection name could be used. He also suggested that the 'language group name should be carried by one of the leading families of the tribe'. Naming, he acknowledged, involved immense difficulties, and 'the choice of surname should be discussed with the group concerned [to] ensure that the surname chosen is acceptable to them and will not give rise to complications in any existing social organisation'. The state was determined to impose a new naming system, but Aboriginal people were to be allowed some degree of choice about the names themselves. Perhaps, this derived partly from the pragmatic consideration that familiar names had best chance of taking root, whereas attempts to impose alien names would likely be resisted, thus compounding the bureaucratic difficulties. However, McCaffery dwelt on the need for cultural continuity, stating that the 'surname should be chosen with definite associations with their aboriginal past giving them ties with their aboriginal heritage. This will serve also to preserve names with meaning in Territory aboriginal life.'[61]

Yet, while names could connect people with their Indigenous heritage, naming systems could disconnect them. McCaffery acknowledged that fixed surnames would gain currency only among people who had experienced 'some degree of detribalisation', and correlated the extension of the Western naming system with further detribalisation. He recognised that the new naming system was an active constituent of sociocultural change, not merely an incidental flow-on, observing that 'the acceptance and use of a family surname will counter the normal social organisation of tribal aboriginal society with its associated duties and beliefs'.[62] That is, a family surname would encourage Aboriginal people to orientate their social life around the nuclear family, rather than in the ramifying kinship networks characteristic of 'tribal' society. Ascribing fixed names was far more than a bureaucratic convenience. It was also an induction and invitation into the nuclear family-orientated world of Western modernity and the nuclear family-based sociality of the Australian way of life.

McCaffery's naming program clearly did not entail the effacement of all markers of Indigeneity. Fixed family surnames such as 'Namatjira' and 'Pareroultja' (two examples cited by McCaffery) would be transmitted down the generations, distinguishing their bearers from non-Aboriginal Australians as plainly as their black skins. Yet the meaning and significance of those names would radically be transformed. No longer signifying totemic ancestry or clan affiliation, the name would merely designate a family, just as former Celtic clan names (like McCaffery) had been transformed from signifiers of social obligation and political allegiance into neutral family names — and indicators of the incidental fact of Scottish or Irish descent. This harks back to Hasluck's point that pride in personal ancestry was one of the few residues of Aboriginality that would remain after the tidal wave of modernisation had washed away the substance of an Indigenous way of life.

Similar endorsements of the retention of an attenuated Aboriginal identity, with a limited repertoire of cultural heritage, were expressed in the assimilation propaganda booklets published under Hasluck's ministerial authority. *One people* proclaimed that:

> Assimilation does not mean that aborigines should necessarily lose their identity as aborigines or forgo their proper pride in this identity. It does not mean that aboriginal language, myths and legends, and art forms should be lost — there is a proper and proud place in the wider Australian culture for all of these.

Only two pages earlier, it had quoted with approval the 1961 Native Welfare Conference definition of assimilation, with its persistent reiteration of the essential sameness of Aboriginal and white Australians in manner of living, rights, privileges, responsibilities, customs, beliefs, hopes and loyalties.[63]

This juxtaposition of a demand for sameness and a concession of difference recurred throughout the series of official pamphlets. The 1960 pamphlet asserted that Aboriginal people 'must, to survive and to prosper, learn to live as white Australians do, and to think as white Australians do'. It added that: 'Assimilation does not mean that the aborigines should lose their racial identity, or lose contact with their arts, their crafts and their philosophy.'[64] The 1963 pamphlet defined assimilation in similar terms to the 1961 Conference, stating immediately afterward that: 'Assimilation does *not* mean that aborigines will necessarily lose their identity as aborigines or their pride in their aboriginal ancestry. It does not mean, either, that aboriginal language, arts and customs should be allowed to languish. These can and should enrich the whole Australian culture.'[65] These passages were not contradictory, but rather consistent with Hasluck's conception of assimilation, whereby Aboriginal people might retain a remnant Indigenous identity and heritage but must, in substantive aspects of their social lives, conform to dominant national norms.

The propaganda booklets were quite specific, even prescriptive, about both the maintenance and the repudiation of cultural heritage. They distinguished between the 'best aspects' of Aboriginal culture, which may be retained, and those elements that would be 'a positive hindrance to their advancement', which must be discarded. The latter included 'extravagant sharing' of possessions, a 'tendency to go on "walkabout"', 'primitive standards of hygiene' and 'tribal obligations'.[66] 'On the other hand,' the 1960 pamphlet explained,

> there are many virtues that belong to the aboriginal tribal life, many arts, and many skills, that can well be carried forward into the new life, to enrich it and to provide for the aborigines something of a link with the past and provide them with justifiable grounds for pride in their aboriginal identity …
>
> The aboriginal stockman who plays his didjeridoo to entertain his mates in the drafting camp, the artisan who makes boomerangs for the tourist trade, the enterprising aboriginal man or woman who can build a small business around aboriginal arts and crafts are examples, in a small way, of the carry-through of the aboriginal tradition.
>
> The merit of aboriginal art is now being recognized by designers, aboriginal music and dancing have had some small recognition, and aboriginal myths and legends now form a small part of our tradition in literature. It may well be that further developments of this sort in the near future will provide aborigines with a pride and a unity that they have previously lacked.[67]

During the assimilationist era, elements of Aboriginal cultural heritage (especially aesthetic) were tolerated, even encouraged if they could be commodified and turned to profit. Perhaps to supplement the paucity of Australian nationalist symbols, Aboriginal people were induced to dance corroborees, throw spears and play didgeridoos for the entertainment and edification of visiting dignitaries, including the Queen in 1954. However, in social norms, values and deportment they were enjoined to forsake the old and subscribe to the new, in the form of the Australian way of life.

While Hasluck accepted the retention of a residue of Aboriginality, he did not value Aboriginal culture as a contributor to the assimilatory process. Nor did he put a positive value on Aboriginal groups as vehicles for the transition into the national community. If assimilated people retained a pride in their Indigenous ancestry and some scattered remnants of their cultural heritage, to Hasluck that was inconsequential. What mattered was that they placed primacy on their membership of the Australian nation and conformed to its norms and values. Other assimilationists concurred on the need for national inclusion, but as the next chapter shows, many were highly critical of Hasluck's failure to appreciate the contribution Australia's Indigenous heritage could make to achieving that goal.

Chapter 6

Assimilation and Integration

When AP Elkin censured the *Welfare Ordinance* in 1953, he did so not only for its demeaning term 'ward' but also for its impoverished conception of assimilation. 'The Bill,' he stated,

> is not satisfactory, basically because it underestimates the *importance of being Aboriginal*.
>
> 1. *The Aborigines — a Distinct Group*
>
> The Aborigines are racially different from us, and recognizably so. In spite of the economic, religious, social and political assimilation at which we aim, they will be a distinct group, or series of groups, for generations to come. Indeed, they will develop pride in their own cultural background and distinctness while at the same time being loyal and useful citizens.[1]

According to Elkin, Hasluck jeopardised assimilation by discounting Aboriginal people's embeddedness in their own social groups, as well as their attachment to their own cultural heritage. As he had observed in a review of the 1951 conference at which the *Welfare Ordinance* had its genesis: 'The Aborigines must move up in groups.'[2]

In his criticisms of the Ordinance, Arthur Ellemor pushed further, questioning the advisability of 'the term "assimilation" itself as a policy aim'. Ellemor's critique moved, sometimes confusingly, between the word 'assimilation' and the content of the policy pursued under that name. He appreciated that assimilation signified a 'progressive' and 'absolutely sound' 'change in policy *direction*'; he endorsed 'economic assimilation' and 'political assimilation'. However, he was apprehensive about what he called 'social assimilation' for its 'denial of worth to Aboriginal culture'.

Policies premised on such denial, he feared, would result in 'the complete breakdown of all existing tribal sanctions', causing 'resentment on the part of our full-bloods' and possibly *'extinction* for the remaining Aboriginal tribes'. As a policy label, Ellemor recommended 'amalgamation' instead of 'assimilation', since the former term encompassed

> the recognition of Aboriginal culture as an element of continuing worth in the new 'whole' that is being worked out; it leaves the Aboriginal people themselves to work out the modification of their culture and to adapt themselves to the European challenge; and it leaves the future open, as to where the balance will lie between predominantly Aboriginal and European elements in the final result.

What was needed, Ellemor insisted, was a policy and a policy label 'broad enough to recognise the place of differing cultures within one community'.[3]

Within these early critiques of the *Welfare Ordinance* can be discerned the substantive issues involved in arguments about assimilation over the next two decades: differing assessments of the worth of Aboriginality and the capacity of Aboriginal people to exercise choice — plus, in Ellemor's case, misgivings about the word 'assimilation' itself. Over the course of the 1950s and 1960s, disputation over these issues escalated into demands for the reform or abandonment of government programs of assimilation. Neither of the two critiques cited above was widely publicised; they were confined to private correspondence with the minister (in Elkin's case) and communication among fellow professionals (in Ellemor's case). In the early to mid-1950s, few people publicly censured assimilation.

That changed in the late 1950s. By then, Aboriginal activists and their supporters had become disillusioned at the sluggish pace of reform as the promises of assimilation — rights, respect, opportunity — continued to be compromised by myriad provisos. At this time, too, Aboriginal affairs were given unusually prominent — and negative — publicity. In 1957, film footage of Third World conditions in the Warburton Ranges in central Australia was screened in cities around Australia and broadcast by the new medium of television under the title 'Manslaughter'.[4] Its graphic images of children with swollen bellies, their faces covered with sores and flies, their parents starving and skeletal-thin, revealed to horrified viewers the disjuncture between the high ideals proclaimed by governments and the stark realities of Aboriginal deprivation. A year later, another scandal erupted over the conviction of Albert Namatjira for supplying his kinfolk with alcohol. A man whose paintings adorned homes throughout Australia, who had been formally presented to the Queen in 1954, and who had come to personify the benefits of assimilation, was to suffer the humiliation of gaol. As the Sydney *Daily Mirror* reported, the Namatjira case 'has brought to a head the fantastic laws governing natives in Australia'.[5]

Internationally, the politics of race were gaining a higher profile in the late 1950s. The decolonisation of Africa provided exemplars of black assertiveness and created new states critical of the treatment of colonised peoples elsewhere. Contemporaneously, South Africa's policy of apartheid came under stronger international criticism, escalating into condemnation after the 1960 Sharpeville Massacre. In the United States, racial segregation came under concerted attack from the civil rights movement. Its campaign for school desegregation was given worldwide publicity in 1957 when federal troops were sent into Little Rock, Arkansas, to enforce an antisegregation decision of the US Supreme Court. In principle, assimilation stood opposed to apartheid and segregation, but it was not difficult to find Australian practices analogous to, if less formalised than, these overseas policies. By the early 1960s, Aboriginal leaders were warning that, 'We must abolish apartheid in our own country...or we may find ourselves in a similar situation as South Africa'.[6]

In this context of intensifying disillusionment and dispute over Aboriginal policy, a new word entered the argument: 'integration'. It was taken from ILO Convention 107 of 1957, 'Concerning the protection and integration of indigenous and other tribal and semi-tribal populations in independent countries'.[7] Although the terms of the convention were consistent with the assimilationist stance taken by the ILO since the Second World War, some activists seized upon the word 'integration' as if it marked a major break from assimilation. 'Integration' was taken to refer to a mode of incorporating a minority group into an encompassing nation without destroying the minority's cultural heritage and collective identity. It projected a future for Aboriginal people as Australian citizens, with all the rights and entitlements attached thereto, while at the same time retaining a secure sense of Aboriginality. The alacrity with which some campaigners adopted the slogan was symptomatic of their growing disenchantment with governmental programs and practices carried out in the name of assimilation. 'Integration' offered a slogan under which activists could distance themselves from government programs while still affirming their commitment to national inclusion. This chapter examines the disputes over assimilation and integration, arguing that beneath the terminological disagreement lay fundamental commonalities of aim and aspiration.

Assimilation through tradition

In the 1950s and 1960s, anthropologists were among the most incisive critics of government programs of assimilation. They were also among the staunchest advocates of assimilation. Working within prevailing anthropological paradigms, which presumed the human need for group cohesion and cultural continuity, most anthropologists assumed that assimilation must proceed through Indigenous groups and recognise a role for Indigenous traditions. Well before the slogan 'integration' appeared, anthropologists had advocated collectivist models of assimilation. So had members of other professions who worked with Aboriginal people, notably missionaries. I shall begin my exposition of this variant of assimilation by discussing the views of AP Elkin, Australia's most publicly prominent anthropologist at the time.

Elkin often described assimilation as a process of 'cultural blending'. In 1951, he explained to Henry Wardlaw, Secretary of the Victorian Council for Aboriginal Rights, that assimilation 'does not mean…the breakdown of the Aborigines as a people' or the destruction of their culture; rather, a 'blend of culture is what will appear'.[8] In an article urging the preservation of Aboriginal languages as part of the assimilatory process, he explained that assimilation was a process of 'bridge-building' between Indigenous and non-Indigenous worlds, and the 'bridge, when built, and built by co-operative effort by the Aborigines and ourselves, will be of blended material — of values and interpretations, both old and new, both Aboriginal and European. Therein will lie its strength.'[9]

Because Elkin's version of assimilation entailed a significant measure of Indigenous agency in creating a new cultural blend, he could not specify exactly what the outcome might be. However, a good idea of how he envisaged assimilation proceeding can be gathered from his 1953 proposals for Aboriginal policy in the Darwin area. He acknowledged that after long interaction with outsiders, Aboriginal groups around Darwin had modified their social structures and created 'a new solidarity of expanded groups'. This in no way diminished the viability of their cultural traditions, whose benefits Elkin extolled:

> Above all, the ritual life is retained or revived. This strengthens the authority of the elders, for their power derives from their place in, and knowledge of, the secret life...Further, rituals, which are sacred but not secret, such as some connected with initiation and burial, serve to express, against the background of the 'Eternal Dreamtime', the solidarity of the group in belief and aspiration, as well as in outward association.

'In other words,' he continued, 'the elders hope and plan to cope with the modern process of economic and political assimilation, by strengthening tribal sentiment and loyalty to the secret ceremonial life, with its moral and social implications'. By retaining 'their own sacred and secret sanctions', they were 'developing a pride in themselves as Aborigines, and when they become full citizens of Australia, they will do so as Australian Aborigines, who have worked out their new adaptation'.[10]

Elkin considered this program of cultural adaptation most applicable to northern and central Australian Aboriginal groups whose traditional cultures still flourished. For those in the closely settled south and east, cultural renovation was less viable since, in his view, Aboriginal groups there had lost the integrity — though not the entirety — of their traditional cultures. What remained still had value, he maintained, for it contributed to their group cohesiveness, thereby assisting them to engage positively with the wider society. Assimilation, he asserted, 'did not, and does not, mean that part-Aborigines, in order to realize citizenship, must discard customs and beliefs that they have inherited from the "old people"'.[11] He maintained that, 'Assimilation does not mean that, to be citizens, Aborigines must give up all their kinship customs and their beliefs and rites, or that local groups may no longer think of themselves as closely knit communities'.[12] Rather, assimilation would result in Aboriginal people becoming 'a series of fairly compact social groups, but good Australian citizens, playing a part in our common life'.[13]

Occasionally, Elkin referred to the emergence of a 'dual' or 'plural' Australian society, though usually with a note of equivocation. In 1960 he suggested that 'a dual society is coming into being in Australia — the Aborigines and ourselves — both full citizens and with the boundaries between us neither sharply nor irrevocably marked', though he added that this duality might 'possibly prove to be no more than a transition phase'.[14] Several years later, he predicted that 'for some time ahead Australia will present a picture of a plural, unified society'.[15] Elkin frequently tacked phrases such as 'for generations' or 'for a long time' on to his references to cultural pluralism, suggesting that he thought it might prove transitory. His point, however, was that Aboriginal cultural distinctiveness would long outlast the fluctuating fashions of government policy. Now and for the foreseeable future, Aboriginal people were distinctive; that was all that could be known, and all that need be known for the formulation of policy. As he remarked to Olive Pink in 1954, assimilation did not mean 'the loss of the Aboriginal minority in the general population; that might happen a very long way in the future, but we have not to envisage it'.[16]

After the advent of 'integration' in the late 1950s, Elkin sometimes discussed its relationship with his preferred term, 'assimilation'. Occasionally, he expressed reservations about the possible connotations of the alternative term.[17] Usually, however, he indicated that integration was quite compatible with assimilation, sometimes using the two words interchangeably or explicitly asserting their synonymity.[18] He specified that integration (like assimilation) had different entailments for southern mixed-bloods than for northern full-bloods. The latter could bring to the process a rich and coherent cultural heritage, whereas:

> For part-Aborigines...from southern Queensland to the south-west of Western Australia...[t]his heritage of inspiring belief and duty has been lost in the confusion of racial contact and mixture, and whatever integration may mean for part-Aborigines it can no longer include a living Aboriginal culture ...
>
> If, however, it means association in groups for housing, social or economic purposes so that part-Aborigines will be able to have an identity of their own, and a 'sense of belonging', there need be no conflict with assimilation.[19]

Regardless of policy label, his crucial point was that group solidarities be maintained.

In a paper entitled 'Assimilation and integration', presented to the 1959 ANZAAS Congress in Perth, Elkin publicly aired his disagreement with Hasluck. Against the minister's representation of assimilation as a process of rescuing 'stranded individuals', Elkin argued that 'the advancement of Aborigines will be in *group formation* not as individuals'. Both 'full-bloods and mixed-bloods', he noted, 'want to keep [their own] identity and continuity and sense of belonging as a distinct group', and should be permitted — even encouraged — to do so. It could be expected that they will observe a partial and voluntary segregation — an apartness for an unpredictable period. This will only be partly a reaction to white prejudice, which in any case is slowly being worn down; fundamentally this apartness is a sense of 'belonging'...Our task is to see that the phase of apartness does *not* become *apartheid* but that the Aboriginal integers are truly integrated in the structure of Australia as a whole.

Thus, he declared, 'the Aborigines will be an *integer* or series of integers in a plural society — Australia'. Whether this process be called 'assimilation' or 'integration' was to Elkin inconsequential.[20]

At the 1959 ANZAAS Congress, Elkin's successor as Professor of Anthropology at the University of Sydney, WR Geddes, spoke in support of his predecessor. Drawing on his experience as a New Zealander, Geddes pointed out how the formation of Maori clubs and associations had promoted Maori self-esteem, enhancing their capacity to engage with the wider society.[21] By the next ANZAAS Congress, he had expanded his comments into a full conference paper, in which he urged Australia to reform its policy along the lines already followed across the Tasman. He argued that specifically Indigenous associations should be fostered, not discouraged, 'because it is through groupings that people everywhere achieve their social adaptation'. Geddes did not dispute assimilation as a goal, though he suggested that Australian governments were impeding its achievement by constantly harping on the word instead of devoting themselves to objectives achievable in the short term, such as improved education and housing. What was needed, he argued, was flexibility in the implementation of policy, so Aboriginal people could group and regroup in whatever ways best facilitated their inclusion into the wider society.[22]

TGH Strehlow argued similarly that assimilation could best proceed by encouraging Aboriginal groupings, even to the extent of strengthening tribal structures of authority. In a formulation typical of anthropologists of his generation, he urged his fellow Australians to 'grasp the true core of the assimilation problem and begin to realize that individuals can be assimilated into a human society only through their membership in one or the other of the many small groups which in their totality constitute this society'.[23] Tearing up the fabric of Aboriginal society was a recipe for failure, he stated, because: 'To destroy the old group loyalties, even with the best of intentions, always brings chaos in its train.'[24]

'Many of us,' Strehlow wrote, 'are apt to think that the native problem could be solved if the natives could be made to give up their own human individuality and to copy us in all points'. However, 'we' were not really so morally admirable as to deserve such emulation; 'they' were far from so culturally and socially bankrupt as commonly supposed; and in any case mere mimicry was no solution.[25] It was essential, he urged, to implement 'an assimilation policy that will not involve the complete annihilation of Australian aboriginal culture'.[26]

Other anthropologists propounded similar versions of assimilation. Elkin's protégés, Ronald and Catherine Berndt, broadly followed their mentor's approach, recommending that assimilation proceed through the retention and renovation of Indigenous cultures and social formations.[27] Sociologist Jean Martin argued for 'the group becoming the focus of assimilation rather than the individual'. She explained that throughout the process, the 'cohesion of the group should be kept intact' and the minority should 'bring its own culture, thus contributing to the society in which the minority group finds itself'.[28] A few anthropologists, such as RG Hausfeld, insisted that the word for this process should be 'integration', not 'assimilation'.[29] Most, however, inclined towards Marie Reay's view that the 'label is not important...Policy should be flexible enough to enable [Aboriginal people] to make their own choices without being brainwashed by do-gooders and petty officials'.[30] Reay was quite prepared to accept 'assimilation' as a policy label, but insisted that those administering it must appreciate the vitality and viability of Aboriginal cultures and social groups.

Missionaries were coming to the same view. Although Australian missionaries before the Second World War — especially those of Protestant affiliation — had generally been hostile towards Aboriginal cultures, there were exceptions; and after the war a more culturally appreciative attitude gained ground in missionary circles.[31] With this went a more positive assessment of Aboriginal sociality and a realisation that its maintenance could contribute to the building of Aboriginal Christian communities. Exponents of this view included the Methodist Wilbur Chaseling, founder of Yirrkala Mission in Arnhem Land, and the Presbyterian JRB Love, whose postings included Kunmunya in Western Australia and Ernabella in South Australia.[32] Ernabella, founded in 1936, was probably the most culturally sensitive mission ever established in Australia. At Ernabella, the local Pitjantjatjara people were encouraged to maintain their ritual and ceremonial life, as well as their hunting and gathering economy, while they were gradually introduced to the Western way of life and the Christian faith. The mission's founder, Dr Charles Duguid, was a committed assimilationist who insisted that Aboriginal people themselves should choose the pace and manner in which they adjusted to the modern world.[33]

Duguid was one of the first Australians to publicly demand that Aboriginal policy conform to the United Nations Declaration of Human Rights.[34] In 1952, he compiled a point-by-point list of articles in the Declaration that were violated by laws and administrative practices relating to Aboriginal people.[35] Far from this making him a critic of assimilation, his dedication to United Nations ideals underpinned his commitment to assimilation. In a 1952 BBC radio broadcast, Duguid celebrated the endorsement of assimilation by the previous year's Native Welfare Conference, though he warned that assimilation must be respectful of Aboriginal cultures and attuned to Aboriginal social groups.[36] In his 1963 book, *No Dying Race*, he condemned the practice of taking mixed-descent children from their parents and individualist modes of assimilation more generally, arguing that if 'the policy of assimilation is to succeed', it must be implemented in ways enabling Aboriginal people 'to retain the self-respect and independence they had in tribal days'.[37]

Most Australian missionaries and missionary organisations remained committed to assimilation throughout the 1950s and 1960s. Some — especially those of fundamentalist stripe — continued coercive and culturally repressive methods of conversion;[38] however, mainstream missionary organisations increasingly turned away from such practices, in the process reforming their conception of assimilation. In 1957, the Australian Board of Missions affirmed its support for assimilation, stipulating that this demanded 'a positive attitude to the indigenous culture'. It explained that:

> Respect for the dignity and integrity of the individual Aborigine and his people as Aborigines will be implicit in any process of assimilation acceptable to Christian conscience. The Aborigine's own community is to be recognised and preserved as the proper environment within which we will encourage and assist him to develop a way of life compatible with the general community life of Australia ...
>
> Aboriginal peoples on their old tribal lands have a moral right to possession of that land and its resources. Their right of

possession should be recognised and expressed in appropriate legal measures.[39]

The Board was not the only advocate of assimilation to also endorse Aboriginal title to land.

In 1953, Ted Evans, Acting District Superintendent of the Native Affairs Branch in Alice Springs, recommended that Aboriginal groups be granted 'Ownership of their land' since a 'native people divorced from their land, in my opinion, has little hope of successful assimilation'. This was part of Evans' broader plea for the adoption of a collectivist approach to assimilation in the Northern Territory. 'For any group to survive and progress,' he argued, 'there must be some principle of cohesion holding the members together, and ties with the past giving them continuity as they move forward'. Consequently, the Aboriginal 'family and social pattern', along with their cultural heritage, should be maintained as far as possible; otherwise 'there can be little hope for their survival and successful assimilation'.[40] Evans' views do not appear to have been exceptional among his patrol officer colleagues[41] — which is unsurprising, since Northern Territory patrol officers received training in anthropology at the University of Sydney under Professor Elkin.

An expedient slogan

In the early to mid-1950s, there was substantial Aboriginal support for assimilation, since it promised social acceptance and recognition of human rights.[42] The Aboriginal-Australian Fellowship, founded in 1956 by Aboriginal activists Pearl Gibbs and Herbert Groves and Pacific Islander Faith Bandler, was unexceptional for its endorsement of the 'policy of assimilation', which its founders evidently considered consistent with their objectives of cultivating 'complete social and political equality' and 'the fullest mutual understanding between the Aboriginal and European Australians'.[43] Yet within a year of the Fellowship's foundation, its president, Herbert Groves, was condemning assimilation and extolling integration in its place.[44] In 1958, the Fellowship changed its constitution, substituting 'integration' for 'assimilation'.

The Victorian Aborigines Advancement League made the terminological substitution during the process of its creation. Its draft constitution, dated 29 April 1957, listed as one of its five primary objectives: 'To assist in the effective assimilation of [Aboriginal people] into the larger community.'[45] A few months later, the League adopted a constitution in which this objective was amended to: 'To work toward the complete integration of people of Aboriginal descent with the Australian community'.[46] The League quickly became one of the most astringent critics of assimilation, in 1959 condemning it as 'racial genocide'.[47] How, then, could this organisation have endorsed 'assimilation' in its own draft constitution only two years earlier? There is nothing to suggest that the founders of the League had experienced an intellectual epiphany in the meantime. Apart from substituting the word 'integration' for 'assimilation', the League's final constitution was substantively unchanged from its draft. Both versions demanded 'full citizenship rights' for all 'people of aboriginal descent' and the 'full recognition of the contribution they are able to make' to the Australian community. What changed was the activists' acquisition of a new word by which to distinguish between their own and governmental modes of national inclusion. The dating of the League's constitutional rewording corresponds precisely with the publication of ILO Convention 107.

These anecdotes illustrate the theme elaborated in this section: 'Integration' was a new slogan in Aboriginal affairs, not a new idea. Activist groups such as the Aboriginal-Australian Fellowship and the Aborigines Advancement League had good reason to adopt a new slogan. They may well have been aware of the more culturally sensitive, collectivist models of assimilation propounded by anthropologists and missionaries — some of their members certainly were. But as political activists, their paramount goal was to change governmental practices, for which purpose a neat dichotomy of policy options was expedient. 'Assimilation', in their usage, referred to what governments did in its name, while 'integration' was a handy slogan under which to propound different, less coercive programs attuned to the advancement of Aboriginality as well as Aboriginal people. Not all reformers expressed a preference for the term 'integration', but many did, and it is on them that this section focuses.

Posing a sharp dichotomy between 'assimilation' and 'integration' was politically expedient in the late 1950s and 1960s, but it has left a legacy whereby that dichotomy has been taken at face value by later historians. Some historical accounts purvey the misleading impression that, in contemporary arguments over Aboriginal policy, exponents of assimilation — dedicated to the effacement of Aboriginality and the withholding of civil rights — lined up against the champions of integration, committed to the preservation of Aboriginality and the extension of Aboriginal rights.⁴⁸ In fact, the distinction between assimilation and integration was at best hazy and probably illusory, as many contemporary commentators acknowledged. 'Integration' had the advantage of being less polysemous than 'assimilation'. Although neither single nor stable in meaning, the former word referred to modes of national inclusion on a group basis, respectful of minority heritage and identity. 'Assimilation' ranged more widely in meaning, from that just given for 'integration' through to policies aiming at the effacement of Aboriginality by engineered interbreeding. Even so, between the two words there was more concordance than contradiction. And the problem with having commensurable words as rival slogans was that it could deflect ostensible debates over policy into sterile semantic squabbles. Charles Rowley complained of this as early as 1962.⁴⁹

Rowley's complaint notwithstanding, many advocates of 'integration' recognised that their aims were not so distant from those pursued under the rubric of 'assimilation'. The Aboriginal-Australian Fellowship, although a critic of assimilation since 1957, in 1966 urged the New South Wales government to change policy 'either by adoption of "integration"…or by retaining the word "assimilation" but defining and interpreting it' such that Aboriginal people could 'retain elements of their group and cultural life if that is their choice'.⁵⁰ It was a clear concession that the policy changes it sought were attainable under either label. John Jago, Convenor of the Commission on Aboriginal Affairs in the Methodist Church, expressed a strong preference for 'integration', but also a desire to avoid 'wordy battles about assimilation and integration'. The former word was acceptable, he indicated, because it smoothed communications with governments and could be given the same meaning as 'integration'.⁵¹ These statements by Jago and the Fellowship (and many of their contemporaries) evince a terminological pragmatism that was possible only because the two terms overlapped so substantially. As the Victorian-based lobby group Aboriginal Affairs (which preferred 'integration') acknowledged: 'In practice the distinctions between the two approaches are not always clear.'⁵²

The distinctions were not clear, but the target of integrationists' criticism was. It was what governments did, and tried to do, under the rubric of assimilation. Integrationists condemned programs of assimilation for denying Aboriginal people 'the right to plan their own destiny';⁵³ smashing Aboriginal communities;⁵⁴ facilitating exploitation of Aboriginal labour;⁵⁵ perpetuating restrictive protectionist laws;⁵⁶ making 'our natives a second-rate copy of ourselves';⁵⁷ 'forcing complete cultural extinction';⁵⁸ depriving

Aboriginal people of their land[59] and much else besides. Some integrationists drew attention to the contradictions within government programs, particularly between the inclusionist ideals of assimilation and the reality of segregation in many jurisdictions professing the policy.[60] Kath Walker characterised assimilation as 'the biggest farce since Rafferty himself set up his own particular brand of rules', noting that 'the Governments of Australia have implemented a policy of segregation, which they blithely call and [sic] "assimilation" policy'.[61] Yet, while Walker condemned assimilation as segregation in disguise, other activists maintained that it was a surreptitious attempt at total, biological absorption.[62] 'Assimilation' in this usage was a catch-all term for all practices, programs and objectives, actual and alleged, of governments professing adherence to the policy — which is to say, all Australian governments in the 1950s and 1960s.

Such use of policy terms may be unexceptional, but it meant that contemporary debate over assimilation was clouded by usage of the word in two quite different senses. One is that just instanced, construing the term as governmental practices and programs. The other, discussed in the previous and later sections of this chapter, conceived assimilation more broadly as a process of social inclusion, by whatever means, with whatever entailments. Those using the term in the latter sense could be just as critical of governmental actions as those using it in the former. Indeed, exponents of assimilation made exactly the same accusations against governmental practices as those, listed above, made by integrationists. Arguments about assimilation in the 1950s and 1960s were far from straightforward.

In fact, even integrationists who vehemently condemned assimilation (as government practice) often slipped into the other sense of the term (as social process). Three years after condemning assimilation as 'genocide' in 1959, the Aborigines Advancement League published another statement on 'Assimilation and Integration'. This time, it posed the distinction more temperately, in terms of 'the speed at which social change is to take place'. 'Thus,' it maintained,

> it becomes meaningful to suggest that Aborigines...might be substantially assimilated into a fairly homogeneous Australian community within *two or three hundred years*. Obviously change is weighted toward assimilation in the long run. Further, it is sensible to suggest that the assimilation process can be impeded by an impatient or naive programme which produces resistance or emotional breakdown.

>On the other hand, the process may be expedited in the long run by allowing groups to maintain a 'transitional separation' until their members have been equipped with the knowledge and confidence they will need to deal successfully with the contemporary environment.[63]

In this rendition, integration was simply a slower, more gentle and therefore probably more successful means of achieving the same end as assimilation. The crucial point, however, is that 'assimilation' in this statement denoted the broad process of minority incorporation into a larger social entity, whereas in the League's earlier condemnation of assimilation as genocide, it used the term in reference to governmental practices.

Similar terminological slippage is apparent in one of the first attempts to counter 'assimilation' with 'integration'. In his 1957 appeal for the adoption of 'integration', Herbert Groves claimed that assimilation policy manifested a pernicious desire for *'the disappearance of the Aboriginals as a separate cultural group, and ultimately their physical absorption by the European part of the population'*. Assimilation was, he declared, an expression of a 'belief that there is nothing worth preserving in Aboriginal culture'. Yet only two pages earlier in the same document, when criticising the lack of governmental effort to improve the material and legal status of Aboriginal people, Groves complained that 'assimilation is proceeding too slowly — and another generation is falling victim to the *"too little"*, *"too late"* policy.[64] In the first-quoted passage, Groves censured assimilation as government policy. In the second, he upheld assimilation as a social process that governments were doing too little to advance. In some later versions of the second passage, Groves amended it to 'integration is proceeding too slowly'.[65] The easy interchangeability of the words reinforces my point that in most contexts the two terms meant much the same thing.

Many contemporary commentators recognised this near-synonymity, and complained that too much energy was being wasted in terminological dispute. Fay Gale, a postgraduate student at the University of Adelaide, claimed integration to be 'almost synonymous with social assimilation'.[66] Charles Duguid said: 'Let's not talk about integration or assimilation. Those are just words. Let us work simply and go together as citizens of the same country.'[67] A doctoral student from Washington University, James Pierson, after interviewing most of the members of the South Australian Aborigines Progress Association in the late 1960s, stated: 'Arguments about the use of the term "integration" as opposed to the official "assimilation" simply allow the absence of action to be obscured by rhetoric.'[68]

Some Aboriginal activists seem to have agreed with Pierson's sentiments. The emerging young Aboriginal leader Charles Perkins was one. His biographer, Peter Read, seems to have been troubled by Perkins' support for assimilation, suggesting that the young Aboriginal man could have done so only because 'he knew no other policy, and was scarcely aware of the meaning of the word'.[69] But Perkins' endorsement of assimilation did not indicate that he approved each and every governmental practice carried out in its name, and still less that he envisaged the process culminating in biological absorption, as Read suggests it must. Read's account reveals Perkins to have been one of the most astute and assertive Aboriginal activists Australia had yet seen. He endorsed not only assimilation but also integration, often simultaneously.[70] It is not clear whether he regarded the two as distinct though compatible policies, or as more or less synonymous terms, but in my view Perkins was simply determined not to allow his fight against racism to be sidelined into a struggle over slogans.

Definitions and redefinitions

It was not until 1961 that the Commonwealth and state authorities responsible for Aboriginal affairs, meeting as the Native Welfare Council, offered a comprehensive definition of assimilation. This was the definition, quoted in the previous chapter, emphasising the desired sameness of Aboriginal and other Australians in rights, responsibilities, customs, beliefs, hopes and loyalties. Although Native Welfare Conferences had championed assimilation since their inception in 1951, earlier conferences had shied away from rigorously defining the term. The belated definition of 1961 seems to have been intended as a rebuttal of integration and other collectivist models of assimilation then gaining ground among reformers.

The record of the 1961 Native Welfare Conference indicates that there was no dispute among delegates over the formal definition of assimilation. However, in the general business of the conference there was a good deal of dispute, in which delegates did express views revealing divergent understandings of assimilation. None was more bizarre than the statement by the Queensland Minister for Health and Home Affairs, Dr HW Noble: 'The Torres Strait islanders are completely assimilated. They have pride of race. You never see a part-coloured Torres Strait islander because they do not want to live with white people.' If this equation of 'assimilated' with a dislike of living with white people was idiosyncratic, so was Dr Noble's conception of integration: 'We in Queensland aim at reaching complete integration. By that I mean that we are aiming at reaching the stage at which the question of colour will be completely forgotten.'[71] Noble's apparent confusion probably derived from the fact that Queensland, while professing a policy of assimilation, actually pursued strategies of segregation. This was a frequent target of criticism at the time.[72] The Queensland authorities had a fine eye for the inconsequentiality of terminological refinement or definitional rigour. They were happy to use any slogan, in whatever way they pleased, while they pursued a policy trajectory of their own. Queensland took lexical licence further than any other Australian government, but the fact remains that neither the 1961 nor any other Native Welfare Conference achieved consistency of practice among the various governments professing commitment to assimilation.

Perhaps the main consequence of the 1961 Native Welfare Council definition of assimilation was to inflame criticism of government policies. Stan Davey, General Secretary of the FCAA, began his 1963 pamphlet, *Genesis or Genocide?*, by quoting this definition. Bain Attwood nominates Davey's pamphlet as 'probably the most thorough repudiation of assimilation in the late 1950s and early 1960s'.[73] It was certainly a thorough repudiation of the 1961 Native Welfare Council definition and of government programs of assimilation more generally, but Davey did not repudiate assimilation itself. His pamphlet concluded:

> The process of assimilation whereby people of different races intermingle and become more and more closely identified with one another will continue in Australia with aborigines, migrants and Australian born Europeans, no matter what policy is adopted by Australian governments. The concern of this pamphlet has been to show that there are strong and real objections to an assimilation policy which assumes one of the races involved in the process has nothing to contribute to the national character and whose only hope is to 'get lost' in the dominant community ...
>
> A new approach to the policy of assimilation is called for, based on respect for Aborigines as a people with minority group rights.[74]

Davey excoriated existing government programs as unjust, immoral, incompatible with international standards and ineffectual in achieving their ostensible (and, in his view, desirable) objective of bringing Aboriginal people into the national community. But nowhere in this pamphlet did he suggest that assimilation should be abjured or an alternative policy label adopted. His plea was for the reform of assimilation, not its abandonment. The fact that in other contemporaneous statements he made the same plea using the terminology of integration underlines my point that no clear distinction can be made between it and assimilation.

After 1961, those who sought reform under the banner of 'assimilation' increasingly emphasised that the policy must show respect for Aboriginality.[75] In 1963 the National Missionary Council issued two booklets on the topic. The first, *The meaning of assimilation*, opened by asserting that while the Council was 'committed to a policy of assimilation', there was an urgent 'need to clarify what "assimilation" means', particularly in view of some undesirable connotations of the 1961 Native Welfare Conference definition. 'Integration' might be a better term in certain respects, it suggested, but since 'it also has several meanings and usages in Australia', the Council preferred to retain the terminology endorsed by governments. Assimilation, the Council insisted, must always be entirely voluntary on the part of Aboriginal people; must be based on the recognition of Aboriginal people as 'a distinct ethnic group' within the Australian nation; and must be 'founded on mutual respect and the mutual recognition of common rights and responsibilities in a land that is shared by two races'. The 'existence of distinctively Aboriginal groups', it explained, 'need not be detrimental to national well-being'. It also asserted that 'assimilation is a two-way process, and the greater initiative rests with the white Australian'.[76]

The Council's second booklet, *Four major issues in assimilation*, began by asserting that Aboriginal people 'have a basic right to land or to compensation for the loss of land', which should be granted 'not as an act of generosity, but as the discharge of an obligation'. 'Assimilation will never take place', it warned, unless Aboriginal people acquired the economic security that came with land ownership. The second issue was language, which the Council designated 'a vehicle of culture'. The 'policy of assimilation', it declared, 'must be so interpreted as to encourage the preservation and development of Aboriginal languages and the cultures they express'. The third issue was legal equality, tempered by recognition that 'there should be particular discriminations in favour of Aborigines in order to offset the disadvantages under which they often find themselves'. The fourth was 'political education and development', which included Aboriginal people's access to 'ways of righting a wrong'.[77] The two National

Missionary Council booklets offered the most comprehensive counter to the 1961 Native Welfare Conference definition so far published. Yet, apart from a single equivocal mention of 'integration', it was framed entirely in the language of assimilation.

The Deputy Secretary of the Department of Territories gave the Missionary Council's arguments a sympathetic hearing, expressing concurrence with most of their propositions and rejecting only those concerning rights to land. He endorsed the Council's central contention that Aboriginal people must be given 'a free choice, either to merge as individuals into the white society or to remain members of their own aboriginal community', adding that:

> It is now fairly widely accepted that a primitive individual is more able to cope with the transition to a modern way of life if he does so from the base, as it were, of his own community. Basically the question involved is that of self-respect...In other words, it now seems necessary to make an attempt to restore the faith of the aborigines in themselves *as aborigines*. It is not sufficient to try and persuade them that it is desirable for them to be like white men; they should be encouraged to believe that they can, as aborigines, enter fully and freely into the modern society.

He recommended that the Council's proposals be discussed at the next Native Welfare Conference. Hasluck rejected the recommendation, not so much out of disagreement with the Missionary Council's arguments as for his freely expressed preference for administrative stability over 'general philosophical debate'.[78]

Hasluck moved portfolio, from Territories to Foreign Affairs, in 1963. The first meeting of the renamed Aboriginal Welfare Council after his departure witnessed a shift in that body's definition of assimilation. The South Australian delegation to the 1965 conference proposed the following:

> The policy of assimilation means that all persons of Aboriginal descent will live as members of the Australian community. It is recognised that the existence of distinctively Aboriginal groups at their wish is not inconsistent with this policy. Likewise it is not inconsistent with this policy that persons of Aboriginal descent retain those cultural activities and social customs which, when blended with other cultures and customs, will enrich the

Australian way of life. The participation of persons of Aboriginal descent in formulating plans for their future is inherent in this policy.[79]

The representatives of other states and the Commonwealth were not entirely comfortable with this, and the definition of 'assimilation' finally agreed to at the 1965 conference was closer to that of 1961. However, the revised definition acknowledged a role for choice on the part of Aboriginal people and deleted the requirement that they adopt the 'same customs' and 'same beliefs' as other Australians. The 1965 redefinition offered, in Rowse's words, 'a frail platform for reformers of government practice'.[80] Yet reformers seized on its 'new permissive note' as an invitation for 'consultation, participation, decision-making by Aborigines to become policy goals'.[81]

By this time, some reformers were proffering additional alternative labels. The Presbyterian minister VW Coombes recommended 'incorporation' as the best term for the 'exceedingly complex' process of including Aboriginal people in the Australian nation without loss of their distinctiveness. 'Already there exists a limited multi-racial nation,' he observed, and looked forward to it becoming more multiracial while still retaining 'an essential unity'. 'Australian Aborigines and Australian Others are,' he wrote,

> two separate and complex communities, each subject to rapidly changing times and each a living organism and consequently adaptable. 'Incorporation' carries clealy [sic] the concept of bringing those two organisms into union or combination to grow into a single organism or Australian Community or Nation. It assumes that each component (ingredient) will make its own peculiar contribution to the whole, but without loss of separate personality.[82]

Coombes' terminological preference aside, his argument was premised on the desirability of pluralist nationhood, an aspiration attracting increasing support by the mid-1960s.

However, both Commonwealth and state governments remained committed to assimilation, and reformers continued to try to squeeze something positive from that commitment. The political scientist Colin Tatz had been a vocal critic of Aboriginal governance throughout the 1960s. Yet in 1967 he declared that the 'assimilation policy is essentially a policy of equality'. Critics of assimilation, he stated, often missed the point since that policy of equality has never really been put into practice, not ever, not by anybody. The ideals of governments, the beautiful polished phrases of government, are something that I think ought not to be condemned but to be respected as reasonable, as attainable goals and ideals and aspirations. The trouble has been in the administration of those policies.

Aboriginal administration, he contended, was excessive, intrusive and often conducted by ill-informed personnel who made little attempt to listen, let alone accede, to Aboriginal desires and aspirations. It was primarily at the administrative interface between government and Aboriginal people, not at the level of policy formulation, that the problems lay.[83]

Charles Rowley was another prominent critic of government programs of assimilation. Their goals, he asserted, were 'nebulous' and 'vaguely defined'.[84] Yet Rowley did not disavow assimilation itself, explaining that what he sought was 'a particular refinement of the assimilation policy, which will make possible the emergence of practical projects on the basis of agreement with Aboriginal groups'. He added that, 'If a slogan is needed, and it probably is, it might be *Aboriginal initiative and development, and assistance on request.*' Slogan-making was evidently not Rowley's forte, but he had little time for 'integration' as an alternative slogan to 'assimilation', stating that there was 'little point in semantic arguments, of the kind which have been common over the last few years'.[85] What mattered, Rowley insisted, was the content of policy, not its name; and while critical of much that had been done under the aegis of assimilation, he was appreciative of its more liberal variants.

Yet by the late 1960s, the word 'assimilation' increasingly was coming into disrepute, to the extent that even governments were becoming circumspect about using the word. The booklet, *Aboriginal advancement and what it takes*, assiduously avoided the word, even though it was the 1967 issue in the propaganda series which Paul Hasluck had begun ten years earlier to promote assimilation.[86] When governments did refer to 'assimilation', they were more likely than before to specify that the policy provided for the maintenance, even encouragement, of Aboriginality. Commonwealth Minister for Territories, CE Barnes, stated that the 1967 Aboriginal Welfare Conference reaffirmed 'the common objective of assimilation', which entailed recognition of:

> the value to Aborigines and to the enrichment of Australian cultural life of encouraging pride and participation in elements of traditional Aboriginal culture in such forms as legend, music, dance and art. It is not the policy of welfare administrations to seek to destroy such cultural elements, but to encourage them, in promoting the advancement of Aborigines in the general community.[87]

More than earlier government statements that had signalled acceptance of a residue of Aboriginality, the minister was now urging cultural retention to promote assimilation.

Although some activists continued to insist that reform was achievable only under the rubric of 'integration', once governments began to use this word it lost whatever edge it once had. As early as 1961, the Select Committee on Voting Rights for Aborigines stated that the 'declared policy of the Commonwealth Government towards the aboriginal people is that they should be gradually integrated into the European community', and that 'any policy other than integration…would be impracticable'.[88] In 1965, Prime Minister Menzies informed the Commonwealth parliament that the aim of his government was 'the integration of the Aboriginal in the general community'.[89] Three years later, WC Wentworth, Commonwealth Minister in Charge of Aboriginal Affairs, issued a policy statement that nowhere used the word 'assimilation', instead looking forward to 'the full integration of Aboriginal and European civilisation in Australia'.[90] By the late 1960s, government statements on Aboriginal affairs flipped between 'assimilation' and 'integration', making no clear distinction between them. Many reformers had effectively done that ever since arguments about assimilation had begun.

Chapter 7

Enriching the Nation

Beneath the arguments about assimilation reviewed in the previous chapter lay differing views on the viability of pluralist nationhood. Advocates of hard-line assimilation opposed pluralism, insisting that nationhood demanded cultural homogeneity, while exponents of collectivist models of assimilation (including integration) sanctioned pluralism, suggesting that greater cultural diversity would enrich the Australian nation. In practice, arguments were not so sharply dichotomised, lying rather on a continuum in which few rejected all manifestations of cultural diversity and even fewer advocated a unconstrained pluralism. Nonetheless, over the course of the 1960s there was a drift toward the pluralist end of the spectrum, as even governments came to cautiously endorse the weaving of an Aboriginal theme into the national fabric.

Change was uneven, but after the Second World War Australia progressively became more cosmopolitan, in outlook as well as in demographic composition.[1] Attitudinal change seeped into Aboriginal affairs, as the Commonwealth's 1965 assimilation propaganda booklet noted: 'Older concepts about the Aborigines have tended to change over the years as the country has become increasingly urbanised, education standards have risen and the post-war influx of migrants has made most people familiar with strangers and with other languages, customs and modes of behaviour.'[2] Yet acceptance of European immigrants and their cultural heritage did not automatically translate into acceptance of Aboriginal people and cultures. Members of the former group, after all, could be accommodated relatively easily within the white Australia ideal. However, Aboriginal people possessed one attribute continental Europeans lacked: they were indisputably, authentically Australian. In an era when Australian conceptions of nationhood were undergoing fundamental change, when the ethnic core of Britishness was being hollowed out of the white Australia ideal, the Aboriginal heritage came to assume a new relevance to Australian nationalism.

Although the Australian nation in the 1950s and 1960s was becoming more open and inclusive, barriers to Aboriginal inclusion remained formidable. This chapter charts the faltering steps by which settler Australians in these decades became more appreciative of Aboriginal people and their heritage, and thereby more willing to accept them into the national community.

Respect and redemption

By the 1950s, settler Australians were increasingly troubled by a sense of guilt about past mistreatment of Aboriginal people. In 1957, Jessie Street noted that, 'Thinking people have a guilty conscience about our treatment of the aborigines and are ready to support measures which will benefit them.' Public opinion had shifted since the war, she suggested, and the shift had accelerated over the 1950s, to the extent that there 'has been an awakening of conscience of the white men during the past few years'.[3] 'Conscience' was the key word in Street's and other campaigners' statements, indicating they believed that the public understood these issues in moral, rather than merely political or legal, terms. In 1960 Gordon Bryant noted that the 'last three years have seen considerable progress in the development of a public conscience' on Aboriginal affairs.[4] A year later, he remarked on the recent growth of 'a tremendous public sympathy towards our First Australians...Most Australians feel that the plight of our aborigines weighs heavily on the conscience of the nation.'[5] FCAATSI president Joe McGinness opened his 1964–65 annual report with the assertion that, 'Never since the white man came to Australia has there been such an awakening of public conscience to the situation of the Aboriginal and Island peoples as during the last 12 months.'[6] These references to the awakening of public conscience may have been motivated partly by a desire to achieve what they ostensibly described, but there is no reason to doubt their veracity in general terms.

Nor is there any reason to suppose that the long-entrenched attitude of indifference had been transcended. Public opinion was shifting, but the shift was slow. Moreover, an awakening of conscience does not necessarily bring a comprehensive transformation of attitudes. Former South African Colin Tatz remarked in 1965:

> Whether white Australians love, like or even respect Aborigines, is difficult to judge. That we do not fear them marks off an essential difference between our administrations and African ones. But the history of white–Aboriginal relations suggests no love, less liking and even less respect. Today we see a national sense of atonement, the bending over backwards, the charity and the do-goodery: the desire to 'do something', to knit, to adopt black babies, to raise funds, start pre-schools, provide scholarships.[7]

The missing factor in white attitudes toward Aborigines was respect — without which, Tatz suggested, Aboriginal people would continue to be treated as the pathetic recipients of well-intentioned, but ultimately demeaning, help and charity.

In the mid-1950s, the National Missionary Council of Australia created a body with the express purpose of fostering respect for Aboriginal people: the National Aborigines Day Observance Committee (NADOC). The Missionary Council specified that NADOC's activities 'would be *expressly and solely directed to the white community*', since the

> one special area which still foiled advance by Aborigines comprised the attitudes and misguided judgements of the white folk. National Aborigines Day would therefore concentrate entirely on winning a changed outlook and consequent changed action on the part of the white community.

As an initiative of civil society, NADOC fitted perfectly with Hasluck's ideas on Aboriginal welfare. So did NADOC's endorsement of assimilation, which it described as the 'complete acceptance of Aborigines by the white community at all stages and standards of their living'. National Aborigines Day was first celebrated, with federal and state government support, in 1957. By 1959, NADOC could report that it had 'succeeded — not in that it has done something to Aborigines, but rather that it has done something to the white community'.[8]

Through the 1960s, NADOC continued to support the pluralist version of assimilation endorsed by the National Missionary Council.[9] Some disputes developed within the committee, particularly between those holding to a narrow interpretation of its educative role and those who wanted to prod governments into more actively promoting the profile of Aboriginal people.[10] Nonetheless, it had considerable success in achieving its objectives. In its 1966 annual report, NADOC could 'humbly claim credit for stimulating' some of the 'deepening interest of the whole community in Aboriginal affairs'.[11] Its members were well aware that the reformation of popular attitudes had a long way to go.

At a 1960 Aboriginal Scholarships National Conference, Reverend John Goodluck, Convenor of the Committee on Part-Europeans in the Methodist Church, argued that the 'Christian concept of unconditional neighbourliness' was essential if Aboriginal people were to be welcomed into the national community. Efforts should be redirected, he urged, 'from changing Aborigines until they become acceptable, to changing Caucasians to allow Aborigines to be accepted as they seek acceptance'. What was needed, Goodluck declared, was 'Reconciliation before Assimilation'.[12] At the same conference, Ian Spalding, founder of the lobby group Aboriginal Affairs, complained that government policies manifested a 'lack of respect' for Aboriginal people. Historically, he claimed, the record was one of continual white Australian 'tramp[ing] across the Aboriginal man's self-respect', and this continued into current practices of assimilation.[13]

Respect for Aboriginal people, Spalding insisted, must be expressed in the words used to refer to them. In 1961 he wrote to Prime Minister Menzies, asking that the word 'Aboriginal' and its derivatives take an initial capital in all government documents, as a token of the 'respect due to a person as the member of a race'. He also requested the word 'native' be dropped from official usage.[14] The Prime Minister's Department replied that his suggestion had been 'noted with interest', but Spalding was not so easily put off. He continued writing to Commonwealth departments on the issue through 1962 and into 1963. Other groups joined the fray. In March 1962, *Smoke Signals* published an article under the heading 'Respect for our Aborigines', urging the capitalised form 'Aborigine' become standard usage[15] (although this journal itself had used the uncapitalised form in all previous issues). Labor member Gordon Bryant raised the matter of the initial capital in parliament, and it was discussed at the 1963 Native Welfare Conference. After this conference, the Department of Territories adopted the capitalised form 'Aboriginal' and dropped use of the term 'native'. Some other Commonwealth departments followed suit.[16] From this time onward, capitalisation of the initial letter of 'Aboriginal', which hitherto had been an idiosyncrasy of individual writers, began to become standard usage.

However, not everyone supported the upper-case 'A'. In her 1964 collection, *Aborigines now*, anthropologist Marie Reay consistently spelled 'aborigine' with a lower-case 'a'. Unlike most, she justified her usage: 'If the aborigines are to have a distinctive name it should be one of their own choosing or at least one that is acceptable to them.' Acknowledging that literate Aboriginal persons generally preferred to see 'Aboriginal' with an initial capital, she noted that in conversation they usually referred to themselves with Aboriginal words that had acquired some regional currency, such as 'Kuri', 'Murree' or 'Jamadji' (words she consistently did capitalise). She argued that for authorities such as government officials and anthropologists to prematurely render 'aboriginal' a distinct ethnic identifier by capitalising its initial letter would impede the evolution of an Aboriginal collective name determined by Aboriginal people: 'To use a general term with world-wide applicability as a distinctive name for a tiny segment of a particular nation seems to me parochial in the extreme. These people will doubtless find a name if they ever develop the kind of social, cultural, or political unity that might inspire a need for one.' In Reay's view, Aboriginal people had not yet reached that point of collective self-consciousness, and until they did it would be best if others refrained from imposing an ethnic label drawn from the English language.[17]

Those seeking public respect for Aboriginal people in the early 1960s also condemned use of the words 'black' and 'blacks' to refer to them. Spalding's lobby group, Aboriginal Affairs, recommended 'the avoidance of all references to skin colour where possible'.[18] In 1964, Barry Christophers published an article under the heading 'Terminology is important', which discussed various 'objectionable' words including 'gin', 'abo', 'nigger' and 'native'. However, he devoted as much space to 'black' as to these other four terms together. 'Black', he claimed, carried connotations of dirt and disgrace, and it was important to avoid a vocabulary 'emotionally charged with prejudice' if racism were to be overcome. 'Using blacks synonymously [sic] with Aborigines,' he warned, 'is pandering to the view that skin colour is important when describing a member of Homo Sapiens'.[19] Only a few years later, young Aboriginal people under the influence of the black power movement would boast of their blackness as a point of pride.

Sporting heroes

Capitalising the initial letter of 'Aboriginal' may have been a mark of respect for those so designated, but winning the respect of the wider community was a more difficult achievement. In a nation that often venerated sport over all other fields of human endeavour, one means of doing so was by demonstrating prowess on the sports field. In 1967, Colin Tatz argued that, for Aboriginal people, 'it has been sporting achievement which has provided the way out of discrimination and the way to social acceptance'.[20] Decades later, in a new role as historian of Aboriginal sport, Tatz qualified that claim but still showed that sport has provided Aboriginal people with a significant, albeit imperfect, route to respect and acceptance by the wider Australian community. Particularly after the Second World War, the sporting profile of Aboriginal people rose steadily higher and they gradually infiltrated an ever-wider range of sporting genres.[21] I shall begin with the sport in which they were already most firmly established: boxing.

In the 1940s and 1950s, Aboriginal heroes of the ring included Elliott ('Elley') Bennett, George Bracken, Jack Hassen and Dave Sands. They were not just Aboriginal heroes, they were heroes to the Australian nation. Dave Sands was perhaps the most revered. In 1946, he held the Australian middleweight and light-heavyweight titles; in 1949, he took the Empire middleweight championship; and by 1950, he was considered the top contender for the world middleweight title.[22] Renowned for his agility and hard hitting in the ring, combined with modesty and devotion to family in his private life, Sands was voted Sportsman of the Year in 1950 and 1951, and would have repeated the achievement in 1952 had he not told the competition organisers to 'give it to somebody else, I've had my day in the sun'.[23] However, neither Sands nor any other Aboriginal boxer of the 1940s and 1950s managed to take a world title. The first to do so was Lionel Rose, who took the world bantamweight title from Masahiko ('Fighting') Harada in Tokyo in 1968.

The Rose–Harada match was publicised around the world, while in Australia people huddled eagerly around their radios. According to a journalist for *Sports Illustrated*, 'women wept over Lionel Rose and men shouted', while for Aboriginal people he was a symbol of hope 'that their own futures might rise beyond futility'.[24] Rose's victory prompted an unprecedented level of national adulation for an Aboriginal sportsman. He was welcomed back to Melbourne by a cheering crowd of 250,000 — more than even the Queen, President Johnson or the Beatles had drawn (see Plate 6). Later in 1968, Rose was awarded an MBE and acclaimed Australian of the Year, the first Aboriginal person to be awarded this honour.

In 1969, Rose published his autobiography, which began with reminiscences of his poverty-stricken childhood in the small Aboriginal community of Jackson's Track in Victoria's Gippsland. It was a fighter's, not a romantic's, view of Aboriginal life and culture: 'To fight was, and still is, the traditional way for the Aborigines...to settle arguments. And the Marquess of Queensberry never enters into the discussion when the men get going.' He recounted how he gradually and grudgingly won the respect of white Australians as he 'began moving up in the boxing world'. Commenting on the adulation he received after winning the world title, he remarked, with characteristic understatement, 'It is difficult to put your finger on the reason, but it could have something to do with being the first Aboriginal to win the world championship at anything and with my assimilation into the white community.'[25]

'I am as proud of my colour as the proudest of dark-skinned men', Rose proclaimed, proud also to see other Aboriginal people succeeding in employment and life. 'The time will come eventually', he predicted, 'when all Aborigines will be assimilated'; however, he equated this not with a loss of Aboriginal identity but with a renewed pride in that identity, 'when an Aboriginal can walk down the street with his head held high and be accepted'. He rejected offers to become 'a sort of political leader' for Aboriginal causes, mainly on account of his youth and the fact that he still had some years of a boxing career ahead of him. When that career was over, he intimated, he would reassess his options, but 'Until then I think I can do more for the Aborigines by setting an example with clean living and being a good citizen.'[26]

Tatz claims that, 'Whenever [Rose] appeared as champion, the speech was: "Ladies and gentlemen, introducing Lionel Rose, a great *Australian*!" His Aboriginality disappeared at those moments.'[27] I read the speech differently. Rose's Aboriginality was never in doubt. The point of proclaiming him a 'great Australian' was not to obscure his Aboriginality but to publicise the fact that an Aboriginal person could be 'a great Australian'. In the late 1960s, white Australians were eager for symbolic affirmations of their inclusiveness toward Aboriginal people, as the 1967 referendum (discussed in the next chapter) attests.

Although Rose rejected the option of using sport as a springboard into politics, some Aboriginal sportsmen took that path. Before his career as an activist, Doug Nicholls had won acclaim as a sprinter and as a winger in the Fitzroy Australian Rules Football Club. For Charles Perkins, who became the most renowned of the new generation of Aboriginal activists in the 1960s, soccer provided his first step into public life. Born into poverty in

1934 at the Old Telegraph Station at Alice Springs, by the age of twenty-one Perkins was among the highest paid soccer players in South Australia. After two years in England, where he played for the Everton and Bishop Auckland clubs, he returned to Australia in 1959. Soon afterwards, he commenced an Arts degree at the University of Sydney, financing his studies through soccer playing and laying the foundations for his political career. John Moriarty followed a similar path, from soccer to university and on to political activism.[28]

Soccer, however, failed to attract many Aboriginal players, at least at the elite level — probably because it was dominated by European immigrant groups and factionalised along European ethnic lines. Perkins and Moriarty played for teams bearing names such as Budapest, Croatia and Pan-Hellenic. Rugby Union also attracted few Aboriginal players in the 1950s and 1960s, since it was a game largely for the privileged classes. In the other two football codes, Rugby League and Australian Rules, things were different.

After the Second World War, the number of Aboriginal players in elite-level Rugby League steadily increased. Queenslander Lionel Morgan became the first Aboriginal person to represent Australia in League, playing in two tests and a World Cup match in 1960. From the mid-1960s, Aboriginal involvement in elite-level Rugby League boomed, with the emergence of stars such as Eric Simms and Arthur ('Artie') Beetson, the latter of whom often captained the Australian team in international matches.[29]

Apart from Doug Nicholls in the 1930s, it was not until after the Second World War that Aboriginal players made an impact in Australian Rules, with stars including Norm McDonald in the late 1940s and early 1950s, Graham ('Polly') Farmer from the late 1950s to the late 1960s, and Syd Jackson from the late 1960s to the mid-1970s. Australian Rules was notable for the extent to which the major Melbourne and Adelaide clubs imported talent from remote Aboriginal communities, particularly in the Northern Territory. Among the stars recruited in this way was David Kantilla, a Tiwi man who played for Adelaide clubs in the early 1960s.[30]

Aboriginal women also began to feature among Australia's elite athletes after the Second World War. Faith Thomas, born on Nepabunna Mission, South Australia, played in the Australian women's cricket team against England in 1958. Cheryl Mullett, born at Jackson's Track (and thus a childhood neighbour of Lionel Rose), represented Australia in international badminton in 1968 and 1969. In the late 1960s, another Aboriginal Victorian, Sharon Firebrace, represented Victoria and Australia in both volleyball and netball. Towards the end of the period covered by this book, a young woman from Barellan in New South Wales emerged as one of Australia's most successful and widely revered Aboriginal sporting heroes. At the age of nineteen, Evonne Goolagong won at Wimbledon and in the French Open in 1971, then went on to amass an impressive list of tennis titles, both Australian and international.[31] She was immensely popular with Australian audiences, her achievements were celebrated in mass-circulation magazines such as *The Australian Women's Weekly*, and in 1971 she was acclaimed Australian of the Year. Although she was criticised by some male activists for her lack of involvement in Aboriginal politics, her sporting success arguably achieved more in raising the public profile of Aboriginal people than any amount of protest could have done.

In 1962, Doug Nicholls suggested that including Aboriginal athletes 'could add glory to Australia in Olympic Games'.[32] Up to that time, no Aboriginal person had competed in any Olympic Games. It was not until the 1964 games in Tokyo that Australia fielded its first Aboriginal Olympic competitor, Michael Ahmatt from Townsville, who was a member of the Australian basketball team. Ahmatt competed again in the 1968 Mexico Olympics, along with the New South Wales-born Aboriginal wrestler John Kinsella.[33] (It was at this Olympic Games that two black American athletes, Tommy Smith and John Carlos, gave their defiant black power salute from the victory podium. Ahmatt's and Kinsella's reactions to the salute are unknown, but Smith's and Carlos's actions were a clear sign of the rising profile of race in sport.)

The importance of sport to Aboriginal people, and of Aboriginal people to Australian sport, was formally recognised in 1969 with the creation of the Aboriginal Sports Foundation, to advise the federal Minister in Charge of Aboriginal Affairs on funding and promoting Aboriginal sport.[34] By this time, an impressive array of Aboriginal sporting luminaries were available for appointment as the Foundation's first directors: Doug Nicholls (Australian Rules and athletics), Lionel Rose (boxing), Darby McCarthy (horseracing), Charles Perkins (soccer), Evonne Goolagong (tennis), Elley Bennett (boxing), Bill Dempsey (Australian Rules), Faith Thomas (women's cricket), George Bracken (boxing), David Kantilla (Australian Rules), Syd Jackson (Australian Rules), Ian King (cricket), Wally McArthur (athletics and Rugby League), Michael Ahmatt (basketball),

Eric Simms (Rugby League) and Reg Saunders (a soldier rather than a sportsman).[35]

It was not only at the elite level that sport promoted the social acceptance of Aboriginal people. Participation at the everyday level of the suburban club could also contribute, and both governments and lobby groups encouraged such participation.[36] The extent to which Aboriginal people in the 1950s and 1960s did participate in everyday sporting events and clubs is difficult to assess, although there must have been a substantial level of participation in at least some sports. The Aboriginal stars of Rugby League and various other sports could have achieved that status only by rising through the ranks in the local club or gymnasium. Popular prejudice doubtless posed impediments, yet it was often white patrons who provided Aboriginal youths with the opportunity to develop as sportspeople, as in the case of Lionel Rose and Cheryl Mullett.

Sporting prowess was a point of pride among Aboriginal people. The Aboriginal newspaper *Origin*, which began publication in 1969, regularly included sports news and photographs among its reportage of political and social issues. Sometimes *Origin* reported on Aboriginal high achievers such as Cheryl and Sandra Mullett; sometimes it was on more modest sports achievers such as the Alice Springs women's hockey team.[37] In either case, *Origin*'s editor, Margaret Koppe, clearly appreciated the role of sport in fostering both Aboriginal self-respect and the acclaim of the wider community. In some instances, sport provided a nucleus for distinctively Aboriginal solidarities, a notable instance being the annual festival, dubbed the 'Black Olympics', held at Yuendumu in the Northern Territory from the late 1950s onwards.[38] Several exclusively Aboriginal sports clubs had been formed, some dating back to before the Second World War. Perhaps the most famous was the Redfern All Blacks Rugby League Club, whose objectives in the 1960s included both 'the advancement of the Aborigines in all fields of sport' and 'their complete integration in the general community'.[39]

While there were exclusively Aboriginal events and clubs, most Aboriginal sporting activity in the 1950s and 1960s, at both elite and non-elite levels, entailed competition with and against non-Aboriginal sportspeople. For most events, too — certainly at the elite level — the majority of spectators were non-Aboriginal. Sport provided an arena in which Aboriginal people could showcase their talents, mental as well as physical, for as every sports follower knows, success in sport depends as much on self-discipline and determination as on muscular strength and coordination. In 1968, HC Coombs lauded 'the natural flair of many Aboriginals for sport — a flair in which we can all take pride'.⁴⁰ National pride in Aboriginal sporting achievement may have been sporadic at the time Coombs spoke but, with few exceptions, this gateway to social recognition had only been opened to Aboriginal people since the Second World War. Once unlocked, Aboriginal people themselves forced it wider and wider open by their own sporting achievements, often against the odds.

Indigenous wisdom

While Aboriginal people won acclaim on the sports field, many white advocates on their behalf preferred to stress the spiritual contribution they could make to the Australian nation. Claims that the Australian community and the wider Western world could benefit from Aboriginal sociality and spirituality were not entirely new, but in the postwar era they were made increasingly frequently and forcefully. The anxieties of the nuclear age, combined with the uncertainties of living in a time of ceaseless and accelerating change, fed into the growing appreciation of a culture once dismissed as a doomed relic of primeval times.

Explaining the relevance of Aboriginal studies to the modern world, in 1956 TGH Strehlow pointed out that this was an era in which World War had followed World War, then a Cold War 'whose antagonisms are backed by atom and hydrogen bombs':

> Our own generation has witnessed the horrors of slave camps, concentration camps, and extermination camps; the ruthless deportation of citizens organised by the rulers of Totalitarian States; and the employment of new weapons of mass destruction, used not against fighting men or installations of war, but against women, children and the residential areas of defenceless cities.

These modern horrors had been spawned by the materialism, greed and competitiveness of a Western civilisation which had lost its spiritual moorings, in response to which, Strehlow pleaded, 'we should strive to advance in point of our moral convictions...More than mere material progress is needed in our times: true civilisation demands civilised minds.' Aboriginal culture offered guidance.⁴¹

Strehlow did not suggest that white Australians should copy Aboriginal social institutions or mimic their rituals; rather, he asked them to cultivate an appreciation of Aboriginal cultures and social systems, from which they might formulate new antidotes to the ills of modernity. The sustaining ideals of Aboriginal societies were, above all, 'the principles of co-operation, not subordination; of differentiation without inequality; of tolerance for the customs of other peoples in their own country; and of respect for the hunting grounds of other tribes'. Strehlow tried to resist relapsing into a romance of the noble savage — not always successfully — but his message was clear: 'A measure of the spirit of co-operation and kinship that once expressed itself in the institutions of our Australian natives might perhaps be helpful in the solution of some of our own problems and those of the modern civilised world.'[42]

Strehlow's political views were decidedly conservative, as were those of many others who urged the modern world to learn from Aboriginal culture. In a 1964 public address, Dr HH Penny, former principal of the Adelaide Teachers' College, lamented that 'we are a rootless people, too heedless, if not contemptuous, of older ways and values, and institutions; restless, even tense and neurotic in our present living; uncertain, if not fearful, of our future'. White Australians, he suggested, had much to learn from the 'tribal aboriginal', especially his sense of 'community of feeling with his fellows'.[43] Like Penny, Mrs ME Langford, secretary of the Queensland government-sponsored One People of Australia League, asserted the value of traditional Aboriginality from a conservative perspective. In 1963, she advised Paul Hasluck that 'we should be prepared to admit that at some points the very real civilisation the Aborigines had was superior to our own'. Hasluck disagreed, responding that 'the aborigines had a culture of their own and that culture was worthy of respect. I would not admit that they had any civilisation.'[44] Nonetheless, the fact that the minister felt obliged to contest this claim by a leader of a conservative assimilationist body, which took its name from Hasluck's own *One people* booklet, suggests that he felt the old certitudes of civilisation to be no longer as secure as they once had been.

In an age when materialism seemed to be running rampant, the non-materialistic outlook of Aboriginal people was often held up for praise. Mr E LeSueur, social worker for the Council of Aboriginal Women of South Australia, maintained that 'many Aboriginal values, particularly their orientation toward human relationships rather than towards material acquisition, are superior to European values'.[45] The visiting American anthropologist Lamont West suggested that white Australians should learn from the ways in which Aboriginal people achieved a balance between material and spiritual fulfilment. This was only one of many benefits West discerned in the Aboriginal heritage, as he promoted what he called 'two-way assimilation' in which white Australians would be as open to Aboriginal culture as Aboriginal people were to Western society.[46]

Admittedly, the lessons to be learned from Aboriginal culture depended on the predisposition of the advocate. In 1969, Bill Wentworth suggested that one modern social problem that Aboriginal knowledge could help resolve was the 'wave of youth unrest' plaguing Western societies, 'particularly at universities'. According to Wentworth, it was 'fairly clear that this comes from a break-down of the sanctions which have been employed over the millennia to channel the energies of youth for the services of the community'. Aboriginal people, more in tune with age-old means of integrating the generations, could offer guidance to modern parents faced with rebellious youth.[47] From a very different perspective, Father Tony Newman, speaking at the 1971 FCAATSI conference in Townsville, observed that, 'Aborigines and hippies have a lot in common in their rejection of materialism. They can teach us to reject materialism.'[48] Although Aboriginality could be invoked for such divergent purposes, the fact that it was increasingly invoked as something positive is indicative of a changing evaluation of its relationship with the modern world.

The idea that familiarity with Indigenous traditions could help strengthen settler Australians' connectedness to the land blossomed in the 1950s and 1960s. Catherine and Ronald Berndt concluded their 1952 book, *The first Australians*, with the assertion that Aboriginal people 'have something to offer us, too…the spiritual heritage of the Aboriginal Way. Enriched by this link with their traditional background, we can become more truly Australian, more deeply a part of this land which we, like the Aborigines, know and love.'[49] The second (1967) edition of this book — which, like the first, was aimed at a general readership — observed that 'because the Aborigines made this Continent their own, because of their especially close association with their natural environment', Aboriginal culture remained 'a vital part of the Australian heritage'.[50] Implicit in these statements was not only the idea that Aboriginal traditions could deepen the national sense of territorial belonging, but also the notion that Aboriginal people were exceptionally sensitive stewards of nature, a notion that accorded with the emergent environmentalism of the 1960s.

In 1968, HC Coombs extolled Aboriginal environmental sensitivity as worthy of emulation. 'The Aboriginal people before the early settlers arrived followed a way of life in harmony with the land and its creatures', he enthused, so they 'can teach us to live in ways which respect and conserve the environment' and thereby make 'our lives richer as well as their own'.[51] In a similar vein, Charles Rowley stated, 'Where there is yet Aboriginal tradition and culture remaining…there is still much that could enrich the Australian community.' He pointed particularly to the need to see the natural environment of Australia in new ways, for which purpose 'we have to go to the Aboriginal tradition'. 'It is my belief', Rowley said, 'that much of what makes Australians Australian comes from contact with Aboriginal people'; he looked forward to their becoming still more Australian through further and closer interactions.[52]

Introducing a collection of Aboriginal myths and legends published in 1965, AW Reed stated, 'We shall not put our roots down into the soil until we have incorporated [Aboriginal] folklore' into Australian literature. Aboriginal people, he claimed, were 'children of nature' who 'lived close to the soil', and from this fact 'a majestic conception of nature was evolved'.[53] However, Reed's manner of presenting the stories was less than majestic, each being recounted in rather flat English prose, with no specification of any story's original purpose or provenance. A year after Reed's collection appeared, the sometime Jindyworobak poet, Roland Robinson, published *Aboriginal myths and legends*, which adhered to different protocols. For each story, the Aboriginal storyteller and his or her tribal affiliations were specified, along with the name of the recorder of the story. Whereas Reed's book was illustrated with line drawings in Western representational style, Robinson's was illustrated with black-and-white renditions of Aboriginal artworks, and again the individual Aboriginal artist's name was specified, wherever known. Robinson's preface was pervaded by an assumption that he was recording an oral literature in decline under the pressures of modernity, but his book is notable for the respectful manner in which that literature was presented.[54]

Perhaps the most successful work in the myths and legends genre was the *Dreamtime* trilogy, comprising *The Dreamtime* (1965), *The dawn of time* (1969) and *The first sunrise* (1971), with text by Charles Mountford and paintings by Ainslie Roberts. Their titles alone convey the message that these were myths of great antiquity, from an ancient people in an ancient land. They were also of enduring cultural value for, as Mountford explained, the 'myths of the Australian aborigines are comparable with those of the ancient civilizations':

> One has only to consider the incalculable influence of the myths of ancient Greece on the literature, drama, and art of the civilized world for over two thousand years, and that of the Nordic myths on the music, drama, and literature of northern Europe, to realize how the living myths of the aborigines, which belong so fully to Australia, could contribute to the cultural life of this country.[55]

Mountford was a self-trained anthropologist who had built up a reputation as a scholar of Aboriginal art. With the *Dreamtime* trilogy, he moved into popularising the Aboriginal heritage for a wider audience. His efforts evidently struck a chord in the contemporary mood, for the first two volumes in the trilogy sold nearly 100,000 copies within a decade of publication.

The work of the sculptor William Ricketts was more overtly didactic, seeking to convey a grand spiritual vision to the world. Ricketts believed that the philosophy of the Aboriginal people expressed a perfect spiritual harmony between humanity and the natural environment. In his clay sculptures of Arrernte, Pitjantjatjara and other desert peoples, he attempted to communicate that harmony to the wider Australian populace — though Ricketts maintained that his works were created not by but through him; they were really creations of the Supreme Essence or the Highest Consciousness. At Mount Dandenong in Victoria, he established a sanctuary where his sculptures were displayed amidst native bushland, rather incongruously setting clay likenesses of people from the arid centre among the towering gums and tree ferns of the dank Dandenong forests (see Plate 7). More incongruously, he scattered through the collection numerous sculptures of his own 'spiritual self' — himself as a young man, adorned with initiation scars across his chest.[56] He seems to have been convinced that he was — or in another life had been — Aboriginal.

Despite — or because of — the eccentricity of his ideas, Ricketts attracted a good deal of attention from the press and public, most of it sympathetic. His supporters included Edith Bolte, wife of the Victorian premier, and through her representations in 1960–61, his collection at Mount Dandenong acquired the protection of the state as the William Ricketts Mountain Gallery Sanctuary National Park. It was opened to the public three years later, attracting busloads of tourists, not all of whom may have appreciated Ricketts' mystical ideas of the oneness of humanity and nature. Nonetheless, it was one among a growing number of expressions of the worth of Indigenous culture and the environmental wisdom it embodied. Moreover, Ricketts' work was esteemed not only by white Australians; it was admired by his friend and near-neighbour, the Aboriginal activist and craftsman Bill Onus, and Bill's son, the artist Lin Onus, who said of Ricketts: 'I think he's Australia's greatest sculptor, there's no two ways about that.' According to Lin Onus, Ricketts' greatest achievement lay in fostering public awareness of Aboriginal people and appreciation of Aboriginal culture.[57]

Appreciation and appropriation

Appeals of the kind examined in the previous section contributed to the growth of more appreciative attitudes towards Aboriginal culture. However, the grander aspiration of infusing Aboriginal spirituality and philosophy into the Australian outlook was not realised. The national culture was changing, but whatever influence Aboriginality had upon it was dwarfed by the cultural stimuli emanating from America, from the new immigrant communities and from global transformations in communications, entertainment, values and expectations. Aboriginal cultural influences were minimal, except in one domain: the aesthetic.

The 1950s was a decade of unprecedented interest in traditional Aboriginal art. Exhibitions were mounted more frequently than ever before, while state art galleries (rather than just museums) began building collections of Aboriginal artworks. A UNESCO publication of the mid-1950s, *Australia's Aboriginal paintings: Arnhem Land*, copiously illustrated with colour reproductions of rock art and bark paintings, outsold all other books on Australian art.[58] Over the following decade, the level of exhibition, collection and public interest in Aboriginal art intensified. The inaugural (1960) Adelaide Festival of Arts included Aboriginal artworks in its program. In 1960–61, an exhibition of traditional art — most of which had been collected in Arnhem Land a couple of years earlier by the artist Tony Tuckson and collector Stuart Scougall — toured state art galleries to widespread acclaim. Philip Jones observes that these exhibitions at the beginning of the 1960s marked a milestone in the 'Australian art establishment's serious acceptance of Aboriginal art, as well as the art's wider popular appreciation'.[59]

Plate 1: AO Neville claimed that all signs of Aboriginal ancestry could be 'bred out' within three generations. His claim was given photographic veracity in this image, showing the desired trajectory from the unacceptably dark half-caste woman on the right to her apparently white grandson on the left. Yet all three figures are equally Westernised in dress, deportment and all apparent features except complexion and physiognomy. For Neville, as for other advocates of absorption, acculturation to Western norms was not enough. To become acceptable to white Australians, the descendants of Aboriginal people had to shed all outward markers of their Aboriginal ancestry. Source: AO Neville, *Australia's coloured minority*, Currawong Publishing, Sydney, c.1947.

Plate 2: Margaret Preston's 1941 work, *Still life: fruit* (*Arnhem Land motif*), exemplifies her use of Aboriginal themes and designs in her paintings. Her palette is restricted to black, white, brown and various shades of ochre, as in the bark paintings of Arnhem Land. The ground on which the basket rests features geometric shapes adapted from the designs on north Queensland Aboriginal shields, rearranged in ways reminiscent of contemporary cubism. The fruit and basket are reduced to basic forms, with a prominent use of dots highlighting the connection with Aboriginal artistic styles. While such works are often criticised today for their appropriations of Aboriginal aesthetic traditions, Preston made a major contribution to white Australians' receptiveness to the beauties of Aboriginal art. Source: © Margaret Preston/Licensed by Viscopy, 2011.

Plate 3: Originally published in *Man* magazine, this photograph of some of the leaders of the 1938 Day of Mourning was reproduced on the cover of the April 1938 issue of *The Australian Abo Call*, a newspaper with an Aboriginal editor, Jack Patten, and aimed at an Aboriginal readership. The men are, from left to right, Tom Foster, Jack Kinchela (partly obscured), Doug Nicholls, William Cooper and Jack Patten. Their political program, set out in this issue of *The Australian Abo Call*, included the demand '*to raise all Aborigines throughout the Commonwealth to full Citizen Status*' and civil equality with the whites in Australia'. Source: *The Australian Abo Call*, April 1938.

Plate 4: *Mt Hermannsburg* is one of several paintings of this striking landform by Albert Namatjira. Like other Hermannsburg artists, Namatjira often painted those features of his country which held special spiritual significance in Arrernte tradition. At the same time, he and other Hermannsburg artists captured the beauty of central Australian landscapes in ways which were easily accessible to the wider Australian public. Thereby, they provided a bridge between Aboriginal and Western modes of apprehending Australian lands, although at the time of their greatest popularity, in the 1940s, 1950s and 1960s, white Australians tended to see the bridge as leading only one way, from the Aboriginal to the Western. Source: Albert Namatjira Arrernte (Aranda) people 1902–1959, Mt Hermannsburg c.1946-51, Watercolour over pencil on smooth wove paper, 25.8 x 37.2cm, Acc. 1:1653, Bequest of Cedric Powne 1979, Collection: Queensland Art Gallery, © Legend Press.

Plate 5: This photograph of two mechanics adjusting the tappets of an engine provided the frontispiece for the 1961 assimilation propaganda booklet, *One people*. By positioning the white man as instructor, the black man as apprentice, the image could be taken as symbolic of a relationship of supremacy and subordination which had reigned since European colonisation. However, by juxtaposing the image next to the words 'One People', it gestured toward an inclusiveness which would transcend that historical relationship. Characteristic of postwar assimilation policies, it suggested that Aboriginal and settler Australians could become 'one people' regardless of differences of skin colour. Source: *One people*, Department of Territories, Canberra, 1961. Courtesy National Archives of Australia, file A452, 1961/2364.

Plate 6: Huge crowds lined the streets of Melbourne to welcome home Lionel Rose (standing in lead vehicle) after he won the world bantamweight title in 1968. In the same year, he was awarded an MBE and voted Australian of the Year. No Aboriginal person had previously won such a level of national adulation. His achievements were hard-earned in the boxing ring, but in the late 1960s white Australians were eager to proclaim their willingness to accept Aboriginal people into the national community. Source: Lionel Rose, *Lionel Rose: Australian: the life story of a champion*, Angus & Robertson, Sydney, 1969. Courtesy HarperCollins Publishers.

Plate 7: William Ricketts hoped to enlighten the world on the spiritual oneness of humanity and nature. Believing that Aboriginal people possessed a deep understanding of that spiritual truth, he created a vast array of clay sculptures to convey the message to the public. The central figure in this work, entitled *Earthly Mother,* was modelled on a real Aboriginal woman (probably from either the Pitjantjatjara or Pintubi language groups). Likenesses of her and numerous other Aboriginal people from the central deserts were set in the lush surrounds of Ricketts' sanctuary at Mount Dandenong in Victoria, where they drew large crowds of admirers and tourists from the early 1960s onward. Source: © Looking Glass, 2010.

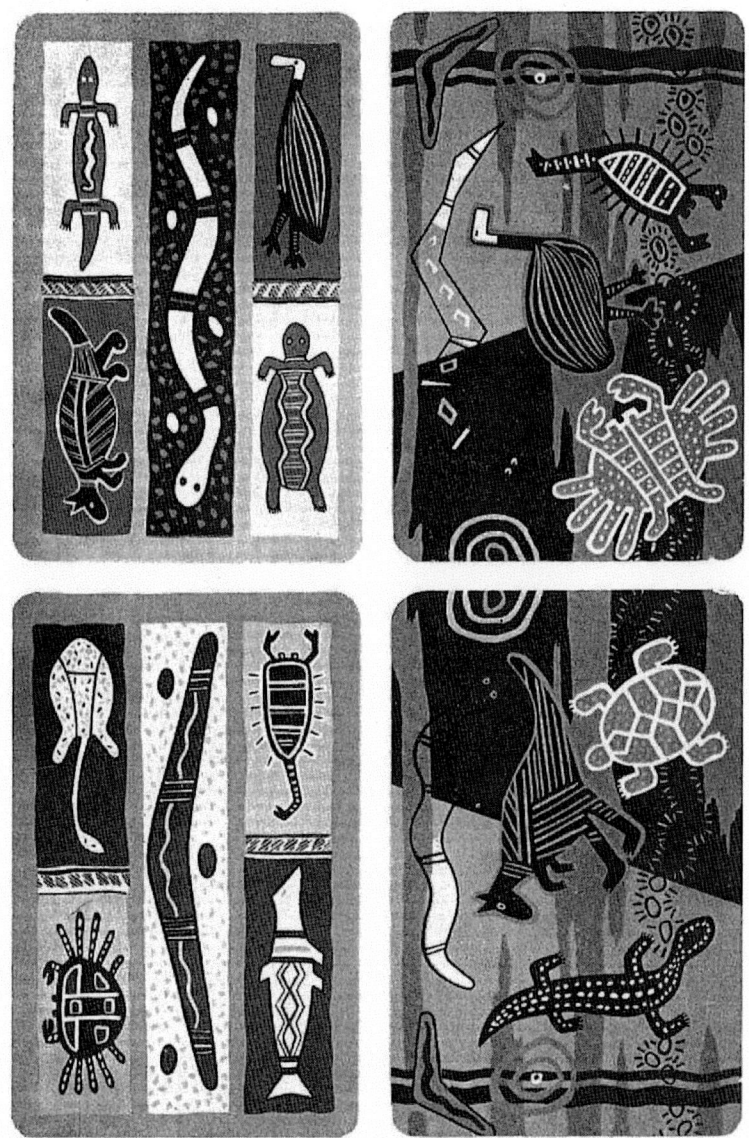

Plate 8: In the 1950s and 1960s, Aboriginal motifs became increasingly common in Australian commercial art and design. The backs of these playing cards were designed by Lloyd Piper of Sydney, using figures and images from Aboriginal rock and bark paintings. The predominant colours are those of traditional Aboriginal painting, black, white and ochre, enlivened with a dash of modern chrome-green. Through such items, white Australians in the postwar era became habituated to Aboriginal art and design – albeit at second-hand. Source: Roman Black, *Old and new Australian Aboriginal art*, Angus & Robertson, Sydney, 1964, p.148. Courtesy HarperCollins Publishers.

Plate 9: At a 1965 demonstration in Sydney's Martin Place, Faith Bandler and her daughter Lilon appealed to the imperative of national unity as grounds for amending the Australian Constitution. The words 'one people' on their placard had been a slogan of Australian nationhood since the 1890s. To the left of Faith and Lilon are the Reverend George Garnsey and an unidentified woman. Source: Faith Bandler, *Turning the tide*, Aboriginal Studies Press, Canberra, 1989, p. 4.

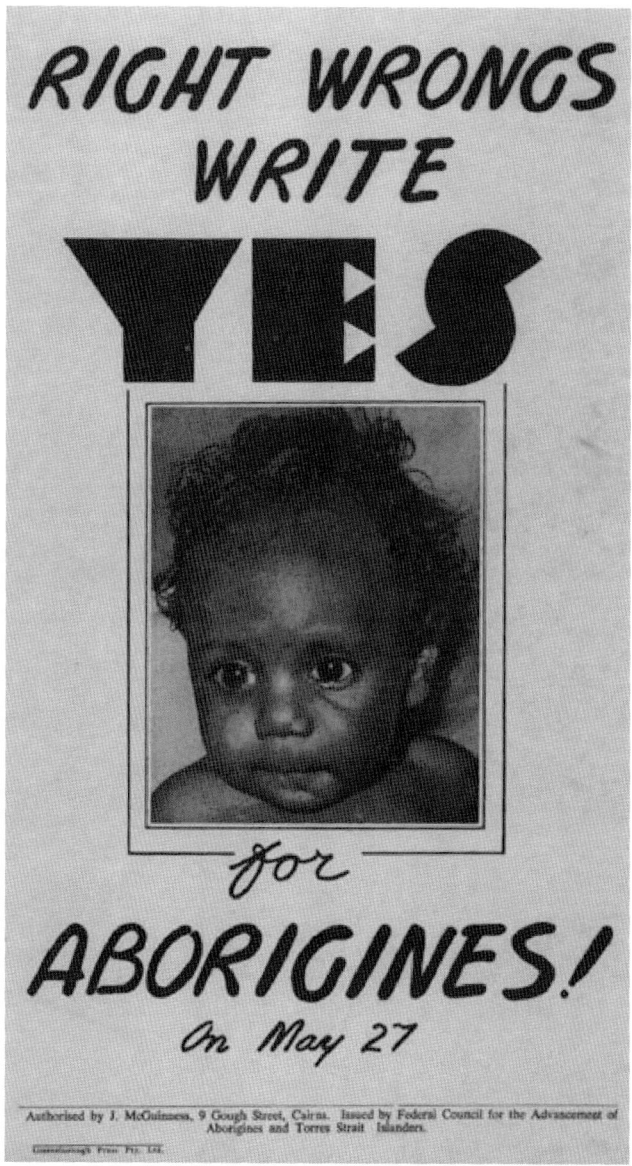

Plate 10: Many of the posters and leaflets promoting a Yes vote in the 1967 referendum used images of Aboriginal children and babies. The campaigners were attuned to the emotional impact of such images, and to the additional implication that the issues at stake were vitally important to future generations. Like this poster, much of the publicity material for a Yes vote was couched in broad terms of rectifying past wrongs, rather than focussing on the specifics of the two sections of the Constitution to be amended. Source: Gordon Bryant papers, box 175, National Library of Australia, ms.8256.

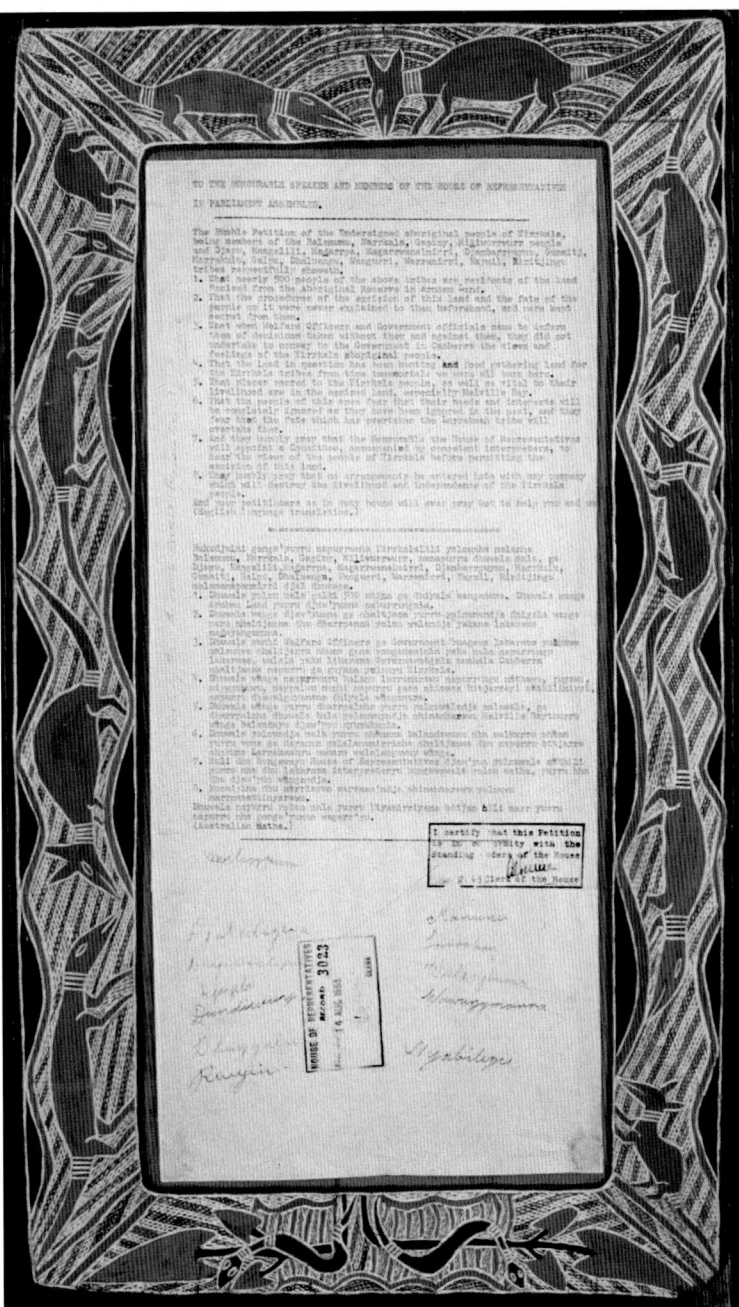

Plate 11: Since the mid-nineteenth century, Aboriginal groups had developed a tradition of seeking redress for wrongs suffered at the hands of settlers by formally petitioning the Crown or Australian parliaments. However, the Yolngu bark petition, presented to the Commonwealth House of Representatives on 14 August 1963, marked a departure from convention in two respects: it was written in an Aboriginal language (Yolngu-matha) as well as English, and it expressed the Yolngu people's title to their lands not only in words but also through the medium of traditional art. Source: Petitions of the Aboriginal people of Yirrkala, *Yirrkala Bark Petition*, replacement papers glued to stringbark sheet with design painted in pipeclay, charcoal and ochre, 14 August 1963, House of Representatives, Canberra. Courtesy Parliament House Art Collection.

Plate 12: At the ceremony installing Pastor Doug Nicholls as head of the National Tribal Council in 1970, he was fitted with the regalia of a *Bapu Mamus* (Great Father or Great Chief) according to Torres Strait Islander custom. Nicholls was a Yorta-Yorta man from Victoria; his adoption of symbols of authority from the Torres Strait Islanders expressed the strengthening ties among Indigenous Australians at this time. Source: *Origin*, vol.3, no.1, 25 September 1970, p. 1.

Plate 13: When first established on 26 January 1972, the Tent Embassy did not fly the Aboriginal flag but the two flags shown here. The one on the left features symbols of traditional Aboriginality in the black, white and ochre colours of bark-painting. The green, black and red tricolour on the right symbolises international black solidarity. Equally symbolic is the joining together of the two flags, since the Embassy represented a fusion of distinctively Aboriginal aspirations with ideas and ideologies drawn from the contemporary global black struggle. Source: © The Australian Institute of Aboriginal and Torres Strait Islander Studies.

Popular appreciation extended well beyond the refined spaces of art galleries. Aboriginal-style designs adorned items in everyday use in suburban homes in the 1950s and 1960s. Much, though not all, of this material was produced by non-Aboriginal artists and artisans, many of them recent European immigrants. Cups and bowls bore depictions of kangaroos and barramundi in the X-ray style of Arnhem Land; curtain fabric and table linen featured Mimi figures, shield designs and concentric dot patterns; playing cards were decorated with adaptations of Aboriginal rock art and bark painting (see Plate 8). Advertising designers found new uses for the ritual insignia of Aboriginal ceremonies; Qantas Empire Airways decorated its tablemats and menu cards with Aboriginal-style designs, while the Orient liner *Orcades* displayed a large mural, by the white artist Douglas Annand, that incorporated variations on X-ray art, Mimi figures and shield designs. Some artists, such as Tony Tuckson, deplored the 'visual horror' of this decorative use of Aboriginal motifs, while others, such as the visiting British-Polish painter Roman Black, lauded it as a 'breath of fresh air [which provided] something that is different, that is typical of the country, that is good'.[60]

Use of Aboriginal styles and motifs was not confined to the visual arts. In the 1940s, John Antill composed a suite, *Corroboree*, combining Western orchestration with Aboriginal rhythms and melodies in an attempt to produce a distinctively Australian musical idiom. It was first performed under Eugene Goosens' baton in 1946. Four years later, Rex Reid choreographed a ballet to this score, which toured Australian capital cities to a generally positive reception from both critics and the public.[61] A few years after that, an American dancer, Beth Dean, choreographed another version of *Corroboree*, excerpts from which — performed by an all-white cast of dancers — were included in the Royal Gala Performance for Queen Elizabeth's 1954 Royal Tour. It was acclaimed as the highlight of the Royal Performance. The *Sunday Telegraph* reviewer praised it as an 'elementally Australian' ballet, which 'transcends mere local interest and belongs to the world', while another reviewer lauded it as the achievement of 'an American who shows, as even our best writers have not been able to do, what is basically Australian'.[62]

As these examples attest, white Australians were not only becoming more appreciative of the Aboriginal artistic heritage, they were also showing an increasing appetite for appropriating parts of that heritage for their own purposes. I shall not attempt here to address the vexed question of where (or whether) a distinction can be drawn between legitimate and illegitimate forms of cultural interchange.[63] Unquestionably, however, in the 1950s and 1960s non-Aboriginal artists, designers and performers drew freely on Aboriginal aesthetic traditions for financial gain as well as nationalist and artistic purposes, without permission from, or compensation to, the original custodians of those traditions. Some scholars condemn these cultural appropriations as manifestations of a continuing colonial relationship whereby white Australians regarded Aboriginal cultures as theirs to ransack as they pleased.[64] Certainly, the cultural exchanges of the 1950s and 1960s were embedded in colonialist power relationships. Ultimately, all exchanges between Aboriginal and non-Aboriginal Australians were embedded in such relationships, as they had been since the beginning of colonisation. Arguably, they remain so today. But while the cultural appropriations of the 1950s and 1960s may have failed to transcend colonial relationships of power, that does not necessarily mean that they failed to transform the relationship between Aboriginal and non-Aboriginal Australians in significant ways.

The cultural politics of artistic appropriations are always ambivalent. As anthropologist Nicholas Thomas observes: 'If appropriations do have a general character, it is surely that of unstable duality. In some proportion, they always combine taking and acknowledgement, appropriation and homage, a critique of colonial exclusions, and collusion in imbalanced exchange.'[65] The duality is readily apparent in the Australian artistic appropriations of the 1950s and 1960s. Settler Australians took what they wanted from the Aboriginal artistic heritage, apparently with little regard for its original cultural significance. Yet it was precisely the Aboriginality of these appropriated elements that rendered them valuable in their new national Australian context. Contemporary white Australians considered that they were honouring the Aboriginal heritage by incorporating elements of it into the national culture. Yet the honouring was on terms set by white Australians. By grasping at those parts of the Aboriginal heritage they found attractive, white Australians manifested a degree of arrogance as well as possessiveness. Yet contemporary Aboriginal activists encouraged the nation to be receptive to their artistic heritage.[66] From their perspective, white Australians' new-found interest in Aboriginal art marked a major advance over earlier attitudes of disdain.

The prevalence of artistic appropriations in the 1950s and 1960s should not be allowed to obscure the extent to which Aboriginal people themselves engaged in cultural production for wider Australian consumption. By the beginning of this period, there were already small, local enterprises specialising in traditional arts, notably the bark-painters of Arnhem Land. With the booming demand for these works, especially from art galleries, the Arnhem Landers stepped up their production. Collectors and connoisseurs were well aware that bark paintings were increasingly being produced for commercial sale; some feared that this might be to the long-term detriment of that art.[67] Another manifestation of commercialisation, catering to a different market, was the lively trade in Aboriginal-made objects offered to tourists, particularly in the north and centre of the continent but also around the capital cities. Commercialisation sometimes caused tensions in Aboriginal communities, particularly when secret-sacred imagery was released into the market.[68] However, the pertinent point here is that Aboriginal people were active participants in the commercialisation of their art.

Some historians suggest that the relationship between Aboriginal artists and artisans on the one hand, and their non-Aboriginal counterparts who appropriated their styles and designs on the other, was automatically competitive and conflictual.[69] Doubtless it sometimes was, but in view of the novelty of a mass market for Aboriginal-style products, it is likely that the relationship was often symbiotic, with both groups contributing to the growing public appreciation of Aboriginal aesthetics. White artists, designers and performers probably played important roles as mediators between the public and artistic styles to which they were hitherto unaccustomed. In any case, during the 1950s and 1960s there was a rising demand for both the faux-Aboriginal works of white designers and performers, and the artistic creations of Aboriginal people themselves. One did not preclude the other.

Indeed, the distinction between them was not always clear. In the early 1950s, Bill Onus set up Aboriginal Enterprises in Melbourne, the first Aboriginal-owned business specialising in the production and sale of crafts, ceramics, souvenirs and textiles using Aboriginal designs. However, many of Onus's staff, including senior designers, were white people.[70] And although Onus was of Wiradjuri and Dharug descent (from New South Wales), his business used designs drawn largely from northern and central

Australia, as did the white-owned enterprises producing Aboriginal-style works. Once in the commercial domain, Onus — like other entrepreneurs — had to produce for a market that was dominated not by Aboriginal but by white people. Onus was one of very few successful Aboriginal entrepreneurs at this time, but his success arguably depended on the mutuality between Aboriginal artistic production and its popularisation by white artists and artisans.

Anna Haebich considers it a 'paradox' that enthusiasm for appropriating elements of Aboriginal culture should flourish when assimilation was at its zenith.[71] It is paradoxical only if assimilation is construed as a demand for Aboriginal people to relinquish the entirety of their heritage. This, as earlier explained, was not normally the case. Even staunch assimilationists such as Hasluck not only tolerated, but encouraged, Aboriginal people to retain elements of their culture — particularly aesthetic elements and especially if these could be turned to profit. It was precisely such elements of the Aboriginal heritage, commodified and detached from any ritual or religious context, that were so pervasive in the Australian popular culture of the 1950s and 1960s. That is to say, in the era of assimilation, elements of Aboriginal culture were to be made available to all Australians, Aboriginal and non-Aboriginal alike. Just as Aboriginal people would (ideally) become part of the national community, a residue of their culture would become part of the national heritage. Government officials were quite frank about this. In 1961, CR Lambert, secretary of the Department of Territories, explained that under the assimilation policy the federal government was determined to preserve aspects of Aboriginal culture, 'not only for the aborigines themselves but as a national heritage'.[72]

It was only in the late 1950s that politicians and public officials explicitly began to endorse the inclusion of elements of Aboriginal culture within the national heritage. Their new-found enthusiasm for Aboriginality, which intensified over the course of the 1960s, doubtless derived from a desire for authentically Australian symbols of nationhood. Incorporating elements of the Aboriginal heritage allowed the nation to claim a deeper temporal connection with the national territory.[73] However, politicians and officials envisaged the inclusion of only a veneer of Aboriginality, supplementing rather than supplanting the Western (and British) heritage that provided the substance of the Australian national culture. The aesthetically appealing surface of Aboriginal cultures would be skimmed off, providing new emblems of Australianness but without penetrating far into the deeper layers of national values, norms and identity. Recognition that Aboriginal cultures possessed an aesthetically appealing surface was itself significant, for even that marked an enhanced level of appreciation of the worth of those cultures. Nonetheless, the level of cultural appreciation was limited, as critics pointed out at the time.[74]

In fact, even those who engaged in artistic exchanges acknowledged the superficiality of their borrowings. Beth Dean admired Aboriginal dance and sought to emulate it on stage, but she recognised that dance movements were mere 'superficial forms' of Aboriginal culture.[75] Dean devoted many years of study to Aboriginal dance, and before choreographing *Corroboree* she and her husband, Victor Carell, embarked on an eight-month tour of northern and central Australia to learn Aboriginal dance directly from its practitioners. She maintained that her choreography remained faithful to Aboriginal styles and movements, but she never pretended that her ballet was an authentically Aboriginal corroboree. Indeed, she drew attention to the fact that her dance was decontextualised from anything sacred or profound in Aboriginal tradition, noting particularly the absence of ritual chanting that accompanied, and gave deeper meaning to, dance in real Aboriginal ceremonies. Her dance, she acknowledged, was a piece of theatre, which she hoped would convey some of the beauty of Aboriginal dance and promote a positive image of Aboriginal people and their heritage.[76] Those were ambitious goals in the 1950s, and perhaps the most remarkable feature is the extent to which she succeeded in achieving them.

Superficiality does not necessarily mean inconsequentiality. A superficial aesthetic appreciation may be a necessary prelude to later, deeper cultural engagements. In any event, recognition that the Aboriginal heritage held much of beauty was a substantial achievement of the 1950s and 1960s. It is true that bits of Aboriginal exotica had been adopted by white Australians before that time, but the extent of admiration and emulation in the later decades — hanging Aboriginal artworks in prestigious galleries, dancing in Aboriginal style before the Queen, decorating homes and homewares with Aboriginal motifs — was of a different order. It is true, too, that the new-found interest in Aboriginality was inspired not only by aesthetic appreciation, but also by nationalist yearnings for authentically Australian emblems and images. Yet that, too, indicates that Aboriginal and Australian were beginning to merge, rather than — as in the prewar period — remaining separate or even antithetical. Although the level of cultural appreciation in the 1950s and 1960s may often have been superficial, and the cultural appropriations self-interested, those developments did not occur in isolation. They were associated, temporally and to a significant extent causally, with a growing realisation on the part of settler Australians that the nation must become more receptive to its Indigenous peoples. One manifestation of that growing realisation, the overwhelming victory in the 1967 referendum, is the focus of the next chapter.

Chapter 8

Fellow Australians

On 27 May 1967, campaigners for Aboriginal rights and status won the most decisive referendum victory in Australian history. Led by FCAATSI, the campaigners sought the deletion of the two references to Aboriginal people in the Australian Constitution. Their removal, campaigners claimed, would inaugurate a new era of acceptance and equality for Aboriginal people. The argument struck a chord with the wider populace, to the extent that on referendum day, 90.77 per cent of the Australian electorate voted for the deletion of the two constitutional references. Ever since, the 1967 referendum has popularly been memorialised as the moment when Aboriginal people gained equal rights with other Australians, even won the right to vote. In fact, the referendum did not achieve those outcomes. Its significance lay not in any expansion of legal rights but in its symbolic affirmation of Aboriginal people's acceptance into the national community. The campaigners for constitutional change represented the issues at stake as vital to Australia's national reputation and self-esteem, converting what could have been a mundane, legalistic tinkering with the Constitution into a plebiscite on Australian nationhood.

The referendum campaigners specified several tangible benefits that would follow from constitutional amendment, in particular an expansion of Aboriginal rights and Commonwealth responsibility for Aboriginal affairs. The overarching campaign theme, however, was the need to bring Aboriginal people into the fellowship of the nation. 'Vote "Yes" for Aborigines, they want to be Australians too' was the opening line of a widely distributed campaign song.[1] Jack Horner, Secretary of the New South Wales Vote Yes Campaign Committee, maintained that a Yes vote was fundamentally an affirmation 'that Aborigines matter as Australian people'.[2]

Archbishop Strong, Anglican Primate of Australia, urged a Yes vote because it would make Aboriginal people 'more completely Australian'.[3] These appeals went beyond legal rights; they demanded attitudinal change on the part of the Australian populace, giving Aboriginal people the honour and esteem due to citizens of the nation. The Yes campaigners were not so naive as to believe that they could secure a change in popular attitudes merely by changing a few words of the Constitution. It was the campaign for change that would serve the educative function. By drawing attention to those words in the founding document of the nation that implied the exclusion of Aboriginal people, campaigners sought to both erase those symbolic exclusions and promote public appreciation of, and respect for, Aboriginal people.

A few days before the referendum, Aboriginal activist Chicka Dixon explained in the Sydney *Sun-Herald* that:

> There's a simple reason why I want a huge 'Yes' vote on the Aboriginal question at next Saturday's referendum:
> *I want to be accepted by white Australians as a person.*
> There are scores of other reasons why the vote should be yes.
> But for most Aborigines it is basically and most importantly a matter of seeing white Australians finally, after 179 years, affirming at last that they believe we are human beings.

Dixon was under no illusion that a Yes vote would instantly heal all discord between Aboriginal and other Australians. He explained that its full benefits would take generations to eventuate, and that 'at first a Yes vote will mean...merely a change of mood by white Australians: acceptance instead of rejection'. This change of mood, he affirmed, was vital to Aboriginal well-being and self-respect.[4] For its proponents, the 1967 referendum was a quest as much for honour and esteem as for legal and institutional reform.

The 1967 referendum had its genesis ten years earlier, when the human rights campaigner, Jessie Street, began lobbying the federal government to put the question of constitutional amendment to the people. By April 1957, she had persuaded the leaders of the Aboriginal-Australian Fellowship to take on the fight for constitutional amendment, and it was this organisation that launched the first petition requesting that a referendum be held on the deletion of the constitutional references to Aboriginal people. A year later, leadership of the campaign passed to the newly formed Federal

Council for Aboriginal Advancement, which in 1962 launched a national campaign entitled 'Towards Equal Citizenship for Aborigines'.

The leaders of the Federal Council (unlike Street) knew that constitutional amendment would not, in itself, expand Aboriginal rights, and that although constitutional amendment could extend Commonwealth powers in Aboriginal affairs, effective action in Aboriginal advancement would remain a responsibility of the various governments. Some Federal Council publicity material explained these points.[5] Much of it, however, did not, simplifying the complexities for public consumption as is usual in political campaigns. Throughout the ensuing campaigns — including that of 1967 — the Federal Council presented constitutional change, national inclusion, Aboriginal rights and the extension of Commonwealth responsibility as a package in which the first of these items was the key to securing the other three. It was partly because of this simplification for publicity purposes that the 1967 referendum came to be mis-remembered as the moment when Aboriginal people won equal rights.

In fact, it was while the Federal Council was lobbying for a referendum to be held that Aboriginal civil rights expanded more substantially than at any other time since Federation. When lobbying began in 1957, both federal and state laws included numerous discriminations, limiting Aboriginal people's access to the franchise and social welfare benefits, their freedom of movement, their control over income, their choice of marital partner and much else besides. By 1967, discriminations had been removed from the statute books at the federal level and in New South Wales, Victoria, South Australia and Tasmania (apart from a few trivial remnants); the same process was almost complete in Western Australia and the Northern Territory; only Queensland lagged behind, and even it was making faltering steps in the same direction.[6] Those lobbying for a referendum were well aware that the process of dismantling legal discriminations was proceeding without any change to the Constitution. After all, it was the referendum lobbyists who also led the protests that spurred governments into repealing discriminatory laws. Yet these campaigners still insisted on the need for constitutional change, partly to augment the rights already attained by Aboriginal people, partly to grant the federal government a greater role in Aboriginal affairs, and partly — and perhaps most importantly — as a public affirmation of Aboriginal acceptance as fellow citizens of the nation.

This chapter begins by discussing the Aboriginal acquisition of two legal rights before the 1967 referendum: the right to vote and the right to consume alcohol. I draw particular attention to the extent to which advocates of those rights framed their arguments in terms of an aspiration for social inclusion and remained faithful to the liberal principle of the legal equality of all citizens. The chapter then discusses the 1967 referendum campaign and the lobbying that preceded it, showing that while the referendum campaigners sought legal rights and expanded Commonwealth powers, of at least equal importance were social acceptance and respect for Aboriginal people.

Voting rights

In April 1961, the Commonwealth House of Representatives set up a select committee to investigate ways of expanding the Aboriginal franchise. There had been no change in Aboriginal people's entitlement to the federal vote since the limited extensions of 1949. Establishment of the 1961 select committee was prompted by a combination of domestic political pressure and the federal government's desire to maintain Australia's international reputation, particularly as South Africa came under increasing condemnation for its racist legislation.[7] The committee itself noted that its deliberations were based on the realisation that Aboriginal people were 'increasing in numbers', and now comprised 'a permanent part of the Australian community. This makes imperative the recognition of their proper status, and the planning of their integration into the Australian community.'[8]

The select committee devoted some consideration to the 'possibility of establishing an aboriginal electorate throughout the Commonwealth… on the model of the New Zealand electorate for Maoris', but ultimately rejected this option.[9] Instead, it recommended that Aboriginal people be enfranchised on the same basis as other Australians. Gordon Bryant, federal Labor MHR and president of the Victorian Aborigines Advancement League, celebrated the recommendation for its affirmation of equality and acceptance:

> The right to vote places the aborigine, for the first time, on an equality with the white man. The humblest citizen when he enters the polling booth is the equal of the most learned, wealthy or powerful person in the Commonwealth…A great barrier has been overcome and both dark and white Australians have an incentive

to work together for the common good and full acceptance of each other.

We are on the way!¹⁰

Less effusively, the chairman of the select committee stated that universal Aboriginal enfranchisement 'will be a large step forward in the assimilation and integration of the aboriginal people'.¹¹ Hasluck agreed, proclaiming that the extension of the franchise was 'one step further towards the ideal of one people in one continent'.¹²

However, in the 1962 amendments to the *Electoral Act*, one difference between Aboriginal and other Australian citizens remained. Whereas for other citizens enrolment and voting were compulsory, for Aboriginal people enrolment was optional. This variation was introduced to avoid the possibility of penalising those people who were 'still in the tribal state, or recently emerged from the tribal state, or not completely integrated into the Australian community' for failing to perform a duty of which they were unaware.¹³

In 1962, Western Australia extended the state franchise to cover all its Aboriginal residents, leaving Queensland the only jurisdiction constricting Aboriginal voting rights. By this time, Queensland had acquired an invidious reputation on Indigenous issues. Yet when the Queensland government considered amending its electoral laws to enfranchise Aboriginal and Torres Strait Islander people, it not only contemplated but actually supported separate Indigenous representation on the Maori model. The committee investigating Indigenous enfranchisement, which handed down its report in 1964, advocated an arrangement whereby Indigenous Queenslanders could choose to vote on the general roll or on a 'Special Roll', as in New Zealand.¹⁴ The chairman of the committee visited New Zealand in late 1964 to investigate how Maori electorates worked there. The separate electorates model got as far as a Bill that made provision for Torres Strait Islanders to elect one member of parliament and Aboriginal Queenslanders to elect another. Never before had William Cooper's proposal for dedicated Aboriginal parliamentary representation come closer to realisation.

But Indigenous Queenslanders in 1964 did not share Cooper's views. The peak state Indigenous lobby group, the Queensland Council for the Advancement of Aborigines and Torres Strait Islanders, argued that separate electoral arrangements implied 'second-class citizenship'.¹⁵ Aboriginal poet and activist Kath Walker condemned the proposed separate representation as 'a denial of democratic rights', which would 'create and uphold segregation'. It was also 'against the Australian way of life', and Walker strongly affirmed the eagerness of Aboriginal and Torres Strait Islander people to adopt that way of life. She explained that 'there should be no barriers between races', so 'the vote must be given to the Aborigine and Torres Strait Islander in the same way as applies to non-Aborigines'. 'It is most desirable that we have in parliament Aboriginal and Island representatives', Walker asserted, but they 'must be elected in the same way as are non-Aborigines by all people voting on [sic] the same election'.[16]

The vehemence of this opposition may have derived partly from distrust of the motives of a government notorious for its oppressive record in Indigenous affairs. It is possible that the Queensland government was attempting to minimise the potential electoral consequences of Aboriginal enfranchisement, as Colin Tatz hinted in 1964.[17] Even so, Walker's diatribe against separate electoral enrolment and special parliamentary representation was entirely in keeping with the liberal anti-racism she and her fellow Aboriginal activists espoused at this time. For Indigenous people in Queensland, more than for those elsewhere, practices and policies based on racial differentiation were facts of their everyday lives. Uncompromising adherence to legal sameness seemed a far preferable option.

The Queensland government dropped the idea of separate Indigenous enrolment and representation in August 1965. Attorney-General Peter Delamothe explained that it did so because 'we, in this State, can not live in a vacuum but must be aware and take heed of public opinion both in Australia and abroad'.[18] The Queensland government may have had additional, less principled motives for abandoning its proposal, but there is no reason to question the validity of Delamothe's assertion. Differentiation in voting and other substantive civic rights was antipathetic to the prevailing orthodoxy on racial equality, internationally as well as domestically.

Racial discrimination had become such a contentious issue that in 1961 the federal government set up a committee to investigate its incidence in Commonwealth legislation. In its report, submitted in April 1964, the Inter-Departmental Committee on Racial Discrimination noted with approval the various United Nations declarations against discrimination; it accepted that to advance the policy of assimilation there was a 'need for the further removal of restrictive protective legislation'; and it 'took special note of the fact that racial discrimination was currently assuming increasing importance as an international issue'. The committee found that Commonwealth legislation included 'a number of provisions that are open to objection on the grounds of racial discrimination', but implied that these were neither numerous nor serious. Its generally positive assessment of the Commonwealth's legislative performance depended on two factors: during the three years between the committee's formation and the submission of its report, the most overtly discriminatory laws (notably those concerning the right to vote) had been repealed; and the committee's terms of reference specified that it would examine instances of discrimination 'in Commonwealth laws but not in administrative practices'.[19] It was primarily in those administrative practices that governmental forms of racial discrimination persisted.

While the Inter-Departmental Committee on Racial Discrimination found few instances of overt racial discrimination in Commonwealth legislation, in the wider Australian society racial discrimination flourished, both overtly and covertly. Less than a year after the committee submitted its report, Charles Perkins led a group of students on a bus tour, dubbed the Freedom Ride, to expose the discrimination endured by Aboriginal people in the towns of northern and north-western New South Wales. Assimilation had been official New South Wales policy since 1940, and by the time of the Freedom Ride in 1965, that state had expunged all racially discriminatory legislation from its statute books — although some discriminatory local council regulations remained in force.[20] More importantly, discriminatory behaviours were inscribed in the everyday social practices and rituals of the towns visited by Perkins and his entourage.[21] So committed were these residents to local segregationist norms that, despite Perkins' attempts to abide by Martin Luther King's strictures against violence, the Freedom Ride was marred by several violent clashes, including assaults on the students who protested against the exclusion of Aboriginal children from the Moree swimming pool.[22] By the mid-1960s, it was primarily at this level of interpersonal behaviour, not in the laws of the land, that racial discrimination could be found (though Queensland still managed to discriminate at both levels).

Drinking rites

Among the last restriction on Aboriginal rights to be removed was the prohibition on drinking alcohol. In most cases, Aboriginal people won the vote before acquiring the right to drink, as if they could be better trusted with the ballot box than with the beer bottle. Partly, the prohibition on alcohol consumption was symptomatic of the continuing assumption of Aboriginal incompetence: like minors, they needed protection from adult vices such as alcohol. Related to this was a prevalent myth that blacks 'couldn't hold their liquor' so were best kept away from it. Partly, the prohibition may have reflected wider Australian ambivalences about alcohol, with attitudes swinging between puritanical demands for abstinence and larrikin revellings in excess.

But more than these were involved. In Australia in the 1950s and 1960s most alcohol was consumed by men in public bars in ritual affirmations of the national ideal of mateship. Aboriginal exclusion from these rituals symbolically excluded them from the community of the (male) nation, and Aboriginal people were acutely aware of the implied insult. Their demand for drinking rights was not so much a demand for access to alcoholic beverages (drink was easy to get despite legal prohibitions) as a demand to 'breast the bar' in demonstration of their equality with other Australians. Prohibition made access to alcohol 'a symbol of equality', or as anthropologist Judy Inglis put it, 'a symbol of citizenship', or in TGH Strehlow's words, a 'symbol of emancipation'.[23] These commentators considered the equation of alcohol with citizenship regrettable, but agreed that the only way to break the connection was to grant Aboriginal people the right to drink.

The prohibition on alcohol consumption was not only a conspicuous restriction on Aboriginal rights; it was implicated in many controversies concerning Aboriginal people. One of the most publicised was Albert Namatjira's incarceration and premature death in 1959. Shortly afterwards, the Victorian Council for Aboriginal Rights published a critique of Northern Territory Aboriginal legislation, including the provision under which Namatjira was convicted for supplying liquor to a ward. According to the council, white Australians had made alcohol into a 'scapegoat' for the Aboriginal dilemma: 'We degrade him and then make available a pain killer — then many have the effrontery to blame the pain killer for his downfall.' Moreover, this attribution of blame to alcohol carried the 'inference that they are an inferior race', incapable of holding their liquor. 'This is not so,' the council protested, since 'the pharmacological action of alcohol is unaffected by skin colour'.[24]

Before the Namatjira controversy had subsided, another famous Aboriginal Territorian, Robert Tudawali, star of the film *Jedda*, was sentenced to six months' gaol for the same offence. Criticism of the alcohol laws, which had been vigorous after Namatjira's conviction, intensified in the Tudawali case. An acerbic account in the *Guardian* highlighted the disjuncture between the law and the Australian ideal of mateship:

> To get into the police news in a big way, the white man has to commit murder, assault, forgery, arson or theft on a rather impressive scale.
>
> An Aborigine does it a little more easily. He only has to offer his mate a beer (penalty — six months in jail) …
>
> This ban on Aborigines' drinking…has become a means of enforcing and consolidating that subjection [of blacks by whites]. To gather in a bar or at home for a convivial drink has become just another of the privileges the 'master race' reserves for itself, to the exclusion of the 'lesser breeds'.[25]

Other newspaper reports made similar points, usually less scathingly. Hasluck, however, was adamant that prohibition would remain because there was 'no single cause greater than intoxicating liquor contributing to the degradation of the primitive and ignorant aborigines'.[26]

Convictions under the Territory law criminalising the supply of alcohol to a ward continued into the early 1960s. So did public condemnation of the law. In early 1961, Wargaitj man Bruce Pott, a non-ward and acclaimed footballer, received six months' imprisonment for the offence. Doug Nicholls commented:

> The first thing a man in Melbourne does when you call is open the fridge and ask what you'll have. When a full citizen aborigine in the Territory does this, he goes to gaol.
>
> This law is destroying the aboriginal citizen.
>
> We put him in the white man's social structure, and when he acts like a white man we gaol him.[27]

Early the following year, a member of the Northern Territory Council for Aboriginal Rights, Peter Australia, was sentenced to twelve months' imprisonment for the same offence. Council secretary Davis Daniels mounted a spirited defence, declaring that in opposing the liquor laws, 'We are fighting for the right to act and be treated like free Human beings.'[28] Convictions continued until Northern Territory legislation was comprehensively overhauled in 1964. Even after that, alcohol could be prohibited in specific areas such as reserves.

In New South Wales, the supply of alcohol to Aboriginal people was prohibited under section 9 of the *Aborigines Protection Act*. Aboriginal residents of that state had complained of this curtailment of their rights in the 1950s, but the level of protest escalated sharply around 1960, possibly prompted by the well-publicised Northern Territory cases discussed above. Elkin, as Vice-Chairman of the Aborigines Welfare Board, had argued throughout the 1950s for the repeal of section 9 on the grounds that it was inequitable and unjust to apply restrictions to a category of citizens on the basis of their race. At a July 1960 meeting of the Board, he formally moved a recommendation to the Chief Secretary that section 9 be rescinded. The Board voted in favour of Elkin's motion.[29] However, it was another three years before parliament acted on the Board's recommendation. In the meantime, lobby groups, most prominently the Aboriginal-Australian Fellowship, kept up the pressure.

Fellowship secretary Jack Horner argued that 'prohibition segregates the two races' and 'makes the task of assimilating the Aborigines much more difficult'.[30] In October 1960, the Fellowship circulated a letter to all members of the New South Wales parliament pointing out that granting the right to drink 'follows logically upon [the government's] policy of assimilation of the Aboriginal people as citizens'.[31] 'Lifting the liquor ban', the Fellowship declared, would help 'end all forms of discrimination and secure equality and acceptance for our Aboriginal people'.[32] A 1961 petition, for signature by 'persons of Aboriginal descent' only, cited section 9 as 'evidence of racial discrimination...subjecting us to unwarranted humiliation and segregation'.[33] The Victorian Aborigines Advancement League condemned the New South Wales liquor ban as 'humiliating', and advised that its repeal 'should help assimilation'.[34] Anthropologists such as JH Bell added their voices to calls for the repeal of section 9.[35] Despite the energetic campaigning, and despite the urging of its own Aborigines Welfare Board, the New South Wales government was inordinately slow to act — probably because it gave the same low priority to this as to all other matters concerning Aboriginal people. Section 9 was eventually repealed in March 1963. South Australia, Western Australia and Queensland were even slower to act, lifting their prohibitions on Aboriginal access to alcohol only in the mid- to late 1960s, and all retaining the power to prohibit alcohol on reserves.³⁶

Most campaigners for Aboriginal rights and welfare in the 1950s and 1960s, even teetotallers like Charles Duguid, insisted that equal citizenship must include equality of access to alcohol.³⁷ Some, however, expressed scepticism about both the motives for, and the consequences of, Aboriginal people acquiring the right to drink. In 1964, Kim Beazley claimed that changes in the legal status of Aboriginal people were typically done on the cheap, citing their acquisition of the rights to drink alcohol, buy methylated spirits and 'fornicate' with white people. He warned, 'You are not going to solve the infant death rate with drinking rights, methylated spirits rights or fornicating rights. However important those "rights" may be, we must recognise they solve nothing.'³⁸

Further complicating the alcohol issue, in some areas Aboriginal people sought not the right to drink but the power to exclude alcohol. This was the case at Yirrkala in Arnhem Land, where the community leaders considered their way of life threatened not only by a massive bauxite-mining venture but also by the alcohol miners brought with them. In a 1968 submission on Yirrkala, Elkin argued that alcohol would 'add a disastrous factor to the contact process', and that the local elders were right in seeking to avoid 'the moral and social breakdown' that typically followed its introduction.³⁹ In Elkin's view, the Yirrkala elders' call for the right to forbid alcohol was as worthy of respect as demands by New South Wales Aboriginal people for the right to drink. He recommended that the decision on alcohol at Yirrkala be left to the local leaders. More generally, Elkin contended that Aboriginal communities should exercise the normal powers of local government authorities, an empowerment he regarded not as compromising assimilation but as fulfilling it.⁴⁰

Right wrongs, write yes

In the referendum on 27 May 1967, voters were asked two questions. The first concerned Aboriginal affairs, with voters being asked whether they approved the deletion of the two references to Aboriginal people in the Australian Constitution. Section 51(xxvi) specified that the Commonwealth parliament could make laws with respect to the 'people of any race other than the aboriginal race in any state, for whom it is deemed necessary to make special laws' (the proposed amendment was deletion of the words 'other than the Aboriginal race in any state').

Section 127 stipulated that in 'reckoning the numbers of the people of the Commonwealth, or of a State or other part of the Commonwealth, aboriginal natives shall not be counted' (deletion of the entire section was proposed). On the referendum paper, both these amendments were combined into a single question. The second question on the referendum paper had nothing to do with Aboriginal affairs. It concerned the so-called 'nexus issue' on the number of senators relative to the number of members of the House of Representatives.

On the Aboriginal question, two features stand out. One is the magnitude of the affirmative vote. No other Australian referendum question has achieved anywhere near so massive an affirmative majority as 90.77 per cent. In fact, most have failed to achieve an affirmative majority at all. On the Aboriginal question in the 1967 referendum, the Yes vote exceeded 95 per cent in some electorates, and in none was it under 70 per cent — a result as close to consensus as can be expected in a democratic contest. The other unique feature of the Aboriginal question in the referendum was the absence of an organised campaign for a No vote. Even the federal government broke with convention by providing, in the official advice issued to voters immediately before the referendum, only the case for Yes. It would be reasonable to posit a connection between the extraordinarily high affirmative vote and the absence of a No campaign, but most histories of the referendum fail to do so. Indeed, most make no more than fleeting mention of the fact that there was no campaign for a No vote, as if this were inconsequential.[41] That it was not inconsequential is indicated by the fate of the question on the nexus issue, against which a strong campaign was mounted. It received a nationwide Yes vote of only 40.25 per cent.

The absence of a No campaign on the Aboriginal question suggests either that the Australian public was already convinced of the rightness of the constitutional amendments when the holding of a referendum was announced in February 1967, or that the case for Yes was presented in such a way as to preclude open opposition to the recommended amendments. Most likely, it was both. The key factors seem to have been the growth of more positive popular attitudes toward Aboriginal people and cultures, and growing concerns that a poor race relations record would damage Australia's international status. South Africa's sullied image was a constant reminder.

Changes in popular attitudes have been discussed in the previous chapter. Referendum campaigners sometimes referred to these changes.

In early 1967, FCAATSI's National Campaign Committee acknowledged that, 'Over the past ten or more years there has been a general awakening on the part of the Australian public to the tragic needs of the Australian Aborigines.'[42] Attitudinal change, however, was partial and uneven. Indifference remained prevalent, not only among the Australian people but among their parliamentary representatives as well. When Faith Bandler, as a member of a FCAATSI delegation, met with Menzies in 1965, she gained the impression that the Prime Minister 'had never given a thought to the Aboriginal situation' and had no idea about the plethora of discriminatory laws in some states.[43] On the eve of the referendum, the Aborigines Progressive Association remarked on both an 'awaking of conscience' and 'the general indifference of the white community' toward Aboriginal people.[44]

In countering the indifference of both people and parliament, the most powerful weapon available to campaigners was concern over Australia's international reputation. It was this concern that eventually persuaded the federal government to hold a referendum on both constitutional references to Aboriginal people.[45] Additionally, in 1966 Menzies had been replaced as prime minister by Harold Holt, who was more attuned to international sensitivities about race. Soon after assuming office, he made the most sweeping changes to Australia's immigration policies since Federation, effectively dismantling the white Australia policy; he also signed the United Nations *International convention on the elimination of all forms of racial discrimination*. For years, Menzies had thwarted the campaign for a referendum by insisting that only section 127 be put to a vote. Once in office, Holt agreed to both sections being put, as another placatory gesture of racial good intentions so Australia could evade opprobrium of the kind heaped upon South Africa.

Having persuaded the government to hold the referendum, campaigners played the international reputation card strongly in their appeals to the public. 'Vote Yes Australia, Vote Yes Australia, the eyes of the world are upon us today', ran a campaign song to the tune of 'Waltzing Matilda'.[46] A press release by Kath Walker warned that, 'Should the public vote "No" on the Aboriginal question, Australia stands condemned in the eyes of the world.'[47] A FCAATSI publicity statement asserted that, 'The eyes of the world — particularly African and Asian eyes — will be on Australia on May 27th. A "no" vote to the Aboriginal rights question will brand this country racist and put it in the same category as South Africa.'[48] It is doubtful whether, two decades earlier, most Australians would have cared how African or Asian eyes saw Australia. By 1967 it was a matter of serious public concern, for as the federal government's statement of 'The Case for YES' pointed out, Australians lived 'in a world in which racial issues are being highlighted every day'.[49]

Redemption of Australia's international reputation depended on the Australian people welcoming their Aboriginal compatriots into the national community. As Faith Bandler told the readers of *The Australian Women's Weekly*, a Yes vote 'will tell the world at large that there is only one Australian, and his colour doesn't matter at all'.[50] A campaign song urged people to 'Vote "Yes" and show the world the true Australian brotherhood'.[51] In these appeals to the Australian public, the image Australia needed to project abroad corresponded closely with Australians' self-conception as an egalitarian and tolerant people. Effectively, 'we' had to show the world what 'we' already really were: a people committed to the ideals of democracy and equality. The empirical accuracy of the characterisation might be open to question, especially on issues of race, but it made effective propaganda — so effective that it was difficult to make a counter-case without implicitly impugning Australia's national self-image and self-esteem. At this point, it is apposite to consider further the absence of a negative campaign in the 1967 referendum.

Not only was there no organised campaign for the negative, there were very few published statements by individuals explicitly advocating a No vote.[52] Occasionally — though instances were few — individuals expressed misgivings about the constitutional amendments and the manner in which the Yes case was presented. In a letter to the editor of the *Sydney Morning Herald* on 16 May 1967, Canon JRL Johnstone worried that the amendment of section 51(xxvi) 'would allow a future centralised Commonwealth Government to pass legislation discriminating against Aborigines on racial grounds', a statement that was legalistically accurate. However, he did not advocate a No vote.[53] SB Page of Brisbane, in a letter published in *The Australian* on 26 May 1967, also pointed out the danger of an amended section 51(xxvi) allowing 'discriminatory legislation of the South African kind'. However, his or her primary complaint was that the democratic process had been compromised by 'the fact that the official pamphlet...gives the case only for one side concerning the proposal on the Aboriginals; and, so far as I can observe, scarcely a word for No has been published in the Press...in all fairness I think the case for No should have been put.' Yet, far from advocating a No vote, he or she stated that, 'Personally I shall vote Yes because the Yes case leads on points.' What irked Page was the conduct of the campaign, not its objective.[54]

Johnstone's and Page's point about the amendment to section 51(xxvi) potentially facilitating legal discrimination had been raised by Prime Minister Menzies in 1965, as an argument against amendment of this section.[55] Yet, when the official advice to voters was prepared less than two years later, not only did it fail to mention this or any other argument for a No vote, it suggested that the case for Yes was so compelling as to be self-evident, whereas the case for No was so insubstantial as not to warrant consideration. 'We have yet to learn of any opposition being voiced to [the amendments] from any quarter', it stated.[56] Perhaps governmental memories are short. Or more likely, having failed to restrict the referendum to a single constitutional clause (as Menzies preferred), the government had a vested interest in ensuring a Yes vote on the combined question, both to mollify international opinion and in the hope that an affirmative vote on the Aboriginal question would carry over to the controversial nexus question.

In this referendum, even the perennial chestnut of Australian politics — that any increase in Commonwealth powers would imperil the federal compact — failed to arouse political passions. Expansion of Commonwealth powers, as was entailed by the amendment of section 51(xxvi), would normally have generated a torrent of states' rights rhetoric. For the 1967 referendum, there was no more than a feeble trickle. An editorial in *The West Australian*, for example, raised the possibility of 'interference in State affairs', but went on to hope that instead there would be increased 'Federal–State cooperation' and recommended, with some equivocation, a vote for Yes.[57] Rarely, if ever, in referenda involving changes to the Commonwealth–state relationship has the states' rights argument been so muted.

Rarely, too, have Australian referenda generated such a profusion of misunderstandings about the consequences of the proposed changes. In response, some commentators issued correctives. In an article published in *The Canberra Times*, constitutional lawyer Geoffrey Sawer explained that the 'substantive importance [of the constitutional amendments] has been much exaggerated' by Yes campaigners, and that improvement in the legal and social status of Aboriginal people did not require constitutional change. He still recommended a Yes vote.[58] Elkin published an article in

The Sydney Morning Herald, affirming that 'I shall vote Yes though not for some of the reasons given by campaigners'. He pointed out that the desirability of constitutional amendment 'does not mean that Aborigines have not been counted hitherto (they have been), or that they will receive the franchise (they have it), or that the Federal Government will henceforth be free to legislate for Aboriginal welfare to a degree not possible up to date'. Rather, the compelling reasons for a Yes vote were that 'the two clauses are out of date, and are misrepresented both in Australia and abroad', and the amendment of section 51(xxvi) would give greater impetus to Commonwealth–state cooperation in Aboriginal affairs.[59]

One of the most sceptical assessments of the proposed constitutional changes was published a year before the referendum by the Victorian lobby group Aboriginal Affairs. It maintained that the arguments for amendment of section 51(xxvi) 'are strong ones but they are not overwhelming', pointing out that Aboriginal legislation in each state ('with the exception of Queensland') had been made substantially congruent without any change to the Constitution and that the Commonwealth could exert a major influence over state policies 'by giving the States Federal financial grants for specified purposes'. It added that the 'record of the Commonwealth government in the complex Aboriginal field over the years does not stand out as clearly superior to that of the States'. However, Aboriginal Affairs' most challenging suggestion lay in its question of 'whether there is not somewhere a thoughtful and hesitant Aboriginal opinion which wishes to see preserved the one minute suggestion of ethnic separateness which is written into the newcomer's Constitution'.[60] The fact that such scepticism was voiced by a body committed to Aboriginal advancement shows that there were already doubts about the wisdom of trying to promote Aboriginal inclusion in the nation by deleting all references to them from the Constitution.

However, the 'ethnic separateness' to which Aboriginal Affairs referred was precisely the target of referendum campaigners' public pronouncements. A 1964 FCAA press release stated that the constitutional amendments 'would help eliminate the Aborigines' feelings of being "different" people in the eyes of the Australian Mother Parliament'.[61] At a protest rally in Sydney's Martin Place the following year, Faith Bandler and her daughter Lilon carried a placard reading 'Count Us Together Make Us One People' (see Plate 9).[62] In April 1967, Faith Bandler stated that, 'All the Aborigines were seeking was to be made, legally and statistically, "one people" with white Australians.'⁶³ In 1961 'One People' had provided the title for a Commonwealth assimilation propaganda booklet. Bandler, it seems, was challenging the government to act on its own inclusionist rhetoric.

Making Aboriginal and other Australians into 'one people' required their having equality not only of legal rights, but also of status and respect. A great deal of campaign effort was devoted to the latter objective. Vote Yes leaflets castigated section 127 as 'an insult to the original Australians', since it implied 'that Aborigines are not worth counting'; its repeal would give Aboriginal people 'the dignity of full citizenship'.⁶⁴ Arguments for the amendment of section 51(xxvi) were more likely to be expressed in instrumental terms, such as the claim that an expansion of Commonwealth powers would allow more resources to be devoted to Aboriginal affairs. Yet arguments for the amendment of this section, too, were frequently couched in terms of national inclusion and social status. In a 1967 newspaper article, Faith Bandler maintained that by the discriminatory provisions of section 51(xxvi), Aboriginal people were 'made to feel a race apart in the land of their birth'.⁶⁵

Yet much publicity material made no mention of the constitutional sections to be voted on, instead representing the referendum as a means to address Aboriginal problems in general and to redress past misdeeds. 'Right Wrongs Write Yes' was emblazoned above a photograph of a cute Aboriginal baby in a widely distributed poster (see Plate 10). Faith Bandler told voters that 'when you write Yes in the lower square of your ballot paper you are holding out the hand of friendship and wiping out nearly 200 years of injustice and inhumanity'.⁶⁶ Hyperbole is not unusual in political campaigns, but what was unusual in this instance is that there was no organised opposition to contest the claims of the Yes campaigners or to counter them with equally extravagant rhetoric for the negative. Without an organised opposition, the hyperbole of the Yes campaigners was seldom subjected to critical scrutiny, and they encountered few constraints in representing the issues at stake as matters of great national moment.

The referendum result revealed that the great majority of white Australians had turned away from an ethnically closed conception of their nation towards a more open understanding of nationhood. This does not mean that those who voted Yes necessarily wanted to have closer personal dealings with Aboriginal people; they were accepting them into the abstract community of the nation, not into the face-to-face community of home and neighbourhood. Nonetheless, it was on the inclusion of Aboriginal people in the national community that the referendum campaign was fought and won. Shortly after hearing of the massive Yes majority, Doug Nicholls proclaimed that it was 'evidence that Australians recognise Aborigines are part of the nation'.[67] As a man whose activist history went back to the 1930s (he was a protégé of William Cooper), Nicholls knew that securing acceptance of Aboriginal people as members of the nation was the culmination of a long, hard struggle. Yet the referendum victory affirmed only the broad principle of national inclusion. On how that principle might be translated into practice, the referendum result was silent.

Special assistance or minority rights?

The front cover of the May 1967 issue of *Smoke Signals* carried the injunction, 'End Discrimination – Vote "Yes" on May 27'. Over the page, it advanced an argument for positive discrimination, 'to enable Aborigines to overcome their disadvantages'.[68] As in almost every instance where campaigners called for positive discrimination, the precedent invoked was the provision of special entitlements to former military personnel under the *Repatriation Act*. It was a modest precedent, but it shows that the referendum campaigners appreciated the need for special provisions for Aboriginal people. In fact, that ambition had been on the campaigners' agenda since the early 1960s.

During the 1962–63 campaign for constitutional amendment, Shirley Andrews, a communist member of the FCAA executive, expounded the benefits of 'special legislation'. She acknowledged that many Aboriginal people, 'who have suffered bitterly from the present discriminatory legislation', had strong misgivings about positive discrimination and preferred an uncompromising adherence to legal sameness. Against those misgivings, Andrews argued that 'special legislation [might] offer the Aborigines a better chance of ensuring that their special needs are properly met'. She suggested the *Repatriation Act* as a model, adding that in 'any modern community there are various groups who are entitled to special privileges without loss of their civil rights. Why not Aborigines?'[69]

By 1964, the Victorian Aborigines Advancement League had adopted a policy of 'preferential assistance' for Aboriginal people. This was 'justified (a) as compensation to descendants of original inhabitants, (b) as essential to enable a people, deprived of equal opportunities for so many generations, to catch up with the rest of society'. Emphasis on the 'catch up' function is evident in the forms of 'special assistance' recommended by the League: 'low interest, long term repayment loans to individuals or groups for housing, business enterprises, farming, etc'; scholarships for the education and training of both youths and adults; special adult education and vocational training courses; and the provision of social workers 'to provide guidance and assistance'. Conventionally, the League pointed to 'Servicemen's Rehabilitation Schemes' as appropriate models in Aboriginal affairs.[70]

In 1965, in response to Prime Minister Menzies' defence of section 51(xxvi) as a safeguard against discrimination, Stan Davey countered: 'Unfortunately not only does it prevent *discrimination against* but also *discrimination in favour of*' Aboriginal people. Davey instanced himself as a beneficiary of 'discriminatory legislation enacted by the Commonwealth Government' in the form of the '*Rehabilitation Act* for ex-servicemen', saying that, 'It is this type of discriminatory legislation the Commonwealth Government must be entrusted to implement for Aborigines if in fact they are to be enabled to catch up with the rest of society to permit a true integration of our people.' He explained that:

> Due to their present economic, educational and social position, most Aborigines see themselves as 'a race apart'. Not until they have been enabled to bridge the gulf between themselves and the rest of the Australian community are they likely to see themselves as being 'one' with other Australians. To this end, for some years, it will be necessary to provide special facilities for them as 'a race apart'.[71]

Positive discrimination, in Davey's recommendation, was an interim measure to expedite the incorporation of the minority into the majority. Frank Engel, secretary of the National Missionary Council, similarly argued that without positive discriminatory measures, 'integration will be further delayed or retarded'.[72]

Sue Taffe argues that the 'vote Yes' campaigners in the 1967 referendum sought 'rights outside the civil rights paradigm'.[73] Perhaps so, but special entitlements to compensate for disadvantage were not at all outside the tradition of social liberalism that had pervaded Australian social policy since Federation. The principle was manifested not only in the *Repatriation Act*, but in numerous items of legislation concerning the unemployed, elderly, disabled, immigrants, mothers and other groups with special needs. Referendum campaign literature occasionally referred to provisions made for these other special-needs groups.[74] Repatriation benefits differed from most in that the beneficiaries could include not only the individual ex-serviceperson but also his or her spouse and children. That may have been a reason for their choice as the primary precedent in the referendum campaign, although repatriation benefits were more likely specified because they resonated with nationalist ideals of sacrifice and duty. Moreover, repatriation benefits were not regarded as a form of charity (as, for example, unemployment benefits could be), but as the fulfilment of an obligation to those to whom the nation owed a special debt.

Hitherto, most special laws in regard to Aboriginal people had abridged their rights. Yet there were items of special legislation that were beneficial to Aboriginal people and enhanced their rights. In 1964, Davis Daniels, Northern Territory State [sic] Secretary of the Council for Aboriginal Rights, instanced three Territory laws that 'give Aboriginals special privileges or rights which other people do not have'. One was the *Intestate Wards (Distribution of Estates) Ordinance* (which enabled the property of a deceased Aboriginal person to pass to his or her spouse or children despite the lack of a will); the second was the *Wildlife Conservation and Control Ordinance* (which freed Aboriginal hunting from the restrictions of faunal protection laws which applied to other people); the third was the *Native and Historical Ordinance* (which forbade non-Aboriginal, but not Aboriginal, people interfering with burial sites and rock paintings).[75] The instances may have been minor, but they exemplify the fact that special beneficial legislation was not a radical innovation of FCAATSI and kindred activist groups.

From the mid-1960s, arguments for positive discrimination began to shift, as some activists came to conceive special Aboriginal entitlements not as mere temporary 'catch-up' provisions but as the enduring rights of an Indigenous minority.[76] As Tim Rowse puts it, 'Conceding indigenous Australians' special but temporary claims in social policy began in the late 1960s to ripen into a recognition of their fundamental, unique and ongoing rights as indigenous peoples.'[77] Rowse attributes this shift to an increasingly positive evaluation of Indigenous cultures and an intensification of Aboriginal claims to land ownership. I shall have more to say about these matters in the next chapter. For our present purposes, the pertinent point is that, although this shift from temporary expedient to enduring rights had begun before 1967, the referendum campaign evinced very little sign of it. Instead, campaigners continued to invoke the precedent of repatriation benefits, with the clear implication that mere 'catch-up' provisions were entailed.[78] Although FCAATSI was a staunch supporter of land rights, it carefully kept its land rights lobbying separate from the referendum campaign.

It was, of course, tactically prudent for campaigners to avoid controversial issues such as land rights. Temporary remedial measures, by contrast, were widely accepted components of Australian social policy — indeed, of the social policy of most liberal democratic states. Unsurprisingly, the referendum campaigners cast their arguments for special Aboriginal entitlements in these terms. Tactical considerations doubtless came into play here, though we must remember that the campaigners faced no organised opposition. The referendum campaigners seem to have judged, rightly, that the Australian public was willing to support special benefits to compensate for Aboriginal disadvantage. After all, the campaigners had managed to present the referendum itself as a means by which the public could demonstrate their acceptance of Aboriginal people as fellow Australians.

Chapter 9

After the Referendum

Although the 1967 referendum has been mythologised as a foundational moment for Aboriginal rights, its immediate consequence among Aboriginal activists was to foster disillusionment with mainstream political processes and disenchantment with the referendum campaigners' avowed objective of equal citizenship. After the referendum, the federal government sat on its hands, while members of the general public seem to have assumed that, having cast their ballot, their duty was done. For many Aboriginal people, it was a deflating experience. Activist Kevin Gilbert explained that 'disillusionment after 1967 hit hard', since Aboriginal people had been 'short-changed after a period of hope'.[1] Kath Walker had been a prominent referendum campaigner from the early 1960s through to 1967; by 1969, she was so disillusioned as to claim that the massive Yes vote brought no benefits to Aboriginal people but merely 'eased the guilty conscience of white Australians'. Aboriginal people involved in the campaign (including, implicitly, herself) had been mere 'stooges of the white Australians working in the interest of white Australians'.[2]

Walker, like many activists, adopted an increasingly radical stance after 1967. In the early to mid-1960s, her self-proclaimed goal had been Aboriginal acceptance into the Australian community as civic equals. In 1965, she had asserted that, 'We cannot advance unless we are taught the white man's way with the white man's help and guidance.'[3] By the end of the decade, she was advocating 'Aboriginal independence', urging other Aboriginal leaders to 'unite your people, and bring them out fighting!'[4] 'Only fools and dreamers', she proclaimed, 'convince themselves that races in Australia can become one people'.[5] Her 'Black Commandments', published in 1969, were a riposte to Australia's 'one people' ideal. They included:

1. Thou shalt gather thy scattered people together.

2. Thou shalt work for black liberation.

3. Thou shalt resist assimilation with all thy might.

...

9. Thou shalt find peace and happiness in a stable black society.

10. Thou shalt think black and act black.

11. Thou shalt be black all the rest of thy days.[6]

Walker's political transition exemplifies a more general shift among Aboriginal activists, away from the quest for inclusion in the Australian nation into stronger affirmations of Aboriginal identity and solidarity. It was a shift of emphasis, not a total reconfiguration of the Aboriginal agenda, but profoundly significant nonetheless.

Not all Aboriginal people travelled down the path of radicalism. Many remained politically moderate, like Neville Bonner who in 1971 became the first Aboriginal member of the federal parliament as a Liberal Party senator for Queensland. Yet the radicalism of the era was palpable, in Aboriginal affairs as elsewhere. Closely associated with this was the unprecedented prominence of youth, which probably constituted a more dramatic change within the Aboriginal community than in the wider Australian society.

Young Aboriginal people had long been involved in political action, but the leaders of earlier times, from William Cooper and Bill Ferguson in the 1930s to Bert Groves and Kath Walker in the 1950s and early 1960s, had been middle-aged or older when they assumed positions of authority. From the mid-1960s, young Aboriginal men and women acted independently for the first time as spokespersons for their race, as leaders of activist groups, as initiators of protest action and as editors of a burgeoning array of Aboriginal newsletters and journals. By their words, actions and appearance, the new generation of Aboriginal activists proclaimed themselves part of the wider phenomenon of youth rebellion. Some openly denigrated their elders,[7] though this seems to have been less common than among their white counterparts. In any event, the political and cultural initiative was passing to a new Aboriginal generation — younger, more brash, better educated and impatient for change.

Educated youth provided the nucleus of a nascent Aboriginal nationalist movement. I have argued elsewhere that the Aboriginal nationalism of the late 1960s and early 1970s was strongly cultural in orientation, concerned with the spiritual and cultural regeneration of the Aboriginal people rather than with establishing a state of their own.[8] Nonetheless, the emergence of Aboriginal nationalism unsettled the relationship between Aboriginal people and the wider Australian community. Growing numbers of Aboriginal people, especially among the young, were coming to see themselves less as an excluded group seeking inclusion and more as a colonised people seeking liberation. The increasing prominence of land rights fed into this reconfiguration of Aboriginal aspirations. These two issues — land rights and Aboriginal nationalism — are examined in the second and third sections of this chapter. First, I shall look at the immediate aftermath of the 1967 referendum and the governmental lethargy that provoked such frustration and disillusionment.

Dream time in Canberra

Warnings that a referendum victory may prove hollow had been sounded over the course of the campaign, particularly in its later stages. An editorial in the Melbourne *Age* two days before the referendum expressed misgivings about the paucity of concrete aims and the profusion of vague promises in the publicity for a Yes vote. 'It will be an empty victory', the editor warned, 'if a Yes majority in the referendum benefits Aborigines only to the extent of acknowledging, in token fashion, their right to be called Australians'.[9]

Two days after the referendum, in an article headed 'Dream time in Canberra', journalist Douglas Wilkie expressed similar views more acerbically. Characterising the massive Yes vote as a mere 'collective conscience-comforter', he claimed that the prime minister was

> glad to be able to use the referendum result to 'prove' to our critics that the ordinary Australian is not really a blood brother of the white racists of the world.
>
> As for us ordinary Australians, we've 'proved' to ourselves, by the simple act of marking a ballot paper, how far we've progressed since our founding fathers thinned out the tiresome blacks with musket balls and arsenic.

Wilkie argued that symbolic gestures and legal rights 'can be meaningless unless accompanied by a measure of assimilation'. For him, assimilation meant the provision of educational and vocational opportunities, without which 'it is nonsense to talk about Australians having "accepted" the aboriginal into the white man's community'. If the referendum were to bring any practical benefits, he insisted, the federal government had to 'draw up an enlightened policy of aboriginal welfare' and coerce the states into conforming to it.[10] He was sceptical about the likelihood of either.

Wilkie's scepticism was well founded. Prime Minister Holt stated that before the referendum, Cabinet had decided to 'leave responsibility for administration largely with the States...Our original purpose was to remove apparently discriminatory references to Aborigines from the Constitution, and not to wrest power from the States.' He acknowledged that the 'remarkably large "YES" vote' had put his government under pressure to adopt 'a rather more active Commonwealth role', but recommended that the status quo in federal–state responsibilities for Aboriginal affairs be maintained as far as possible. He also advised that 'we should not magnify the Aborigine problem out of its true reality'. Cabinet agreed with this and with the Prime Minister's submission that no substantive new initiatives need be taken in Aboriginal affairs.[11]

Not all government members were content with this determination to maintain the status quo. Bill Wentworth, Minister in Charge of Aboriginal Affairs, pressed the point that the referendum result indicated a 'public expectation that the Commonwealth would move decisively for Aboriginal advancement'. Failure to do so, he advised, 'could have quite serious repercussions for us, both internally and internationally', including the likelihood that communists would use it to their advantage. Wentworth set out a comprehensive program for Aboriginal advancement, which included the provision of

> certain benefits for Aboriginals beyond those generally available to Australian citizens. This principle seems inherent in the Referendum mandate, and it should also be remembered that Aboriginals are under-privileged in many ways, even in respect of Government expenditure ...
>
> As already suggested, however, to the extent that our policy of Aboriginal advancement succeeds, it will be possible to phase out these special benefits.[12]

Cabinet sent Wentworth's submission to an Inter-Departmental Committee for further deliberation.

In July 1968, Cabinet issued its decision on Wentworth's submission. It 'declared firmly that the ultimate objective would continue to be assimilation — a single Australian community'. This Cabinet statement is unusual among government documents of the day for the fervour with which it reiterated the government's commitment to assimilation, as if members were concerned that Wentworth's proposal might sway it from that path. Cabinet wished 'to avoid proposals which…are likely to have the effect of acknowledging and establishing a policy of continuing separate development', though it acknowledged that, as a long-term process, assimilation may require 'transitional arrangements which would help Aboriginals to overcome social and other handicaps'.[13] There was nothing new in that, or in anything else in this Cabinet decision. The tepid support it gave Wentworth's proposals, hedged around with provisos and qualifications, amounted to little more than a placatory gesture with no promise of action to follow.

The only significant administrative change prompted by the referendum was the creation of the Council for Aboriginal Affairs, an advisory body comprising public service mandarin HC Coombs, former diplomat Barrie Dexter and anthropologist William Stanner. Coombs' biographer, Tim Rowse, remarks that just as the 1967 referendum 'did not reject assimilation in favour of a new policy philosophy' nor did the members of the council. They continued to endorse assimilation, although this owed more to their appreciation of the capaciousness of the word and its capacity to smooth communications with government, than to any commitment to existing governmental practices.[14] Despite their terminological conservatism, the council was — or tried to be — a conduit through whom new ideas in Indigenous affairs could flow into the domain of governments.

In 1968 Coombs stated that his council had three fundamental aims:

> firstly, to strengthen the sense of Aboriginal Australians as a distinctive group within our society with a distinctive contribution to make to the quality of our national life; secondly, to develop the means whereby Aboriginal citizens can look forward to a secure future, a security which will derive not from handouts but from the results of their own efforts; and thirdly to open the doors of opportunity in all fields of endeavour…to try to develop the means whereby Aboriginal citizens, whether as individuals or as groups or communities can increasingly make the decisions in their own affairs.

Aboriginal policy, he explained, should aim primarily to 'open ways [for Aboriginal people] to solve their own problems…with their human dignity preserved'.[15]

Coombs and his council did their best to initiate reform in Aboriginal affairs at the federal level in the late 1960s and early 1970s. Though working under the rubric of assimilation, they sought to cultivate an Indigenous leadership with firm roots in local communities, and through these leaders advance the Aboriginal people's capacity for self-determination. They tried to stay attuned to the varied aspirations of the vast diversity of Aboriginal groups they considered it their duty to represent. Their efforts were not entirely fruitless.[16] Yet the federal government, dominated by a coalition of the Liberal and Country Parties, was extraordinarily slow to move, so much so that a 1971 FCAATSI memorandum to the United Nations complained that, 'Very little has been done, or even attempted, since the Federal Referendum of 1967.'[17]

FCAATSI was acutely aware of the public indifference underpinning governmental lethargy. Its 1971 Report on Racism in Australia to the World Council of Churches began with the word 'Apathy' and the entire report pivoted on the assertion that this attitude pervaded interactions between Indigenous and non-Indigenous Australians. Racism in Australia, FCAATSI explained, was normally manifested in 'cold, callous indifference to Aborigines, rather than intemperate hatred'.[18] Peter Hastings, a columnist in *The Australian*, agreed. Writing on Australian racism in May 1970, he noted that the 'majority view seems to be one of sheer, appalling white indifference', which gave mere 'lip service assent to the notion of doing something about the problem' of Aboriginal disadvantage.[19] Hastings' colleague, Ian Moffitt, similarly remarked that, 'Australian racism is not a blow in the face. It is a back turned, a pious face averted.'[20] An insidious indifference perpetuated governmental negligence and allowed well-meaning platitudes to take the place of effective action.

On Australia Day 1972 — the last of the Coalition's twenty-three years in government — Prime Minister McMahon issued a statement of Commonwealth Aboriginal policy. He reiterated the ideals that had by then become standard in such policy declarations: Aboriginal people should possess equal rights and responsibilities with other Australians; 'they should be encouraged and assisted to preserve and develop their own culture, languages, traditions and arts so that these can become living elements in the diverse culture of the Australian society'; they should exercise 'effective choice about the degree to which, and the pace at which, they come to identify themselves with [the wider Australian] society'. The federal government, McMahon declared, would 'encourage and strengthen [Aboriginal people's] capacity increasingly to manage their own affairs — as individuals, as groups, and as communities at the local level'; it would take 'special measures' to 'increase their economic independence' and improve standards in 'health, housing, education and vocational training'.[21] These accorded with the aspirations of Aboriginal and pro-Aboriginal lobby groups. But many in these groups, especially their younger members, had become impatient with grand statements of intention. They were particularly dismayed by the Prime Minister's rejection of what they had come to regard as an essential foundation for Aboriginal material and cultural well-being: land rights. McMahon's statement prompted the most audacious Aboriginal protest so far witnessed in Australia.

On the evening of McMahon's address, four young Aboriginal men, Michael Anderson, Billy Craigie, Bert Williams and Tony Coorey, set up a beach umbrella labelled 'Aboriginal Embassy' on the lawns outside Parliament House in Canberra. Over the next few days, the umbrella was upgraded to a tent, more activists joined the embassy, and what had begun as a land rights protest ballooned into an affirmation of Aboriginal identity and solidarity. The protestors' claims extended to Aboriginal ownership of 'certain areas of certain cities', as well as an initial compensation payout of six billion dollars 'plus a percentage of the gross national income per annum'. More confronting was the fact that by constituting themselves an embassy the protestors implied that Aboriginal people comprised a distinct nation within Australia. In line with this, they demanded political autonomy in the form of 'Full state rights to the Northern Territory under Aboriginal ownership and control'.[22] It was not a call for secession, since an Aboriginalised Northern Territory/state was envisaged as remaining within the Australian federation, but it was a demand for Aboriginal people not merely to own land but to take a share of sovereignty over a substantial tract of Australian territory. The Tent Embassy encapsulated the two ideals — land rights and Aboriginal nationalism — then coming to the fore and complicating, though not contradicting, the quest for inclusion in the Australian nation. The following sections consider these two ideals in turn.

Land rights

Demands for land predate the establishment of the first Aboriginal political organisations in the interwar years. However, as Bain Attwood argues, it was not until the 1960s that 'land rights' emerged as a coherent political discourse. In that decade, new relationships and channels of communication were forged among political campaigners and Indigenous landholders, allowing what were previously regarded as merely local land claims to be subsumed into a continent-wide land rights agenda. Attwood draws particular attention to the ways in which, in 1963, the land claims of the Yolngu in Arnhem Land were linked with those of the Aboriginal inhabitants of Lake Tyers in Victoria, creating a common moral and political basis for asserting rights to land on the grounds of indigeneity. Not until then did the Lake Tyers and other southern Aboriginal groups represent their land claims in terms of traditional rights to 'tribal' lands, along the same lines as title was claimed by Aboriginal groups in remote Australia.[23] From that time onward, these became the paradigmatic terms in which land rights were articulated.

Highlighting tradition as the foundation of their claims to land, when the Yolngu sent the Commonwealth parliament a petition in mid-1963, it was written in a local language, Yolngu-matha, inscribed within a bark painting in traditional Arnhem Land style (see Plate 11). The bark petition, as it was dubbed, attracted enormous media attention. The Yolngu style of bark painting was already well known, after several decades of white Australian interest in Aboriginal art, but this art was now deployed for a purpose with which it had not hitherto been associated. Not merely an ensemble of decorative motifs or an instance of primitive aesthetics or an ethnographic artefact, the bark petition was a political claim addressed to the paramount political institution in Australia. Traditional artistic expression and modern political demands came together as never before.

As the 1960s progressed, land rights assumed ever greater prominence on the Aboriginal agenda. In 1966, Aboriginal stockworkers on several Northern Territory cattle stations went on strike over the Conciliation and Arbitration Commission's decision to defer implementation of its equal wages determination for almost three years. At Wave Hill station, the strike escalated into a land claim by the local Gurindji people, whose cause was publicised by the communist writer, Frank Hardy.[24] Meanwhile, the Yolngu at Yirrkala, far to the north of Wave Hill, continued their campaign to regain title to their lands. In late 1968, Yolngu elders lodged a claim for their lands in the Supreme Court of the Northern Territory, the first such claim in Australian history to come before a court. Over the following several years, these two land claims — from the Gurindji at Wave Hill and the Yolngu at Yirrkala — were the iconic land rights struggles. There were other land rights claims, some in southern Australia, but publicity for land rights focused on Aboriginal claims in remote Australia, not only in the mainstream media but also in the newsletters, press releases and statements of Aboriginal and pro-Aboriginal activist groups.

Some land rights supporters suggested that the issue may be raising unrealisable expectations. In his 1968 Boyer lecture, 'After the Dreaming', William Stanner warned that land rights held political dangers, since most Aboriginal people would be unable to prove traditional attachment to specific tracts of land, and non-Aboriginal Australians would likely resent land being granted on any basis other than an unambiguous demonstration of ancestral ownership of such tracts.[25] Aware of popular unease about land rights, campaigners in the 1960s often specified that the land in question was limited in extent, usually citing existing Aboriginal reserves and settlements, as well as 'tribal territory' in those areas 'where tribal consciousness still exists'. They also specified that land so acquired would be put to productive use as farms, pastoral stations, tourist enterprises, and so forth.[26]

The federal government was sympathetic toward Aboriginal people acquiring land as a means of improving their economic prospects, but not to land rights as an entitlement on the basis of indigeneity. In August 1968, Commonwealth Minister for the Interior, PJ Nixon, stated that the 'government is in favor of Aboriginals gaining title to land but believes that this should be under the land tenure system which applies to the rest of the community'. He opposed 'measures which are likely to set Aboriginal citizens permanently apart from other Australians through having their development based on separate or different standards'. Government opposition derived largely from its assessment that if 'areas of land [were] granted to groups of Aboriginals in remote places…we could end up with a series of depressed Aboriginal communities tied to a form of substandard living with a barrier between them and the rest of the Australian community'. Most Aboriginal people in remote areas already lived under such circumstances, but Nixon preferred to hold out the promise of 'the assimilation of Aboriginal Australians as fully effective members of a single Australian society'.[27] In pursuit of that promise, new legislation in 1969 enabled Northern Territory Aboriginal people to acquire leasehold title to restricted areas on stringent conditions.

Even if the 1969 legislation had been more generous, leasehold title could never satisfy the demands for land rights. For one thing, land rights connected with an ideal of Aboriginal autonomy, whereby security of title would give Aboriginal groups the power to engage with mining, pastoral and other enterprises on terms which allowed them to assert their own interests. No longer to be pushed aside at the whim of governments or developers, Aboriginal landowners possessing secure title would be able to negotiate terms favourable to themselves, and even veto projects if that were their choice. Land rights would bring about fundamental change in the power relations between Indigenous and non-Indigenous Australians. Leasehold arrangements merely tinkered around the edges.

Equally importantly, land rights were bonded to Aboriginal culture, identity and dignity. FCAATSI president Joe McGinness explained that a primary purpose of land rights was to assist Aboriginal people 'to regain some of their lost culture, identity and pride'.[28] Even conservative Aboriginal leaders took this view. Senator Neville Bonner argued for land rights on the grounds that land was 'the foundation of our being'.[29] Kevin Gilbert, writing in 1968, emphasised that land rights would meet 'the psychological and emotional needs of true justice and status within the community'. For Aboriginal people, he claimed, 'the status of dignity and pride, can only come after our land claims are recognised'.[30] Some years later, Gilbert stated that the 'crux of the Aboriginal question is *land*. The original theft of all Aboriginal land is the root-cause of the whole complex of ills that go to make up the "Aboriginal Problem".' If that root-cause were remedied, he suggested, all other Aboriginal problems would be solved.[31]

A 1968 statement by the Aborigines' Progressive Association put the case more effusively:

> This land, this claim for justice is one that represents a symbolic being, a oneness, a complete belonging to the land, to the nation who recognises our just claim, to the land of our fathers.
>
> It is also an assuagement to hurt sensibilities. It is a land tie, an identification to ourselves and with our fathers. It is, above all, a recognition of our fathers' title.

> It is more: for today, it can well mean the recognition, and our bond of place within the Australian community. It can mean that pride of Race, pride of nationality, pride of entry into the Australian community in a dignified manner can be accorded us, our children, and the generations to come.[32]

Land rights, in this rendition, would both bolster an Aboriginal identity — even a distinct Aboriginal nationality — and promote Aboriginal membership in the wider community.

Land rights campaigners were quite prepared to appeal to popular Australian nationalism. 'The Gurindji Blues', a song written by former Northern Territory welfare officer Ted Egan, and sung by him and a young Yolngu man named Galarrwuy Yunupingu on a 1971 RCA recording, resonated with the popular Australian ideal of a 'fair go', constantly repeating the refrain, 'Poor bugger me, Gurindji' and reiterating the wrongs suffered by this people.[33] Its identification of the primary wrongdoer as Lord Vestey seems to have been calculated to appeal to both an Australian love of 'pommy-bashing' and the contemporary antagonism toward foreign ownership of Australian resources. Some other land rights propaganda took an anti-foreign-ownership slant. In 1968 FCAATSI claimed that the 'major objections' to the recognition of land rights 'come from the spokesmen of overseas companies who have no direct interest in Australia's social welfare'.[34] The veracity of the claim is dubious, but its insinuation against foreign big-business interests appealed to the contemporary mood.

Land rights advocates also argued that the possession of land would expedite the incorporation of Aboriginal people into the Australian nation. A pamphlet issued by FCAATSI and Abschol (a committee of the National Union of Australian University Students) in 1968 stated that by providing Aboriginal people with capital resources, land rights 'should lead to a lessening of the economic barriers between the races and thus to a faster eventual integration between Aborigines and non-Aborigines'.[35] Barrie Pittock maintained that 'social equality and ultimately integration or even assimilation, depends greatly on economic equality', which could best be achieved by Aboriginal people acquiring ownership of land. 'Without land rights', he claimed, 'there will always be some bitterness and resentment, and people with chips on their shoulders'. He added that Aboriginal people had developed what the American sociologist Oscar Lewis called a 'culture of poverty', a self-perpetuating cycle that could be broken only through their acquiring capital assets.[36] Similar arguments, invoking the 'culture of poverty' thesis and claiming that land offered a platform for both economic advancement and national inclusion, were propounded in the course of FCAATSI's 1968 national land rights campaign.[37]

Intensifying demands for land rights induced shifts in the Aboriginal agenda. Land rights promoted a diagnosis of Aboriginal disadvantage emphasising dispossession over discrimination, thus pushing the agenda beyond legal equality. By asserting Indigenous entitlement to land on grounds that could not be claimed by other Australians, land rights emphasised Aboriginal distinctiveness. By rendering Indigenous tradition into title deeds, land rights promoted attentiveness to the deep past of Aboriginal societies and the recovery of traditional culture. These were shifts of emphasis rather than fundamentally new ideas or aspirations. Although it tended to demote the quest for inclusion in the Australian nation and added new complications to that quest, the land rights agenda did not run counter to the goal of Aboriginal membership of the Australian community. The emergent Aboriginal nationalism had a similar pertinence.

An Aboriginal nation

The rudiments of a pan-Aboriginal consciousness can be discerned as far back as the late nineteenth century,[38] although it was not until the interwar years that activists deliberately began cultivating that consciousness. For them, as for their successors, pan-Aboriginality had both geographic and demographic dimensions, as they sought to create solidarity not only between widely dispersed groups but also between those of differing degrees of Aboriginal ancestry. This solidarity grew slowly but steadily through the postwar years. Contemporary anthropologists commented on the phenomenon, usually approvingly, although they noted that the sense of solidarity was confined largely to 'southern mixed-bloods', who conceived a bond among themselves and to their 'northern full-blood' compatriots that was not reciprocated by the latter group.[39] This view was by no means confined to white observers. In 1973, the self-styled 'Aboriginal patriot', Kevin Gilbert, lamented that, 'Even today the northern full-bloods do not consider that the southern blacks are Aborigines.' He added, more optimistically, that 'a Pan-Aboriginal feeling is on the move'.[40]

Rising literacy levels facilitated the interconnectedness essential for pan-Aboriginal solidarities. So did the creation of organisational links among Aboriginal groups. A crucial development was the foundation of the Federal Council for Aboriginal Advancement (FCAA) in 1958, the first continent-wide lobby group devoted to Aboriginal issues. As a multi-racial and initially white-dominated body, the Federal Council's creation owed little, if anything, to an intention to foster pan-Aboriginality. However, as the first organisation to provide a forum for Aboriginal people from around Australia to air their grievances and compare their situations, it inevitably had that effect. Through the 1960s, the Indigenous groups who came together at the Federal Council's annual conferences grew more determined to gain the strength which came from unity, to become — as reported at the 1969 FCAATSI conference — 'one People instead of various tribal and fragmented societies'.[41] Perhaps the most important contribution the Federal Council made to pan-Aboriginality was in the cultural domain. At the annual council meetings, Aboriginal people from southern Australia met others from the remote north and centre, often for the first time, thereby becoming familiar with their outlooks and with living traditional cultures.[42] Arguably, these cross-cultural encounters among Aboriginal peoples were more consequential than the items on the conference agendas.

Yet, while FCAATSI contributed to the strengthening of pan-Aboriginal connectedness, the organisation itself fell victim to the strains generated by that process. FCAATSI clung to its foundational precept of interracial cooperation, illustrated in its 1967 referendum propaganda showing black and white Australians working together in pursuit of their shared destiny as equal and respected citizens. Behind the facade, however, the council was riven with factionalism and discord. Some FCAATSI leaders, both Indigenous and non-Indigenous, wanted the council to retain a multi-racial leadership, in line with its principle of concordance between black and white Australians. A growing number, however, sought to change the council into an Indigenous-led organisation, in keeping with its principle that Aboriginal people must take control over their own affairs. Those supporting the former line did not dispute the latter principle or the need for Indigenous-only organisations; they merely maintained that FCAATSI, as an umbrella organisation, must remain multi-racial in membership and leadership.[43] Friction between the two views generated a great deal of heat, which boiled over at FCAATSI's 1970 annual conference. The council split, with one faction hiving off to establish the National Tribal Council.

Commenting on events at the 1970 FCAATSI conference, Sue Taffe notes that the 'multiracial coalitions of the 1960s were no longer acceptable to many Indigenous political activists' and that the 'politics of Aboriginal affairs had moved towards separatism'.[44] However, while the Tribal Council demanded organisational separation and the creation of a domain in which Aboriginal people could develop their own social, cultural and political projects, its program was not separatist in the sense of seeking an independent Aboriginal state. To the contrary, the Tribal Council asserted its commitment to the inclusion of Indigenous people in an Australian nation reformed into 'a genuine and voluntary plural society'.[45] Even the organisational separation was regarded by some activists as a reconcilement of differing views rather than a clash of incompatible outlooks. The editor of *Smoke Signals* wrote:

> The formation of the National Tribal Council was a sensible compromise which enables those Aborigines who want to exercise the powers of office in an all black organisation to do so, whilst still allowing those Aborigines who have found nothing much wrong with working with white people in a multiracial organisation to continue to help guide the activities of the F.C.A.A.T.S.I. The functions of the two bodies can be complementary raher [sic] than opposed. There is still plenty of work for both to do.[46]

This, however, does not detract from the importance of the National Tribal Council's creation. The name of the new council flaunted its members' tribal origins, at the same time suggesting that tribal divisions were subsumed within a national unity. The point was vividly illustrated in the ceremony installing Doug Nicholls as head of the council under the title Bapu Mamus. Nicholls was a Yorta-Yorta man from Victoria; Bapu Mamus was a chiefly title from the Torres Strait. At the instalment ceremony, depicted in a full-page photograph on the cover of the September 1970 issue of *Origin* (see Plate 12), Nicholls was honoured with

> a special corroboree and ceremonious presentation of spear, woomera, and killing stick, while Pastor Don Brady played the didgeridoo.
>
> Islanders performed the dance only for their chief and presented a symbolic polished shell worn on the breast, a feathered headdress and a chief's wooden hammer.[47]

In this *mélange* of motifs from around Australia, the Tribal Council expressed both the fusion of the varied strands of Indigenous culture into a harmonious national unity, and the growing importance attributed to traditional culture as a vital constituent of Indigenous identity.

Pan-Aboriginality also drew sustenance from ideologies of pan-blackness. A year before the Tribal Council's foundation, black power came to Australia when the Bermudan, Roosevelt Brown, visited at the invitation of the young Melbourne Koorie, Bruce McGuinness. Fellow activist Bob Maza enthused that the day of Brown's arrival 'was the day that enlightenment came to Australia'.[48] Some among the older generation, including Doug Nicholls, expressed misgivings about black power, but the ideology spurred many young people to adopt increasingly radical stances. The ultimate, perhaps, was the creation in 1970 of an Aboriginal Black Panther Party, closely modelled on its American namesake.

However, black power in Australia was not always inflected in radical mode. Ken Colbung explained the guiding principles of the Western Australian Black Power Group, which he founded and coordinated:

> Principally it is to give the Aboriginal individual a sense of responsibility. Then working up to responsibility to his partner, responsibility to the family unit, responsibility to his Aboriginal race. Responsibility then to his fellow mankind in the multi-racial society that we have in Australia.

Throughout his exposition, Colbung reiterated the point that 'our plans for eventual integration with the multi-racial society must be everpresent'.[49] Against such moderate interpretations of black power might be set some of the Australian Black Panthers' threats of armed insurrection, or Bruce McGuinness' injunction: 'We must think black, we must educate our kids black…and above all we must reject the white education system.'[50] Yet the Australian Panthers, unlike the American originals, never carried their threats of violence into action, and McGuinness's injunction was probably intended as provocative rhetoric rather than practical advice; when he wrote it, he was studying for an Arts degree at Monash University.

Some Australian black power advocates sometimes gave priority to international black solidarity over specifically Aboriginal aspirations.[51] For most Aboriginal activists, however, black power was a source of precepts and ideas to be selectively drawn upon to bolster Aboriginal rights, pride and status. Bruce McGuinness defined black power as 'Koorie power, Aboriginal autonomy'.[52] For Kevin Gilbert, black power was an affirmation of Aboriginal people's 'humanity, rights, justice, dignity and right to self-determination'.[53] Neither of these men — nor the vast majority of other Aboriginal black power advocates — conceived autonomy and self-determination as entailing an independent Aboriginal state. Gilbert opposed even the Tent Embassy's calls for the creation of an Aboriginal state within the Australian federation.[54] They sought autonomy within the Australian state, enabling them to advance the collective interests of Aboriginal people and secure a domain wherein Aboriginal identity and culture could flourish. This entailed closing ranks against white hegemony; however, few — if any — envisaged a total closure in the manner of, say, the Nation of Islam in America.

Even among black power devotees, secession had few supporters. The Australian Black Panthers demanded 'a United Nations-supervised plebiscite to be held throughout the black colony in which only black colonial subjects will be allowed to participate, for the purpose of determining the will of the black people as to their national destiny'. They added an excerpt from Thomas Jefferson's 1776 Declaration of Independence. However, the Panthers' statement did not explicitly call for secession; rather, it asserted a right to secession. And this assertion was preceded by a string of demands for the federal government to provide a comprehensive array of services for Aboriginal people in employment, housing, education and welfare, on the implicit assumption that Aboriginal people would remain the responsibility of that government.[55] Perhaps secession was a last-ditch strategy, or perhaps — like the Panthers' occasional calls to arms — it was little more than a rhetorical flourish. It seems that even the Panthers, the most radical Aboriginal group of the day, could not easily imagine a political future for Aboriginal people divorced from the Australian state.

Some young Aboriginal activists were openly critical of the quest for inclusion in the Australian nation, attacking not only assimilation — long a target of criticism — but also integration, which activists since the late 1950s had championed as an ostensible alternative to assimilation. Probably drawing on the American black power critique of the civil rights movement's goal of integration, Bob Maza offered a scathing assessment of integrated Aboriginal people as 'lost':

> If there are black integrateds who are playing the part of whites whom you know, then pity them, for in their blindness they

show their desperation to be an accepted people. When all the black people of this country are nationally welded together, the integrates will soon have to identify themselves. To deny your brothers and sisters is treason of the highest degree.[56]

Even so, Maza's antagonism was directed not so much against national inclusion *per se* as against the prioritising of that goal; the cultivation of Aboriginality, he urged, must always take precedence.

Bruce McGuinness extolled black power as 'a turn inward, a rallying cry for a people in the sudden labor of self-discovery, self-naming and self-legitimization'.[57] Yet McGuinness's 'turn inward' was never total; separatism was not on his agenda. He explicitly urged fellow Koories not to 'go it alone', and insisted that to be politically effective, 'we must never alienate ourselves from our main source of support, and that is the white sympathetic followers of the black man'.[58] Like other Australian exponents of black power, he construed the 'turn inward' primarily in cultural terms, as a recovery of lost pride and dignity and as an affirmation of the worth of Aboriginality. Conceived in these terms, black power did not stand opposed to Aboriginal inclusion in the Australian community, although it did mean that inclusion would assume lower priority. Building Aboriginal status and self-esteem came first, and the new generation of activists came increasingly to the view that these could best be achieved through the recovery and revitalisation of Indigenous tradition.

Aboriginal activists had always sought to represent their people's past in positive terms, but from the late 1960s this intensified into a veneration of Indigenous antiquity. A leaflet produced for the protests against the Cook bicentenary depicted pre-colonial Australia as a golden age of peace and harmony, when Aboriginal people 'had a cultural heritage and a religion which was as sophisticated as any known'.[59] Bob Maza proclaimed that pre-colonial Aboriginal 'culture and civilisation' had 'evolved a perfect harmony…where every man's want was catered for, and their leaders were honoured, respected and listened to'.[60] Kevin Gilbert observed that before the arrival of Europeans, 'the Aborigines had land, a proud stone-age culture, a rich spiritual heritage, satisfaction and self-sufficiency'.[61] He claimed that most Aboriginal people

> believe that the tribal way of life was a superior way of life, devoid of the competitive, sharking ruthlessness required in white society. We believe that the old Laws were just and wise and good and

provided an umbrella for the growth of the human spirit. Certainly most of us believe that it was not until the white man came that greed, lust, arrogance and meanness came to the Eden that was Australia.[62]

More tersely, the Black Rights Committee stated that, 'We used to have a beautiful way of life before the white man came along.'[63]

A golden age is part of the repertoire of all nationalisms. Its purpose is not mere nostalgic remembrance of past greatness but to inspire moral and cultural regeneration in the present and future.[64] It was in this spirit that Bob Maza urged Aboriginal people to recover 'pride and dignity' in the ancient culture and history 'which lies in your ancestry'. Maza invoked not the ancestry and culture of any particular Aboriginal group, but a generalised pan-Aboriginal ancestry and culture:

> You need the knowledge of the wonderful way of life that the old Aborigines had. You need to know the height of his honour, integrity and unique self-discipline. You need to know of his high moral code and religious ethics, so that in some small way you can build within yourself a national pride. You can then look back with dignity and know that you come from an honourable people.[65]

Finding virtue in traditional culture was not new. What was new was the extent to which the recovery of that culture was harnessed to building an Aboriginal national consciousness.

Accompanying this was an intensified demand for cultural authenticity as an essential component of identity. On this assumption, the National Tribal Council called for the establishment of

> programmes, seminars, and courses which aim at the reacculturation of Aborigines and Islanders. There is a growing desire by many people of Aboriginal and Islander descent for study programs which will teach them what they need to know in order to find their true identities as Aboriginal and Islander Australians.[66]

Implicitly, these true identities had been smothered by false ones, which could be stripped away only through the determined effort of newly self-aware Indigenous people.

This bonding of cultural authenticity to Aboriginal identity was an innovation of the late 1960s. Earlier activists had sought respect for traditional Aboriginal culture and the preservation of certain of its elements. However, they had not regarded the Aboriginal identity (which they cherished) as dependent on traditional Aboriginal culture (which most acknowledged they had lost). As shown in Chapter 3, the Aboriginal activists of the 1930s had explicitly advocated the supplanting of traditional by modern Western cultures, even putting themselves forward as emissaries who should convey the benefits of civilisation to their primitive compatriots in remote Australia. Exemplifying their attitude toward traditional cultures, in 1936 William Cooper stated that his Australian Aborigines' League 'does desire the preservation of the best features of aboriginal culture and feels that the preservation of certain corroboree dances, in the way the old World peoples have retained their folk dances, is in harmony with this', but went on to warn that 'great care should be exercised till such time as the native race is so fully civilised that the outlook on the corroboree is just that of the Old World civilisation on their folk dances'.[67] In 1962, Cooper's protégé, Doug Nicholls, bluntly stated that in Victoria the 'old culture is lost'. What survived was 'an attitude, an outlook', which Nicholls clearly esteemed; however, he expressed no unease at his lack of the 'old culture'.[68] Activists of the late 1960s and early 1970s, particularly the young, construed this lack quite differently: as a loss that must be remedied.

In 1972, Paul Coe explained that, 'We want to relearn and relive...the wisdom of our ancestors if possible, learn the cultural, the spiritual values of the Aboriginal people — our ancestors.'[69] He outlined a strategy for doing so: 'We're trying to invite tribal people to come to Sydney to teach young kids. Even if they don't teach us the culture of our particular tribes, at least we'll be able to learn aspects of the Aboriginal culture from certain other tribes — which will be invaluable.'[70] Alternatively, urban people might visit their tribal compatriots. A 1973 Workshop on Aboriginal Culture and Identity recommended:

> That the tribal Aboriginals should help those Aboriginals who have lost their culture to find out more about the Aboriginal way of life and customs.
>
> That the best way for Aboriginals who have lost their identity as Aboriginals to regain it would be for such families to come and live in tribal communities for two or three years so that they could learn about the Aboriginal way of life and grow up with it.[71]

It was a reversal of William Cooper's 1930s project, whereby civilised Aborigines would bring cultural enlightenment to their tribal compatriots.

Like other nationalists, the Aboriginal activists of the late 1960s and early 1970s imbued particular tracts of territory with special significance, laden with cultural and spiritual meaning for the nation. Their favoured special place was the Northern Territory. Paul Coe declared that the Northern Territory could become an Aboriginal 'spiritual homeland', analogous to what 'Israel is now to the majority of Jews' or 'the Aboriginal's sort of Mecca'.[72] Michael Anderson proclaimed, 'I look to Arnhem Land as a place where we can start to dig our roots in and restore the pride of the Aboriginal culture.'[73] John Newfong called Arnhem Land 'our Israel'.[74] None of these men had traditional associations with anywhere in the Northern Territory; rather, they took the Territory as emblematic of traditional Aboriginality, a place where the culture and customs of their forebears still flourished and from which the spiritual rejuvenation of the Aboriginal nation could flow. However innovative their program may have been in other respects, theirs was a conventional view of the Northern Territory as the primary repository of Aboriginal culture, an image it had acquired at the beginning of the twentieth century through the pioneering ethnographies of Baldwin Spencer and Frank Gillen.

Elaborating on the Tent Embassy's demand for the Northern Territory to become an Aboriginal state, Bobbi Sykes explained that this followed from their superiority of numbers there. Paul Coe observed that a democratic Northern Territory would automatically become 'a black controlled state, because by definition the blacks up there outnumber the Europeans by an extent of seven to one'.[75] There seems to have been an element of hopefulness in this, as if these activists needed to imagine some part of Australia where Aboriginal people still predominated. Their demographics were mistaken. In fact, by 1972 non-Aboriginal outnumbered Aboriginal Territorians by a factor of three to one.[76] However, the ultimate significance of the Northern Territory had little to do with demographic statistics. The Tent Embassy protestors chose it as the primary site of Aboriginal autonomy because it was the repository of authentic Aboriginality, a place from which a cultural renaissance could be initiated to reinvigorate the Aboriginal nation.

The Embassy protestors chose their emblems partly from the repertoire of traditional Aboriginality. One of the two flags they first flew featured stylised images of a churinga, a spear and a campfire hearth in the ochre, black and white colours of traditional bark-painting. The other flag was quite different: it was the red, black and green tricolour of international black solidarity (see Plate 13).[77] The combination expressed the distinctively Aboriginal character of the protest alongside its embeddedness in a larger struggle for the liberation of all the black peoples of the world. It was not until several months after its establishment that the embassy flew the now-familiar red, black and yellow Aboriginal flag. Although that flag had been designed the previous year by Luritja man Harold Thomas, it seems not to have been well known among Aboriginal activists when the embassy was first set up. It was the embassy itself, after it adopted this flag around April 1972, that propelled the Aboriginal flag into prominence as a symbol of Aboriginal nationhood.

Even before adoption of the flag, Aboriginal activists increasingly adopted the vocabulary of nationalism, including the term 'self-determination'. The term had been used earlier, but the increasing invocation of 'self-determination' from the late 1960s onwards signalled the maturing of Aboriginal nationalism. Even so, the self-determination sought was self-determination within an overarching Australian nation. In early 1972, Kevin Gilbert asserted that 'true dignity can come only by the granting of real self-determination to Aboriginal communities', but he went on to explain that this meant that 'the Aboriginal people could begin to redefine their role in Australian society'.[78] For Gilbert, as for generations of Aboriginal activists before him, dignity and esteem were as important as rights and entitlements. For Gilbert, as for his predecessors, the Aboriginal future was envisaged within a wider Australian nation. Where he and growing numbers of Aboriginal people differed from their antecedents was in configuring Aboriginal people themselves as a nation, with intensified demands for the typically nationalist aspirations for autonomy, unity and identity. These aspirations already existed, but their intensification from the late 1960s shifted the foundations on which Aboriginal people claimed membership of the Australian nation.

Epilogue

Unfinished Business

Three decades after Jack Patten and Bill Ferguson issued the declaration with which this book began, demanding Aboriginal people be included 'fully and equally...in the body of the Australian nation', Australians voted in a referendum on just this issue. The referendum result — an affirmative majority of over 90 per cent — would have been inconceivable in Patten and Ferguson's day. The fact that a referendum was held in 1967 can be credited to the tenacity of FCAATSI and kindred lobby groups, but the magnitude of the referendum victory had deeper roots. It lay in the transformation, over the middle third of the twentieth century, of settler Australian attitudes towards Aboriginal people, Aboriginality and their own nationhood. Myriad factors impelled that transformation, ranging from government-sponsored assimilation propaganda to oppositional agitation for integration; from Aboriginal demonstrations of their artistic creativity to anthropological expositions of Aboriginal sociality; from a global recoil against racism to a new diversity in the national immigrant intake. These catalysts were not always completely congruent, but together they moved the nation to a greater openness towards Aboriginal people. So far had this trend progressed by 1967 that the extraordinary affirmative vote in that year's referendum, together with the absence of a negative campaign, suggests that the Australian people were not merely willing but eager to demonstrate their inclusiveness towards Aboriginal people.

Yet the aspirations of Patten, Ferguson, Cooper and other Aboriginal activists of the 1930s had not been attained. They had sought inclusion in the Australian nation on terms providing economic security, political representation and a respected role in the life of the community. They strove to avoid the pitfall of marginalisation along the route to national

Epilogue

incorporation. Despite the advances of the following three decades, at the end of the 1960s Aboriginal people still remained on the margins of Australian society, still impoverished, still with limited access to political power, still the 'Aboriginal problem' rather than, as William Cooper had hoped, an 'Aboriginal asset'. By the 1960s, the 'Aboriginal problem' was of far greater concern to settler Australians than it had been in the 1930s, and in selected domains — notably aesthetic heritage and sport — Aboriginal assets were coming to be recognised. Yet, while the indifference of earlier times was being eroded, the slowness and unevenness of the process left apathy still prominent in the landscape of Aboriginal affairs. Even the culminating moment in the quest for inclusion — the 1967 referendum — was pervaded by a peculiar combination of indifference with professions of good intentions, a combination that continues to pervade settler Australian attitudes towards Aboriginal people today. In 1967, the Australian public plainly showed their goodwill towards Aboriginal people; and having shown it, they retreated to comfortable complacency.

After the referendum, and partly out of disillusionment with its meagre gains, came an upsurge of Aboriginal nationalism. For the next three decades, self-determination was the lodestar in Indigenous politics. Self-determination sometimes veered towards separatism — although, as Noel Pearson remarks, Aboriginal separatism typically has been invoked as a 'tactical device', a rhetorical underlining of Aboriginal identity and solidarity, rather than as a realistic political strategy.[1] Throughout the period from the 1970s to the early 2000s, 'self-determination' was generally understood to denote some form of Indigenous autonomy within the national state of Australia, not secession from it. Indeed, throughout those years a demand for Aboriginal inclusion in the Australian nation continued to interweave through advocacy of self-determination, as attested by the calls for a treaty (or *makarrata*) between Indigenous and other Australians that gathered force from the late 1970s onwards, and even more by the reconciliation movement that dominated the 1990s. Defending a domain of Indigenous autonomy and shoring up a bastion of Indigenous identity now assumed greater prominence than they had in the 1950s and 1960s, but a similar dynamic continued, between on the one hand a desire for union between Indigenous and non-Indigenous Australians and on the other a demand for the recognition of distinctiveness. Differing priorities in the eras of self-determination and assimilation should not be allowed to obscure the continuities. The first item in the celebrations to mark the centenary of Federation in 2001 was a traditional Arrernte ceremony of invitation. Rosie Ferber, one of the Arrernte dancers, explained that through this ceremony, 'we are asking non-indigenous people to include us Aboriginal people with all Australian people'.[2]

Since the beginning of the twenty-first century, policies and practices pursued under the aegis of self-determination have come under increasing attack for failing to remedy Indigenous poverty, ill-health and educational deficits, or to offer Indigenous people the opportunities available to other Australians. Linguist Peter Sutton makes the further point that over-commitment to a doctrinaire version of self-determination has tended to obscure the reality of Aboriginal suffering.[3] Indifference in Indigenous affairs, it seems, can take strange twists. Yet, while interrogating policy and its implementation is essential, some recent criticisms of self-determination barely rise above calumny. Gary Johns, for example, condemns self-determination as no more than a white Australian-induced fantasy for the perpetuation of Aboriginal primitivity.[4] The irony is that, in his polemical style, Johns follows in the footsteps of the devotees of self-determination whom he condemns. Just as partisans for self-determination in the late twentieth century bluntly condemned assimilation as devoid of any positive attributes or aspirations, now denunciators of self-determination, like Johns, lambast that policy as morally vacuous and lacking any redeeming qualities. Posing issues in sharply dichotomous terms may be common practice in Australian politics, but it does nothing to advance our understanding of those issues. Instead, it incites a combativeness that may be exhilarating to political protagonists but offers little benefit to those people whose betterment is the ostensible objective.

Today, more than ever, we need to transcend the polarised polemics that have bedevilled discussion of Indigenous affairs in Australia. I offer this book in that spirit, as a contribution to a more nuanced understanding of relations between Indigenous and settler Australians. The much-maligned era of assimilation was far from devoid of positive achievements; it was a dynamic era in which the foundations of national inclusiveness towards Indigenous people were laid, even if those foundations were built upon shifting sands. Assimilation itself was not the morally bankrupt proposition it is commonly represented as; it was a discourse of competing ideals holding aspirations for a brighter future, even if its implementation was imperfect and often insensitive. By the same token, we need to honour the positive aspirations and achievements, as well as the shortcomings, of the subsequent period when self-determination was in the ascendant. Blanket condemnations of either era do justice to neither. Both assimilation and self-determination were flawed prescriptions for a better future for Indigenous people and their relations with their non-Indigenous compatriots. There was never a time when either option held uncontested sway over Indigenous affairs; there was always contestation over how far and in what ways maintaining an Indigenous domain might be reconciled with membership of the national community.

As policy-warriors in Indigenous affairs today seem to be drawing new battle-lines, for and against self-determination, I take heart from the advocacy of a new generation of Aboriginal activists whose most prominent and articulate member is Noel Pearson, a Guugu Yimithirr man from Hopevale in North Queensland. Pearson himself has sometimes indulged in combative polemics, but his central endeavour is to transcend the battle-lines — to pursue, as he puts it, a 'quest for a radical centre'. While critical of the failures of policies pursued in the name of self-determination, Pearson does not repudiate self-determination itself, but seeks to build its achievements — recognition of Indigenous title to land and cultural integrity, a toehold on political power — into a program of Aboriginal advancement within the Australian nation. His recommendations weave together strands of Aboriginal advocacy extending back to the interwar years. The failure of Aboriginal people to secure an honoured place in the Australian nation, Pearson argues, has deepened their disadvantage and constricted their opportunities both to perform in the modern economy and to sustain a viable Indigenous domain. His writings on this theme, along with his assertions of an Aboriginal 'right to take responsibility', echo William Cooper's pleas seventy years earlier.[5] The continuities are testament to both the incompleteness of the realisation of Cooper's ambitions and the embeddedness of Pearson's proposals in a long tradition of Indigenous politics.

Australians today are exhorted to 'close the gap', a slogan that implies Indigenous people's interests lie not only in overcoming disadvantage in health, education, employment, housing and so forth, but also in bridging a gulf, of misapprehension or lack of empathy, between Indigenous and other Australians. If we are to successfully do so, we might reflect on the efforts of those in the past who also sought to 'close the gap'. History provides no template for resolving present dilemmas, but historical awareness might provide a depth of perception that will allow us to see beyond the crude caricatures which too often pass for reality in disputes over Indigenous affairs in Australia. It might even inject a note of humility into those disputes, converting them into genuine debates that might offer, in place of grand gestures, realistic means of bridging the gap which still yawns between Indigenous and other Australians.

Notes

Preface

1. JT Patten & W Ferguson, *Aborigines claim citizen rights! a statement of the case for the Aborigines Progressive Association*, The Publicist, Sydney, 1938, p. 5. Emphases in all quoted passages in this book follow emphases in the original documents.
2. Here, I build on the work of other historians, notably Tim Rowse and Rani Kerin. See especially Tim Rowse, *White flour, white power: from rations to citizenship in central Australia*, Cambridge University Press, Cambridge, 1998, Ch. 7; Tim Rowse (ed.), *Contesting assimilation*, API Network, Perth, 2005, particularly the Introduction and Ch. 9; Rani Kerin, 'Charles Duguid and Aboriginal assimilation in Adelaide, 1950–1960: the nebulous "assimilation" goal', *History Australia*, vol. 2, no. 3, 2005, pp. 85.1–85.17.
3. See especially John Chesterman & Brian Galligan, *Citizens without rights: Aborigines and Australian citizenship*, Cambridge University Press, Melbourne, 1997; John Chesterman, *Civil rights: how Indigenous Australians won formal equality*, University of Queensland Press, Brisbane, 2005.
4. Anthony Smith, *Nations and nationalism in a global era*, Polity Press, Cambridge, 1995, p. 99; Anthony Smith, *The nation in history: historiographical debates about ethnicity and nationalism*, University of New England Press, Hanover, NH, 2000, pp. 4, 25–6.

Prologue

1. *Official record of the proceedings and debates of the Australasian Federation Conference, 1890*, Government Printer, Melbourne, 1890, pp. 41–2; *Official record of the proceedings and debates of the National Australasian Convention, 1891*, Government Printer, Sydney, 1891, p. 32.
2. WB Spencer, 'Totemism in Australia', Report of the tenth meeting of the AAAS, 1904, p. 376.
3. WB Spencer & Frank Gillen, *The native tribes of central Australia*, Macmillan, London, 1899, pp. 17–18.
4. Lyn Spillman, *Nation and commemoration: creating national identities in the United States and Australia*, Cambridge University Press, Cambridge, 1997, p. 54.
5. Charles Pearson, *National life and character: a forecast*, Macmillan, London, 1893.

6. Garran to AP Elkin, 22 July 1944, Elkin papers, box 73, item 1/12/205.
7. Hugh Mahon, 'The native races under the new constitution', *The Austral Light*, vol. 3, no. 3, 1 March 1902, pp. 198–9.
8. John Chesterman & Brian Galligan, *Citizens without rights: Aborigines and Australian citizenship*, Cambridge University Press, Melbourne, 1997, pp. 70–3.
9. Russell McGregor, *Imagined destinies: Aboriginal Australians and the doomed race theory, 1880–1939*, Melbourne University Press, Melbourne, 1997.
10. Russell McGregor, 'The necessity of Britishness: ethno-cultural roots of Australian nationalism', *Nations and Nationalism*, vol. 12, no. 3, 2006, pp. 493–511.
11. Quoted in John Lack and Jacqueline Templeton (eds), *Sources of Australian immigration history*, vol. 1, History Department, University of Melbourne, Melbourne, 1988, p. 11.
12. See, for example, Myra Willard, *History of the white Australia policy to 1920*, Melbourne University Press, Melbourne, 1923; WK Hancock, *Australia*, Ernest Benn, London, 1930, pp. 66–8. See also John Kane, 'Racialism and democracy: the legacy of white Australia', in Geoffrey Stokes (ed.), *The politics of identity in Australia*, Cambridge University Press, Cambridge, 1997, pp. 117–31.
13. *CPD*, 1902, vol. 9, pp. 11580–1.
14. ibid., pp.11586–7.
15. ibid., pp. 11594–5.
16. ibid., pp. 11929–30, 11975–80.
17. ibid., vol. 10, p. 13003.
18. ibid., pp. 13003–7.
19. Pat Stretton & Christine Finnimore, 'Black fellow citizens: Aborigines and the Commonwealth franchise', *Australian Historical Studies*, vol. 25, no. 101, 1993, pp. 523–9; Chesterman & Galligan, pp. 74–9, 105–8.
20. Chesterman & Galligan, pp. 91–2.
21. Mahon, p. 201.
22. See, for example, CEC Lefroy, 'The future of the Australian Aborigines', Report of the thirteenth meeting of the AAAS, 1911, pp. 453–4.
23. McGregor, *Imagined destinies*, pp. 135–6

Chapter 1

1. Jens Lyng, *Non-Britishers in Australia: influence on population and progress*, Macmillan, Melbourne, 1927, pp. 204–5.
2. John Chesterman & Brian Galligan, *Citizens without rights: Aborigines and Australian citizenship*, Cambridge University Press, Melbourne, 1997, pp. 18–20.
3. Peter Read, *The stolen generations: the removal of Aboriginal people in New South Wales 1883 to 1969*, NSW Ministry of Aboriginal Affairs, Sydney, 1981, pp. 5–8; David Hollinsworth, *Race and racism in Australia*, 2nd edn, Social Science Press, Katoomba, 1998, pp. 121–4; Heather Goodall, 'New South Wales', in Ann McGrath (ed.), *Contested ground: Australian Aborigines under the*

British Crown, Allen & Unwin, Sydney, 1995, pp. 76–7; Richard Broome, 'Victoria', in McGrath, pp. 140–1.
4. Katherine Ellinghaus, *Taking assimilation to heart: marriages of white women and Indigenous men in the United States and Australia, 1887–1937*, University of Nebraska Press, Lincoln, NB, 2006, pp. 190, 205–8.
5. Anna Haebich, *For their own good: Aborigines and government in the southwest of Western Australia, 1900–1940*, University of Western Australia Press, Perth, 1988, pp. 348–51; Pat Jacobs, *Mister Neville: a biography*, Fremantle Arts Centre Press, Fremantle, 1990, pp. 240, 262.
6. Keith Windschuttle, *The fabrication of Aboriginal history: volume three — the stolen generations 1881–2008*, Macleay Press, Sydney, 2009, pp. 383–98.
7. Tony Austin, 'Cecil Cook, scientific thought and "half-castes" in the Northern Territory 1927–1939', *Aboriginal History*, vol. 14, no. 1, 1990, p. 115; Haebich, pp. 318–19, 331; Jacobs, pp. 195, 260–1; Russell McGregor, *Imagined destinies: Aboriginal Australians and the doomed race theory, 1880–1939*, Melbourne University Press, Melbourne, 1997, pp. 173–80.
8. JA Carrodus, *Report on the Northern Territory*, 20 November 1934, NAA, A1, 34/10021.
9. Brown to Minister, Interior, 3 November 1933, NAA, A659, 40/1/408.
10. Jacobs, pp. 186–7; Haebich, pp. 353–4; Andrew Markus, *Governing Savages*, Allen & Unwin, Sydney, 1990, Ch. 2.
11. Australian National Missionary Conference (NMC), *Report*, NMC, Sydney, 1937, p. 70.
12. *Aboriginal welfare: initial Conference of Commonwealth and State Aboriginal Authorities*, Government Printer, Canberra, 1937, p. 11.
13. Russell McGregor, '"Breed out the colour" or the importance of being white', *Australian Historical Studies*, vol. 33, no. 120, 2002, p. 289; Haebich, pp. 352–6; Markus, p. 93.
14. *Bringing them home: report of the National Inquiry into the Separation of Aboriginal and Torres Strait Islander Children from Their Families*, Human Rights and Equal Opportunity Commission, Sydney, 1997.
15. Quoted in Haebich, p. 317.
16. Notes on Conference Regarding Payment of Halfcastes and Aboriginals in Country Districts, 9–13 May 1930, NAA, A1, 38/329.
17. *Aboriginal welfare*, pp. 16, 21.
18. ibid., p. 11.
19. Ernest Renan, 'What is a nation?' (1882), in Geoff Eley & Ronald Suny (eds), *Becoming national*, Oxford University Press, Oxford, 1996, pp. 44–5. Benedict Anderson points out that Renan could not have meant 'forget' to be taken literally: see Anderson, *Imagined communities: reflections on the origin and spread of nationalism*, rev. edn, Verso, London, 1991, pp. 199–201.
20. *Aboriginal welfare*, pp. 13–14.
21. ibid., pp. 8, 18, 20. See also JW Bleakley, 'The control and care of half-caste children in Queensland', in *The half-caste Aborigines of North and Central Australia: suggestions towards solving the problem*, APNR, Sydney, 1930, pp. 7–11; JW Bleakley, 'The Aborigines: past and present treatment by the state', in JS Needham (ed.), *White and black in Australia*, National Missionary Council, London, 1935, pp. 38–62.

22. Cook to Administrator, NT, 27 June 1933, NAA, A659, 40/1/408.
23. Quoted in Patricia Jacobs, 'Science and veiled assumptions: miscegenation in WA, 1930–1937', *Australian Aboriginal Studies*, no. 2, 1986, p. 18. See also David Paul, '"A man of many parts": Cyril Phillips Bryan and Western Australian Aboriginal affairs policy in the 1930s', in Martin Crotty, John Germov & Grant Rodwell (eds), *'A race for a place': eugenics, Darwinism and social thought and practice in Australia*, University of Newcastle, Newcastle, 2000, pp. 91–9.
24. Cook, Half-caste housing policy, 1932, NAA, A452, 52/414.
25. Cook to Administrator, NT, 7 February 1933, NAA, A659, 40/1/408; Cook to Administrator, NT, 27 June 1933, NAA, A659, 40/1/408.
26. Cook to W Morley, 28 April 1931, NAA, A1, 36/6595.
27. Cook to Administrator, NT, 27 June 1933, NAA, A659, 40/1/408.
28. Cook, 'Report of the Chief Protector of Aboriginals, 1934', CPP, no. 138, 1934–7, p. 12.
29. Quoted in Humphrey McQueen, *A new Britannia: an argument concerning the social origins of Australian radicalism and nationalism*, rev. edn, Penguin, Melbourne, 1986, p. 39.
30. Curtis to Secretary, Interior, 19 August 1934, NAA, A452, 52/420.
31. Russell McGregor, 'An Aboriginal Caucasian: some uses for racial kinship in early twentieth century Australia', *Australian Aboriginal Studies*, no. 1, 1996, pp. 11–14; Lucinda Aberdeen, 'Australian scientific research, "Aboriginal blood" and the racial imaginary', in Crotty et. al., pp. 101–11.
32. Herbert Basedow, *The Australian Aboriginal*, FW Preece and Sons, Adelaide, 1925, p. 59.
33. Norman Tindale, 'Survey of the half-caste problem in South Australia', *Proceedings of the Royal Geographical Society of South Australia (South Australian Branch)*, vol. 42, 1940–41, pp. 66–161. See also 'Lecture by JB Birdsell to the Anthropological Society of South Australia', 24 July 1939, Cleland collection.
34. Mary Bennett, *The Australian Aboriginal as a human being*, Alston Rivers, London, 1930, p. 13.
35. Tindale, pp. 68–9, 116–20, 125–58.
36. WK Hancock, *Australia*, Ernest Benn, London, 1930; Tim Rowse, *Australian liberalism and national character*, Kibble Books, Melbourne, 1978.
37. McGregor, *Imagined destinies*, pp. 227–9.
38. Tindale, pp. 71–81.
39. Pat O'Malley, 'Gentle genocide: the government of Aboriginal peoples in central Australia', *Social Justice*, vol. 21, no. 4, 1994, pp. 52–3.
40. See, for example, Patrick Wolfe, *Settler colonialism and the transformation of anthropology: the politics and poetics of an ethnographic event*, Cassell, London, 1999, p. 11; Robert Manne, *In denial: the stolen generations and the right*, Schwartz, Melbourne, 2001, p. 39.
41. 'Would you welcome marriage with a half-caste?', *Health and Physical Culture*, 1 July 1937, pp. 20–1, 24.
42. See Carroll's journal, *The Science of Man*, any issue [it was published monthly between February 1898 and December 1912].

Notes (pages 11–16)

43. Stephen Garton, 'Writing eugenics: A history of classifying practices', in Crotty et. al., p. 11.
44. Austin, pp. 106–7, 112–13, 119; see also Jacobs, 'Science and veiled assumptions', pp. 19, 21.
45. Daniel Kevles, *In the name of eugenics: genetics and the uses of human heredity*, Penguin, London, 1986, pp. 75, 319; Diane Paul, *Controlling human heredity: 1865 to the present*, Humanities Press, Atlantic Highlands, NJ, 1995, pp. 111–14.
46. Nancy Stepan, *'The hour of eugenics': Race, gender, and nation in Latin America*, Cornell University Press, Ithaca, NY, 1991.
47. Cook to Administrator, NT, 27 June 1933, NAA, A659, 40/1/408.
48. Tindale, p. 124.
49. Cleland to Minister, Interior, 4 October 1932, Cleland collection.
50. W Morley, 'Association for the Protection of Native Races: twenty-seventh annual report, Year 1937–38', *Aborigines' Protector*, vol. 1, no. 6, 1939, p. 22.
51. 'Review of the Chief Protectors' conference at Canberra, April 1937: with comments and criticism from the viewpoint of the APNR', *Aborigines' Protector*, vol. 1, no. 5, 1938, p. 17.
52. Tom Wright, *New deal for Aborigines*, Forward Press, Sydney, 1939, p. 19; Alison Holland, 'Saving the race: critics of absorption look for an alternative', in Tim Rowse (ed.), *Contesting assimilation*, API Network, Perth, 2005, pp. 89–92.
53. Cooper to Paterson, 16 June 1937, NAA, A659, 1940/1/858.
54. Cooper to McEwen, 19 April 1939, NAA, A659, 1940/1/858.
55. JT Patten & W Ferguson, *Aborigines claim citizen rights! A statement of the case for the Aborigines Progressive Association*, The Publicist, Sydney, 1938, p. 11.
56. ibid.
57. See, for example, Wolfe, p. 11.
58. See, for example, John Murphy, *Imagining the fifties: private sentiment and political culture in Menzies' Australia*, Pluto Press/University of NSW Press, Sydney, 2000, pp. 8, 171; Julie Wells, 'Welfare colonialists: contexts and encounters on government settlements', in Tony Austin & Suzanne Parry (eds), *Connection and disconnection: encounters between settlers and Indigenous people in the Northern Territory*, Northern Territory University Press, Darwin, 1998, p. 279.
59. Chesterman & Galligan, p. 148.
60. *Aboriginal welfare*, p. 3.
61. Scott Bennett, *White politics and black Australians*, Allen & Unwin, Sydney, 1999, pp. 20, 59.
62. AP Elkin, 'The Australian Aborigines to-day', typescript of an address, c.1963, Elkin papers, box 109, item 1/17/53. See also AP Elkin, 'Background and present position of the Aborigines in Australia', 1967, Elkin papers, box 109, item 1/17/56; CD Rowley, 'Aborigines and other Australians', *Oceania*, vol. 32, no. 4, 1962, p. 251.
63. Conference of Commonwealth and State Aboriginal Welfare Authorities, 3–4 February 1948, NAA, A431, 1951/866; Record of the Native Welfare

Conference, Canberra, 3–4 September 1951, Hasluck papers, box 33; Native Welfare Council: Meeting at Canberra, 29 September 1952, Hasluck papers, box 32.
64. See, for example, Catherine Kaye, 'Another Aborigine goes to gaol', *Advocate* (Melbourne), 7 January 1960, clipping in Christophers papers, box 1.
65. See, for example, Herbert Groves, 'Editorial: assimilation and the Aborigines', *Churinga*, vol. 1, no. 11, December 1969–February 1970, p. 1.
66. Rowley, p. 251.
67. Kim Beazley, *Dispossession and disease — or dignity*, Provocative Pamphlet no. 115, Federal Literature Committee of the Churches of Christ in Australia, 1964, p. 7.
68. See especially CD Rowley, *Outcasts in white Australia*, Penguin, Melbourne, 1972.

Chapter 2

1. Katherine Susannah Pritchard, *Coonardoo*, Jonathan Cape, London, 1929.
2. Xavier Herbert, *Capricornia*, The Publicist, Sydney, 1938.
3. Tom Griffiths, *Hunters and collectors: the antiquarian imagination in Australia*, Cambridge University Press, Cambridge, 1996; Sianan Healy, '"Years ago some lived here": Aboriginal Australians and the production of popular culture, history and identity in 1930s Victoria', *Australian Historical Studies*, vol. 37, no. 128, 2006, pp. 18–34.
4. Neville Green, *The Forrest River massacres*, 2nd edn, Focus Education, Perth, 2008.
5. J Cribbin, *The killing times*, Fontana, Sydney, 1984.
6. Tigger Wise, *The self-made anthropologist: a life of AP Elkin*, Allen & Unwin, Sydney, 1985, pp. 124–31.
7. Geoffrey Gray, *A cautious silence: the politics of Australian anthropology*, Aboriginal Studies Press, Canberra, 2007; H Kuklick, *The savage within: the social history of British anthropology, 1885–1945*, Cambridge University Press, Cambridge, 1991; GW Stocking, 'The ethnographic sensibility of the 1920s and the dualism of the anthropological tradition', in GW Stocking (ed.), *Romantic motives: essays on anthropological sensibility*, University of Wisconsin Press, Madison, WI, 1989, pp. 208–76.
8. AR Radcliffe-Brown, 'Editorial', *Oceania*, vol. 1, no. 1, 1930, pp. 1–4; AR Radcliffe-Brown, 'Applied Anthropology', *Report of the twentieth meeting of ANZAAS*, 1930, ANZAAS, Canberra, pp. 267–80.
9. AP Elkin, *The Australian Aborigines: how to understand them*, Angus & Robertson, Sydney, 1938.
10. Elkin to RD Moseley, 21 March 1934, Elkin papers, box 64, item 1/12/86; Elkin to R Schenck, 21 March 1934, Elkin papers, box 64, item 1/12/86.
11. AP Elkin, 'The Aborigines: our national responsibility', *Australian Quarterly*, vol. 6, no. 3, 1934, p. 56; Elkin, *The Australian Aborigines*, p. 152. See also Russell McGregor, 'From Old Testament to New: AP Elkin on Christian conversion and cultural assimilation', *Journal of Religious History*, vol. 25, no. 1, 2001, pp. 39–55.

12. AP Elkin, 'Missionary methods and the Aborigines', *The Missionary Review*, vol. 5, February 1934, p. 19.
13. See, for example, AP Elkin, 'The function of religion in society', *Morpeth Review*, no. 2, June 1931, pp. 8–16; AP Elkin, 'The present social function of religion', *Morpeth Review*, no. 2, December 1931, pp. 23–33.
14. AP Elkin, *Society, the individual and change, with special reference to war and other present-day problems*, R Day & Son, Sydney, 1941.
15. Frederic Wood Jones, *Australia's vanishing race*, Angus & Robertson, Sydney, 1934, pp. 17, 29, 39–40.
16. Donald Thomson, 'Recommendations of policy in native affairs in the Northern Territory of Australia, December, 1937', *CPP*, no. 56, 1937–40.
17. JB Cleland, 'The native of central Australia and his surroundings', *Proceedings of the Royal Geographical Society of Australasia, South Australian Branch*, vol. 35, 1933–34, pp. 75–7. See also Cleland to Minister, Interior, 7 September 1936, NAA, A1, 36/8795.
18. Norman Tindale, 'Survey of the half-caste problem in South Australia', Proceedings of the Royal Geographical Society of South Australia (South Australian Branch), vol. 42, 1940–41, pp. 79–80.
19. Robert Turner & Milton Boyce, *Australian Aboriginal signs and symbols for the use of boy scouts*, PR Stephensen & Co., Sydney, 1934.
20. PR Stephensen, *The foundations of culture in Australia: an essay towards national self respect*, WJ Miles, Sydney, 1936, pp. 12, 98–9.
21. Rex Ingamells, *Conditional culture* (with commentary by Ian Tilbrook), FW Preece, Adelaide, 1938, pp. 4–6, 16–17.
22. Kosmas Tsokhas, 'Romanticism, Aboriginality and national identity: the poetry and prose of Mary Gilmore', *Australian Historical Studies*, vol. 29, no. 111, 1998, pp. 230–47.
23. Rex Ingamells, 'Introduction', *Jindyworobak Review 1938–1948*, Jindyworobak Publications, Melbourne, 1948, p. 12.
24. See, for example, Rex Ingamells, 'Moorawathimeering', in Brian Elliott (ed.), *The Jindyworobaks*, University of Queensland Press, Brisbane, 1979, p. 11.
25. Ingamells, *Conditional culture*, pp. 17–18.
26. ibid., p. 16.
27. Humphrey McQueen, *The black swan of trespass: the emergence of modernist painting in Australia*, Alternative Publishing, Sydney, 1979, p. 132.
28. Ann McGrath, 'Europeans and Aborigines', in Neville Meaney (ed.), *Under new heavens: cultural transmission and the making of Australia*, Heinemann, Melbourne, 1989, p. 45.
29. Margaret Preston, 'The Indigenous art of Australia', *Art in Australia*, vol. 11, 3rd series, March 1925.
30. Philip Jones, 'Perceptions of Aboriginal art: a history', in Peter Sutton (ed.), *Dreamings: the art of Aboriginal Australia*, Viking, Melbourne, 1988, p. 168; Peter Sutton, Philip Jones & Steven Hemming, 'Survival, regeneration and impact', in Sutton, pp. 208–9.

Notes (pages 27–33)

31. Ian McLean, *White Aborigines: identity politics in Australian art*, Cambridge University Press, Cambridge, 1998, p. 89.
32. 'Petition: A Model Aboriginal State', November 1926, NAA, A1, 1932/4262.
33. JC Genders, 'The Australian Aborigines', 4 January 1937, Cleland collection.
34. 'Conference of representatives of missions, societies and associations interested in the welfare of Aboriginals to consider the report and recommendations submitted to the Commonwealth government by JW Bleakley', 1929, NAA, A1, 33/8782.
35. JC Genders, *The Aborigines Protection League*, [APL], Adelaide, 1929, pp. 1–2.
36. Genders to Minister, Home Affairs, 19 December 1929, NAA, A1, 1932/4262.
37. Kevin Blackburn interprets Genders' proposals as entailing a larger measure of Aboriginal sovereignty; see his 'White agitation for an Aboriginal state in Australia (1925–1929)', *Australian Journal of Politics and History*, vol. 45, no. 2, 1999, pp. 157–80.
38. 'Petition: A Model Aboriginal State'.
39. Mark Mazower, *Dark continent: Europe's twentieth century*, Allen Lane, London, 1998, pp. 51–63; Patrick Thornberry, *International law and the rights of minorities*, Clarendon, Oxford, 1991, pp. 38–52; Michael Banton, 'Self-determination', in Athena Leoussi (ed.), *Encyclopaedia of nationalism*, Transaction, New Brunswick, NJ, 2001, p. 272.
40. 'The Proposed Aboriginal State: Manifesto', c.1926, NAA, A1, 1932/4262.
41. Benedict Anderson, 'Introduction', in Gopal Balakrishnan (ed.), *Mapping the nation*, Verso, London, 1996, pp. 3–4; Otto Bauer, 'The nation', 1924, in Balakrishnan, pp. 39–77.
42. 'The Proposed Aboriginal State: Manifesto'.
43. Genders, 'The Australian Aborigines'.
44. 'The Aboriginals and half-castes of Central Australia and North Australia: report by JW Bleakley, 1928', *CPP*, no. 21, 1929, p. 30.
45. *The Workers Weekly*, 24 September 1931, p. 2, *Reason in revolt: source documents of Australian radicalism*, viewed 19 January 2011, <http://www.reasoninrevolt.net.au/pdf/a000219.pdf>.
46. Fiona Paisley, 'Federalising the Aborigines? Constitutional reform in the late 1920s', *Australian Historical Studies*, vol. 29, no. 11, 1998, pp. 248–66.
47. AP Elkin, *A policy for the Aborigines*, St John's College, Morpeth, 1933, pp. 8, 10.
48. David Unaipon, *Australian Aborigines*, AFASA, Adelaide, 1930.
49. See for example Constance Cooke, 'The status of Aboriginal women in Australia', in *Proceedings of the second pan-Pacific women's conference*, 1930, pp. 129–30; Edith Jones, 'Conference of representatives', 1929, NAA, A1, 33/8782.
50. Fiona Paisley, *Loving protection? Australian feminism and Aboriginal women's rights 1919–1939*, Melbourne University Press, Melbourne, 2000, pp. 3, 7–8.
51. 'Notes of deputation…which waited upon the Minister for the Interior, 23 January 1935', NAA, A1, 35/3951.
52. VAG, 'Suggestions for the 1937 conference of chief protectors', March 1937, NAA, A431, 48/961.

Notes (pages 34–40)

53. 'The Northern Territory of Australia: Commonwealth government's policy with respect to Aboriginals', February 1939, pp. 1–2, 8, NLA NP 572.99429 MCE.
54. Elkin to McEwen, 9 February 1939, NAA, A1, 38/31785.
55. Julie Wells, 'The long march: assimilation policy and practice in Darwin, the Northern Territory, 1939–1967', PhD thesis, University of Queensland, 1995, p. 51.
56. AP Elkin, 'Anthropology and the future of the Australian Aborigines', *Oceania*, vol. 5, no. 1, 1934, p. 16.
57. AP Elkin, 'Native policy in Australia', *Historical Studies Australia and New Zealand*, vol. 2, no. 8, 1943, p. 274.
58. Chinnery, 'Qualities which should be possessed by any aboriginal requiring the privileges of a European', 5 April 1939, NAA, A431, 50/597.
59. CD Rowley, *Outcasts in white Australia*, Penguin, Melbourne, 1972, p. 31.

Chapter 3

1. Cooper to Menzies, 5 October 1939, NAA, A461/7, A300/1, part 3; Cooper to Menzies, 3 December 1939, NAA, A461/7, A300/1, part 3.
2. Cooper to Menzies, 19 April 1939, NAA, A461/7, A300/1, part 3.
3. Helen Baillie, 'Report of journey to Dubbo for Aboriginal conference', Elkin papers, box 68, item 1/12/144; Helen Baillie, 'Report of conference of the Aborigines' Progressive Association, Railways Hall, Dubbo', 2 January 1940, Elkin papers, box 68, item 1/12/144.
4. JT Patten & W Ferguson, *Aborigines claim citizen rights! A statement of the case for the Aborigines Progressive Association*, The Publicist, Sydney, 1938, pp. 9–11.
5. Cooper to Paterson, 25 June 1937, NAA, A659, 1940/1/858.
6. John Maynard, *Fight for liberty and freedom: the origins of Australian Aboriginal activism*, Aboriginal Studies Press, Canberra, 2007; John Maynard, '"In the interests of our people": the influence of Garveyism on the rise of Australian Aboriginal political activism', *Aboriginal History*, vol. 29, 2005, pp. 1–22.
7. Peter Biskup, *Not slaves, not citizens*, University of Queensland Press, Brisbane, 1973, pp. 158–60; Bain Attwood & Andrew Markus, *The struggle for Aboriginal rights: a documentary history*, Allen & Unwin, Sydney, 1999, pp. 61–2.
8. Cooper to Menzies, 3 December 1939, NAA, A461/7, A300/1, part 3.
9. Patten & Ferguson, p. 9; *Australian Abo Call*, no. 3, June 1938, p. 1.
10. Cooper to Paterson, 25 June 1937, NAA, A659, 1940/1/858.
11. Cooper, 'From an educated Aboriginal', pp. 1–3, typescript enclosed with letter to McEwen, 21 January 1939, NAA, A659, 1940/1/858.
12. Cooper to Paterson, 31 October 1936, NAA, A659, 1940/1/858.
13. ibid.; Cooper to Paterson, 25 June 1937, NAA, A659, 1940/1/858.
14. Cooper to PM, 16 January 1937, NAA, A461/7, A300/1, part 3.
15. Russell McGregor, 'Protest and progress: Aboriginal activism in the 1930s', *Australian Historical Studies*, vol. 25, no. 101, 1993, p. 555; Russell McGregor, *Imagined destinies: Aboriginal Australians and the doomed race theory, 1880–1939*, Melbourne University Press, Melbourne, 1997, p. 251.

16. Attwood & Markus, p. 12. In a later study, Attwood qualifies his rejection of the 'assimilationist' label: Bain Attwood, *Rights for Aborigines*, Allen & Unwin, Sydney, 2003, p. 68.
17. Cooper, 'From an educated Aboriginal', pp. 2–3; see also Cooper to McEwen, 26 July 1938, NAA, A659, 1940/1/858.
18. Cooper to Paterson, 18 February 1937, NAA, A659, 1940/1/858.
19. 'Report of the board of inquiry appointed to inquire into the land and land industries of the Northern Territory of Australia, 10 October 1937', *CPP*, no. 4, 1937–40, p. 71. Cooper criticised this report for its neglect of Aboriginal people as agents of northern development: Cooper to Paterson, 30 July 1937, NAA, A659, 1940/1/858.
20. Cooper, 'From an educated Aboriginal', p. 3.
21. Cooper to Paterson, 30 July 1937, NAA, A659, 1940/1/858.
22. Cooper to McEwen, 26 July 1938, NAA, A659, 1940/1/858.
23. Cooper to McEwen, 19 February 1938, document 62 in Bain Attwood & Andrew Markus, *Thinking black: William Cooper and the Australian Aborigines' League*, Aboriginal Studies Press, Canberra, 2004, p. 90.
24. Cooper to Paterson, 31 October 1936, NAA, A659, 1940/1/858.
25. Cooper to Paterson, 25 June 1937, NAA, A659, 1940/1/858.
26. Cooper, 'From an educated Aboriginal', p.10.
27. Cooper, 'From an educated black', typescript enclosed with letter to PM Lyons, 31 March 1938, NAA, A659, 1940/1/858. The APA made similar recommendations; see *Australian Abo Call*, no. 1, April 1938, p. 1.
28. Heather Goodall, 'Land in our own country: The Aboriginal land rights movement in south-eastern Australia, 1860–1914', *Aboriginal History*, vol. 14, no. 1, 1990, pp. 1–24; Richard Broome, *Aboriginal Australians: black responses to white dominance, 1788–2001*, 3rd edn, Allen & Unwin, Sydney, 2001, pp. 76–87.
29. Cooper to McEwen, 26 July 1937, NAA, A659, 1940/1/858.
30. Cooper, 'From an educated black'.
31. Cooper to Paterson, 30 July 1937, NAA, A659, 1940/1/858.
32. Cooper to Paterson, 16 June 1937, NAA, A659, 1940/1/858.
33. See Judith Brett, 'Retrieving the partisan history of Australian citizenship', *Australian Journal of Political Science*, vol. 36, no. 3, 2001, pp. 423–37.
34. Attwood, especially pp. 59–69.
35. Cooper to PM, 4 February 1938, NAA, A461/7, A300/1, part 3.
36. 'Petition of the Aboriginal inhabitants of Australia to His Majesty George V', 1933 NAA, A431, 49/1591.
37. Cooper to Paterson, 16 June 1937, NAA, A659, 1940/1/858.
38. Cooper to McEwen, 26 July 1937, NAA, A659, 1940/1/858. See also Cooper to Paterson, 25 June 1937, NAA, A461/7, A300/1, part 3; Cooper to Menzies, 5 October 1939, NAA, A461/7, A300/1, part 3.
39. Attwood, p. 64.
40. Cooper to Paterson, 25 June 1937, NAA, A659, 1940/1/858.
41. GS Knowles, Solicitor-General, Opinion no. 6 of 1938, 14 January 1938, NAA, A461/7, A300/1, part 3.

42. Carrodus, memo, 4 April 1935, NAA, A1, 35/3951.
43. Patten & Ferguson, p. 3.
44. AAL, 'Agenda of proposals', 16 January 1937, NAA, A461, A300/1, part 3.
45. *Australian Abo Call*, no. 1, April 1938, p. 1.
46. *Australian Abo Call*, no. 4, July 1938, p. 1.
47. Patten & Ferguson, p. 10.
48. Cooper, 'From an educated black'.
49. Cooper to McEwen, 3 January 1939, NAA A659 40/1/858.
50. ibid.
51. Ferguson to Premier Mair, 11 March 1940, Elkin papers, box 68, item 1/12/144.
52. Pearl Gibbs, radio broadcast 1941, quoted in Kevin Gilbert, *Because a white man'll never do it*, Angus & Robertson, Sydney, 1973, pp. 13–17.
53. Robert Hall, *The black diggers: Aborigines and Torres Strait Islanders in the Second World War*, Allen & Unwin, Sydney, 1989, pp. 8–9.
54. Ferguson to Menzies, 8 July 1940, quoted in Hall, p. 19.
55. Hall, Chs 3 and 5.
56. ibid., pp. 14–28.
57. ibid., p. 189.
58. Aviel Roshwald, *The endurance of nationalism: ancient roots and modern dilemmas*, Cambridge University Press, Cambridge, 2006, pp. 268–70; Anthony Smith, *The nation in history: historiographical debates about ethnicity and nationalism*, University of New England Press, Hanover, NH, 2000, p. 74.
59. Cooper to Menzies, 31 August 1940, NAA, A659, 1940/1/858.
60. James to Chifley, 20 August 1945, NAA, A461, A300/1, part 4; James to Chifley, 27 August 1945, NAA, A461, A300/1.

Chapter 4

1. EV Raymont, General Secretary, RSSAILA, to Menzies, 12 December 1940, NAA, A431, 1949/822.
2. MF King to Menzies, 14 June 1940, NAA, A431, 1949/822.
3. Robert Hall, *The black diggers: Aborigines and Torres Strait Islanders in the Second World War*, Allen & Unwin, Sydney, 1989, Ch. 4.
4. Ronald Berndt & Catherine Berndt, 'Some aspects of native labour on northern cattle stations', *Aborigines Protector*, vol. 2, no. 2, 1946, p. 11; AP Elkin, 'The future of the Australian Aborigine', *Current Affairs Bulletin*, vol. 1, no. 13, 1948, p. 8.
5. AP Elkin, 'Post war and the Aborigines', 1945, Elkin papers, box 111, item 1/17/123.
6. Coombs to Secretary, PM Dept, 27 September 1945, NAA, A461, A300/1, part 4.
7. Patrick Thornberry, *International law and the rights of minorities*, Clarendon, Oxford, 1991, pp. 133–7.
8. UNESCO, 'Statement on race', 1950, in Ashley Montague, *Statement on race: an annotated elaboration and exposition of the four statements on race issued by the United Nations Educational, Scientific and Cultural Organization*, Oxford

University Press, New York, 1972, pp. 8–10; UNESCO, 'Statement on race and racial prejudice', 1967, in Montague, p. 163.
9. Michael Banton, 'Self-determination', in Athena Leoussi (ed.), *Encyclopaedia of nationalism*, Transaction, New Brunswick, NJ, 2001, p. 272.
10. 'Declaration on the granting of independence to colonial countries and peoples', 14 December 1960, *Audiovisual library of international law*, viewed 19 January 2011, <http://untreaty.un.org/cod/avl/ha/dicc/dicc.html>.
11. Chris Tennant, 'Indigenous peoples, international institutions, and the international legal literature from 1945–1993', *Human Rights Quarterly*, vol. 16, 1994, pp. 4–5, 12–16, 25–7; Makere Stewart-Harawira, *The new imperial order: indigenous responses to globalization*, Zed Books, London, 2005, pp. 77, 121–4, 128–30; Thornberry, pp. 343–53.
12. Tennant, p. 10.
13. Michael Ignatieff, *Human rights as politics and idolatry*, Princeton University Press, Princeton, NJ, 2001.
14. Quoted in RT Appleyard, 'Post-war British immigration', in James Jupp (ed.), *The Australian people: an encyclopedia of the nation, its people and their origins*, rev. edn, Cambridge University Press, Cambridge, 2004, p. 62.
15. Gwenda Tavan, *The long, slow death of white Australia*, Scribe, Melbourne, 2005, pp. 51–70.
16. Andrew Markus, *Australian race relations 1788–1993*, Allen & Unwin, Sydney, 1994, p. 167.
17. Tavan, pp. 36–41.
18. Alan Walker, *White Australia?*, Christian Distributors' Association, Sydney, [1946].
19. AP Elkin, 'Re-thinking the white Australia policy', *Australian Quarterly*, vol. 17, no. 3, 1945, p. 34.
20. AP Elkin, 'Is white Australia doomed?', in WD Borrie et. al., *A white Australia: Australia's population problem*, Australasian Publishing Co., Sydney, 1947, pp. 196–200.
21. 'Churchman attacks "racialism"', clipping from unnamed newspaper, 20 May 1953, Simpson papers, box 80, folder 205.
22. Markus, p. 169.
23. Richard White, 'The Australian way of life', *Australian Historical Studies*, vol. 18, no. 73, 1979, pp. 528–45; John Murphy, *Imagining the fifties: private sentiment and political culture in Menzies' Australia*, Pluto Press/University of NSW Press, Sydney, 2000, Ch. 5.
24. Tim Rowse, 'The post-war social science of assimilation 1947–1966', in Tim Rowse (ed.), *Contesting assimilation*, API Network, Perth, 2005, p. 151.
25. Australian Citizenship Convention, 1951, p. 8, quoted in Brian Galligan & Winsome Roberts, *Australian citizenship*, Melbourne University Press, Melbourne, 2004, p. 60.
26. WD Borrie, 'New and old Australians', in WV Aughterson (ed.), *Taking stock: aspects of mid-century life in Australia*, Cheshire, Melbourne, 1953, pp. 174–5.
27. Sean Brawley, 'Slaying the white Australia dragon', in Nancy Viviani (ed.), *The abolition of the white Australia policy: the immigration reform movement revisited*,

Centre for the Study of Australia-Asia Relations, Griffith University, Brisbane, 1992, p. 2.
28. HC Coombs, 'The predecessors', in *The Whitlam phenomenon: Fabian papers*, McPhee Gribble/Penguin, Melbourne, 1986, p. 57.
29. AP Elkin, *Citizenship for the Aborigines: a national Aboriginal policy*, Australasian Publishing Co., Sydney, 1944, pp. 43, 71.
30. ibid., p. 22.
31. AP Elkin, 'Anthropology and the future of the Australian Aborigines', *Oceania*, vol. 5, no. 1, 1934, p. 18.
32. AP Elkin, 'Race and culture', 25 March 1952, Elkin papers, box 111, item 1/17/127.
33. AP Elkin, *Changes that are upon us*, Presidential address to the Australian Institute of Sociology, Sydney, 1943, p. 8; AP Elkin, *Society, the individual and change, with special reference to war and other present-day problems*, R Day & Son, Sydney, 1941, p. 60.
34. See, for example, Elkin, *Society, the individual and change*, p. 65.
35. Elkin, *Citizenship for the Aborigines*, p. 40.
36. AP Elkin, 'The rights of man in primitive society', in *Human rights: comments and interpretations: a symposium edited by UNESCO*, Allan Wingate, London, 1949, pp. 234–5.
37. ibid., pp. 228–9.
38. Elkin, *Citizenship for the Aborigines*, p. 39.
39. James to Elkin, 16 October 1944, Elkin papers, box 171, item 4/2/119.
40. Ferguson to Elkin, 14 August 1944, Elkin papers, box 170, item 4/2/93; Elkin to Ferguson, 16 August 1944, Elkin papers, box 170, item 4/2/93.
41. AP Elkin, 'Assimilation and integration', address to ANZAAS Congress, Perth, 1959, Elkin papers, box 108, item 1/17/3.
42. AP Elkin, 'Background and present position of the Aborigines in Australia', address given in Brisbane, 1967, Elkin papers, box 109, item 1/17/56; Elkin, 'Assimilation and integration'.
43. Elkin, *Citizenship for the Aborigines*, pp. 45–53.
44. Elkin, 'The future of the Australian Aborigine', p. 13.
45. Russell McGregor, 'Arguing about assimilation: Aboriginal policy and advocacy in Australia', in Bain Attwood & Tom Griffiths (eds), *Frontier, race, nation: Henry Reynolds and Australian history*, Australian Scholarly Publishing, Melbourne, 2009, pp. 264–5.
46. See, for example, VA Leeper, VAG, to Minister, Interior, 16 August 1946, NAA, A431, 1949/822.
47. Elkin to Carrodus, 23 October 1948, NAA, A431, 1949/822. See also AP Elkin, *Aborigines and the franchise*, APNR, Sydney, 1946, pp. 1–2.
48. Chifley to Hanlon (Qld) and Wise (WA), 28 March 1946, NAA, A431, 1949/822; Hanlon to Chifley, 12 April 1946, NAA, A431, 1949/822; Wise to Chifley, 10 May 1946, NAA, A431, 1949/822.
49. Elkin to Carrodus, 23 October 1948, NAA, A431, 1949/822; Elkin to Johnson, 25 October 1948, NAA, A431, 1949/822; Carrodus to Johnson, 28 October 1948, NAA, A431, 1949/822.

50. Rex Battarbee, *Modern Australian Aboriginal art*, Angus & Robertson, Sydney, 1951, pp. 17–18.
51. Roslynn Haines, *Seeking the centre: the Australian desert in literature, art and film*, Cambridge University Press, Cambridge, 1998.
52. Quoted in Philip Jones, 'Perceptions of Aboriginal art: a history', in Peter Sutton (ed.), *Dreamings: the art of Aboriginal Australia*, Viking, Melbourne, 1988, p. 251.
53. Daniel Thomas, 'Albert Namatjira and the worlds of art: a re-evaluation', in Nadine Amadio, *Albert Namatjira: the life and work of an Australian painter*, Macmillan, Melbourne, 1986, pp. 22–6; Jane Hardy, JVS Megaw and M Ruth Megaw (eds), *The heritage of Namatjira: the watercolourists of central Australia*, Heinemann, Melbourne, 1992; Margie West, 'The art of engagement: Indigenous art and outside influence', in Julie Wells, Mickey Dewar & Suzanne Parry (eds), *Modern frontier: aspects of the 1950s in Australia's Northern Territory*, Charles Darwin University Press, Darwin, 2005, pp. 165–82.
54. TGH Strehlow, 1952, quoted in West, p. 169; TGH Strehlow, *Nomads in No-Man's-Land*, AFASA, Adelaide, 1961, pp. 9–10.
55. TGH Strehlow, 'Foreword' to Battarbee, p. 7.
56. ibid., p. 6.
57. AP Elkin, 'A modern Aboriginal artist', *Social Horizons*, vol. 2, 1945, pp. 37–9.
58. Mary Durack Miller, *Child artists of the Australian bush*, Australasian Publishing Co., Sydney, 1952, pp. 8, 64.
59. ibid., pp. 62–3.
60. Jones, pp. 169–74.
61. Arnold Haskell, *The Australians: the Anglo-Saxondom of the southern hemisphere: an historical sketch*, Adam and Charles Black, London, 1943, pp. 119–20.
62. Russell McGregor, 'Bill Harney's yarns', *Journal of Northern Territory History*, no. 10, 1999, pp. 25–9.
63. HE Thonemann, *Tell the white man: the life story of an Aboriginal lubra*, Collins, London, 1949.
64. Alan Marshall, *Ourselves writ strange*, Cheshire, Melbourne, 1948, pp. 319–20.
65. Colin Simpson, *Adam in ochre: inside Aboriginal Australia*, Angus & Robertson, Sydney, 1951, pp. 186–97.
66. BH Watts and JD Gallacher, *Report on an investigation into the curriculum and teaching methods used in Aboriginal schools in the Northern Territory*, Government Printer, Darwin, 1964, pp. 26–9. See also Suzanne Parry and Julie Wells, 'Schooling for assimilation: Aboriginal children in the Northern Territory, 1939–1955', *History of Education Review*, vol. 26, no. 2, 1997, pp. 49–62.
67. Commonwealth Office of Education, 'Provisional syllabus for use in Aboriginal schools in the Northern Territory', 23 June 1950, NAA, A431, 1951/560.
68. ibid.

Notes (pages 76–82)

Chapter 5

1. Paul Hasluck, *Our southern half-caste natives and their conditions*, Native Welfare Council, Perth, 1938; Paul Hasluck, *Black Australians: a survey of native policy in Western Australia, 1829–1897*, Melbourne University Press, Melbourne, 1942.
2. Paul Hasluck, 'A national problem', 1950, in *Native welfare in Australia: speeches and addresses by the Hon. Paul Hasluck*, Paterson Brokensha, Perth, 1953, pp. 5–6.
3. Native Welfare Conference, 26–27 January 1961, 'Verbatim Record of Proceedings', Hasluck papers, box 32. Nine years earlier, in communication with the Government Secretary, Darwin, Hasluck had given an almost identical definition of assimilation: Hasluck to Leydin, 2 January 1952, NAA, A452, 1952/162.
4. Will Kymlicka, *Politics in the vernacular: nationalism, multiculturalism, and citizenship*, Oxford University Press, Oxford, 2001, pp. 244–8; Anthony Smith, *The nation in history: historiographical debates about ethnicity and nationalism*, University of New England Press, Hanover, NH, 2000, pp. 18–19.
5. Smith, p. 101.
6. Native Welfare Conference, 1951, p. 20.
7. Paul Hasluck, 'The native welfare conference, 1951', in *Native welfare in Australia*, pp. 15–16.
8. Paul Hasluck, *Shades of darkness: Aboriginal affairs 1925–1963*, Melbourne University Press, Melbourne, 1988, p. 130.
9. See, for example, Cora Thomas, 'From "Australian Aborigines" to "white Australians"', *Australian Aboriginal Studies*, no. 1, 2001, pp. 22, 24; Tim Rowse, 'The modesty of the state: Hasluck and the anthropological critics of assimilation', in Tom Stannage, Kay Saunders & Richard Nile (eds), *Paul Hasluck in Australian history: civic personality and public life*, University of Queensland Press, Brisbane, 1998, p. 122.
10. Paul Hasluck, *Mucking about: an autobiography*, Melbourne University Press, Melbourne, 1977, pp. 278–9.
11. Paul Hasluck, 'Some problems of assimilation', address to ANZAAS Congress, Perth, 1959, Elkin papers, box 80, item 1/12/295.
12. ibid.
13. Paul Hasluck, 'The future of the Australian Aborigines', 1952, in *Native welfare in Australia*, p. 54; Paul Hasluck, 'Native welfare in Australia', speech on the estimates debate, 6 October 1955, Hasluck papers, box 33.
14. Paul Hasluck, 'The future of the Australian Aborigines', address to ANZAAS Congress, 1958, Hasluck papers, box 38.
15. Paul Hasluck, 'From protection to welfare', in *Native welfare in Australia*, p. 35.
16. Marian Sawer, *The ethical state? Social liberalism in Australia*, Melbourne University Press, Melbourne, 2003.
17. Native Welfare Conference, 1951, p. 21.
18. Wise to Secretary, Territories, 12 August 1952, NAA A452 1952/162.
19. Secretary, Territories to Wise, 4 September 1952, NAA A452 1952/162.

20. *Welfare Ordinance 1953*, s. 8(a).
21. Paul Hasluck, 'The record in the Northern Territory', 1952, in *Native welfare in Australia*, p. 22; Hasluck to Wise, 28 July 1952, NAA, A452, 1952/162.
22. J Willoughby, Assistant Secretary, Territories, 'Citizenship Status: Draft', 23 July 1951, Hasluck papers, box 33; unsigned document headed 'Notes for Conference' [probably by SG Middleton, Commissioner for Native Affairs, WA], c.September 1951, Hasluck papers, box 33.
23. 'Statement by the minister', 6 August 1952, NAA A452 1952/162.
24. Hasluck to Leydin, 2 January 1952, NAA A452 1952/162.
25. Hasluck, 'Some problems of assimilation'.
26. Hasluck to Secretary, Territories, 13 August 1951, Hasluck papers, box 33.
27. Hasluck, 'Welfare policy in the Northern Territory', press statement, 23 September 1953, Hasluck papers, box 33.
28. B Damaso, Secretary, Australian Half-caste Progressive Association, Darwin, to PM, 12 March 1951, NAA A431 1951/899. See also Sue Stanton, 'The Australian Half-caste Progressive Association: the fight for freedom and rights in the Northern Territory', *Journal of Northern Territory History*, vol. 4, 1993, pp. 37–46.
29. Wise to Secretary, Territories, 15 July 1952, NAA A452 1952/162.
30. Quoted in Julie Wells, 'The long march: assimilation policy and practice in Darwin, the Northern Territory, 1939–1967', PhD thesis, University of Queensland, 1995, p. 105.
31. ibid., pp. 106–8; Colin Tatz, 'Aboriginal administration in the Northern Territory of Australia', PhD thesis, ANU, 1964, pp. 22–4.
32. Conspectus of the work of the Welfare Branch of the Northern Territory Administration, August 1954–February 1959, Hasluck papers, box 32.
33. Hasluck to Nott, 20 August 1962, NAA A452 1960/8435.
34. CWW Greenidge, Director, ASAPS, to Hasluck, 17 December 1957, Street papers, box 27, folder 4, item 10/428; Northern Territory News, 14 October 1958, clipping in NAA A452 1958/4955.
35. Julie Wells & Michael Christie, 'Namatjira and the burden of citizenship', *Australian Historical Studies*, vol. 31, no. 114, 2000, pp. 121–2.
36. Hasluck to Secretary, Territories, 18 May 1959, and subsequent correspondence, NAA A452 1960/8435.
37. AP Elkin, 'Post-war and the Aborigines', *The Aborigines Protector*, vol. 2, no. 1, June 1946, p. 6.
38. AP Elkin, 'Wards, not Aborigines, in the Northern Territory: the proposed Ordinance', February 1953, Elkin papers, box 71, item 1/12/187.
39. AF Ellemor, 'Some effects of the policy of assimilation on the full-blood Aborigines', paper presented to Missions-Administration Conference, Darwin, December 1953, NAA, A452, 1953/138.
40. Hasluck to Administrator, 28 July 1952, NAA, A452, 1952/162; Statement by the Minister, 6 August 1952, NAA, A452, 1952/162.
41. Hasluck, *Black Australians*, p. 161.
42. Native Welfare Council, 1952, agenda item 1: 'Citizenship status', Hasluck papers, box 32.

43. *One people*, Department of Territories, Canberra, 1961. See also Russell McGregor, 'One people: Aboriginal assimilation and the white Australia ideal', *History Australia*, vol. 6, no. 1, 2009, pp. 3.1–3.17.
44. See, for example, David Hollinsworth, *Race and racism in Australia*, 2nd edn, Social Science Press, Katoomba, 1998, p. 155; Brian Galligan & Winsome Roberts, *Australian citizenship*, Melbourne University Press, Melbourne, 2004, p. 173.
45. Anna Haebich, *Spinning the dream: assimilation in Australia 1950–1970*, Fremantle Press, Fremantle, 2008, p. 149; Anna Haebich, 'Imagining Assimilation', *Australian Historical Studies*, vol. 33, no. 118, 2002, pp. 61–70.
46. *The Aborigines and you*, Department of Territories, Canberra, 1963, p. 7.
47. *One people*, p. 32.
48. *Our Aborigines*, Department of Territories, Canberra, 1957.
49. Gwenda Tavan, '"Good neighbours": community organisations, migrant assimilation and Australian society and culture, 1950–1961', *Australian Historical Studies*, vol. 28, no. 109, 1997, pp. 77–89.
50. Hasluck, 'The future of the Australian Aborigines', pp. 57–8.
51. Paul Hasluck, 'Aborigines Sunday', press release, 10 July 1958, Hasluck papers, box 33.
52. Paul Hasluck, 'Are our Aborigines neglected?', 12 July 1959, Elkin papers, box 80, item 1/12/294.
53. Hasluck to Leydin, 2 January 1952, NAA, A452, 1952/162.
54. Hasluck, 'Future of the Australian Aborigines' (1952), p. 57.
55. *The skills of our Aborigines*, Department of Territories, Canberra, 1960, p. 19.
56. Hasluck, 'Native welfare conference, 1951', p. 17.
57. Paul Hasluck, 'New hope for old Australians', 14 July 1957, Hasluck papers, box 38.
58. Hasluck, 'The future of the Australian Aborigines', 1958.
59. Hasluck, *Shades of darkness*, p. 30.
60. RK McCaffery, 'Identification and naming of Aborigines', December 1953, NAA, 452, 1953/138.
61. ibid. See also Wise to Secretary, Territories, 15 February 1955, NAA, A452, 1954/617.
62. McCaffery, 'Identification and naming of Aborigines'.
63. *One people*, pp. 10, 12.
64. *The skills of our Aborigines*, p. 23.
65. *The Aborigines and you*, p. 3.
66. *Fringe dwellers*, Department of Territories, Canberra, 1959, pp. 13, 18–22; *The skills of our Aborigines*, p. 30; *The Aborigines and you*, pp. 9–10.
67. *The skills of our Aborigines*, pp. 30–1.

Chapter 6

1. AP Elkin, 'Wards, not Aborigines, in the Northern Territory: the proposed Ordinance', February 1953, Elkin papers, box 71, item 1/12/187.
2. AP Elkin, 'Aborigines and the ministers' welfare council', *Australian Quarterly*, vol. 23, no. 4, 1951, p. 16.

3. AF Ellemor, 'Some effects of the policy of assimilation on the full-blood Aborigines', paper presented to Missions-Administration Conference, Darwin, December 1953, NAA, A452, 1953/138.
4. Jennifer Clark, *Aborigines and activism: race, Aborigines and the coming of the sixties to Australia*, University of Western Australia Press, Perth, 2008, pp. 71–5.
5. *Daily Mirror*, 19 May 1959.
6. Resolutions passed by Aboriginal session, Fourth National Conference of FCAA, 1961, Christophers papers, box 27.
7. Other possible sources of 'integration' are the American civil rights movement and Australia's policies toward immigrants. However, lobby groups who adopted the term in Aboriginal affairs stated that they took it from ILO Convention 107.
8. Elkin to Wardlaw, 12 July 1951, Elkin papers, box 182, item 4/2/313.
9. AP Elkin, 'Aboriginal languages and assimilation', *Oceania*, vol. 34, no. 2, 1963, p. 154.
10. AP Elkin, 'Social and cultural change in the Darwin region, 1953', Elkin papers, box 111, item 1/17/146.
11. AP Elkin, 'Background and present position of the Aborigines in Australia', address given in Brisbane, 1967, Elkin papers, box 109, item 1/17/56.
12. AP Elkin, 'The role of Aborigines in the Australian community', typescript, c.1965, Elkin papers, box 111, item 1/17/143.
13. AP Elkin, 'Do Aborigines get a fair deal?', *Sunday Herald*, February 1953, clipping in Simpson papers, box 80, folder 207.
14. AP Elkin, 'The background of present day Aboriginal policies', in *Proceedings of a conference on welfare policies for Australian Aborigines*, Adult Education Department, University of New England, Armidale, 1960, p. 18.
15. AP Elkin, 'The Australian Aborigines to-day', typescript, 1963, Elkin papers, box 109, item 1/17/53.
16. Elkin to Pink, 26 October 1954, Elkin papers, box 38, item 1/10/7.
17. AP Elkin, *Aborigines and Citizenship*, APNR, Sydney, 1958, p. 26.
18. See, for example, AP Elkin, 'The Aborigines: Australians', typescript for an address c.1960, Elkin papers, box 109, item 1/17/19; AP Elkin, 'The Australian Aborigines', c.1961, Elkin papers, box 109, item 1/17/45; Elkin to Ian Spalding, 6 February 1961, Elkin papers, box 218, item 5/2/24; Elkin, 'The Australian Aborigines to-day'.
19. Elkin, 'Background and present position'.
20. AP Elkin, 'Assimilation and integration', address to ANZAAS Congress, Perth, 1959, Elkin papers, box 108, item 1/17/3.
21. *Smoke Signals*, October 1959, p. 4.
22. WR Geddes, 'Maori and Aborigine: a comparison of attitudes and policies', *Aboriginal Affairs Information Paper*, no. 1, April 1962.
23. TGH Strehlow, *Nomads in No-Man's-Land*, AFASA, Adelaide, 1961, p. 21.
24. TGH Strehlow, *Dark and white Australians*, AALSA, Adelaide, 1958, p. 22.
25. ibid., p. 11.
26. TGH Strehlow, *Assimilation problems: the Aboriginal viewpoint*, AALSA, Adelaide, 1964, back-cover blurb.

27. Ronald Berndt & Catherine Berndt, *From black to white in South Australia*, Cheshire, Melbourne, 1951, p. 21; Catherine Berndt, 'Mateship or success: an assimilation dilemma', *Oceania*, vol. 33, no. 2, 1962, pp. 71–89. See also Tim Rowse, 'The modesty of the state: Hasluck and the anthropological critics of assimilation', in Tom Stannage, Kay Saunders & Richard Nile (eds), *Paul Hasluck in Australian history: civic personality and public life*, University of Queensland Press, Brisbane, 1998, p. 126.
28. Jean Martin, notes from address to the Aboriginal Scholarships National Conference, August 1960, Christophers papers, box 6.
29. RG Hausfeld, letter to editor, *Sydney Morning Herald*, 8 September 1961, clipping in Simpson papers, box 80, folder 207; RG Hausfeld, 'An integration policy for Australian Aboriginal groups', *Oceania*, vol. 34, no. 1, 1963, pp. 32–7.
30. Marie Reay, 'Introduction', in M Reay (ed.), *Aborigines now: new perspectives in the study of Aboriginal communities*, Angus & Robertson, Sydney, 1964, p. xx.
31. Russell McGregor, 'From Old Testament to New: AP Elkin on Christian conversion and cultural assimilation', *Journal of Religious History*, vol. 25, no. 1, 2001, pp. 41–6.
32. Wilbur Chaseling, *Yulengor: nomads of Arnhem Land*, Epworth Press, London, 1957; Andrew Markus, *Governing savages*, Allen & Unwin, Sydney, 1990, pp. 78–9.
33. Rani Kerin, 'Charles Duguid and Aboriginal assimilation in Adelaide, 1950–1960: the nebulous "assimilation" goal', *History Australia*, vol. 2, no. 3, 2005, pp. 85.1–85.17; Rani Kerin, '"Doctor do-good"? Charles Duguid and Aboriginal politics, 1930s–1970s', PhD thesis, Australian National University, 2004.
34. Duguid to General Secretary, UN Association of Australia, 30 June 1950, Duguid papers, series 1, box 1.
35. Charles Duguid, 'The Universal Declaration of Human Rights as it relates to the Aborigines of Australia', 24 November 1952, Duguid papers, series 6, box 7.
36. Charles Duguid, 'The Aborigines' place in the present day life of Australia', text of BBC radio broadcast, 19 February 1952, Duguid papers, series 6, box 7.
37. Charles Duguid, *No dying race*, Rigby, Adelaide, 1963, pp. 184–6.
38. See for example Robert Tonkinson, *The Jigalong mob: Aboriginal victors of the desert crusade*, Cummings Publishing, Menlo Park, CA, 1974.
39. ABM, 'A new policy for Aborigines', November 1957, Elkin papers, box 65, item 1/12/98(f).
40. EC Evans, 'Responsibilities of missions', paper presented to the Missions-Administration Conference, Darwin, December 1953, NAA, A452, 1953/138.
41. See Jeremy Long, *The go-betweens: patrol officers in Aboriginal affairs administration in the Northern Territory 1936–74*, North Australia Research Unit, Darwin, 1992; Kerin, '"Doctor do-good"', p. 177.

42. Marilyn Lake, *Faith: Faith Bandler, gentle activist*, Allen & Unwin, Sydney, 2002, p. 78.
43. Constitution of the Aboriginal-Australian Fellowship, 1956, Christophers papers, box 6.
44. Herbert Groves, 'The case for the Aborigines of NSW and the whole of the Commonwealth of Australia', [1957], Christophers papers, box 27.
45. Draft constitution of the Aboriginal Advancement League, 29 April 1957, Christophers papers, box 6. See also *Council for Aboriginal Rights, Victoria: Bulletin*, no. 10, April 1957, p. 7.
46. Aborigines Advancement League (Victoria) Constitution, c.August 1957, Christophers papers, box 6.
47. *Smoke Signals*, October 1959, p. 4.
48. See especially John Chesterman, *Civil rights: how Indigenous Australians won formal equality*, University of Queensland Press, Brisbane, 2005, pp. 22–3; see also Sue Taffe, *Black and white together: FCAATSI: the Federal Council for the Advancement of Aborigines and Torres Strait Islanders 1958–1973*, University of Queensland Press, Brisbane, 2005, pp. 53–5.
49. CD Rowley, 'Aborigines and other Australians', *Oceania*, vol. 32, no. 4, 1962, pp. 251–2, 254–5, 259–60.
50. AAF, 'Submissions to the joint committee of the NSW Legislative Council and Legislative Assembly upon Aboriginal welfare', January 1966, NAA, A2354, 1968/25.
51. John Jago, 'The Church and the Aborigine in Australia', summary of address to the AGM of CARV, 21 October 1963, pp. 1–2, Christophers papers, box 7.
52. *On Aboriginal Affairs*, no. 14, September 1965, p. 13.
53. CARV, 'Ownership and development of reserves by Aborigines', 28 June 1963, Christophers papers, box 6.
54. *Why Retain Lake Tyers for the Aborigines?*, pamphlet published by the Lake Tyers Campaign Committee, Melbourne, August 1963, Christophers papers, box 6.
55. Davis Daniels, NTCAR circular, 24 March 1962, Christophers papers, box 1.
56. 'Three points of view on Aboriginals', *Australian*, 24 April 1967, clipping in Bryant papers, box 179.
57. Lorna Lippmann, 'Assimilation: does it work?', *Smoke Signals*, vol. 2, no. 1, October 1962, p. 15.
58. Herbert Groves, 'A condensed statement of the "case for the Aborigines"', c.1964, AAF records, box 5.
59. Joe McGinness, 'Aboriginal study in a contemporary situation', 14 November 1973, Christophers papers, box 27.
60. FCAA, 'Government legislation and the Aborigines', February 1964, p. 8, Christophers papers, box 29.
61. Kath Walker, 'Political rights for Aborigines: address delivered to the 12th annual conference of FCAATSI', *Rights and Advancement*, no. 20, June 1969, pp. 3–4.

62. Herbert Groves, 'Assimilation and the Aborigines', *Churinga*, vol. 1, no. 11, December 1969–February 1970, p. 1.
63. 'Assimilation and integration', *Smoke Signals*, vol. 2, no. 1, October 1962, p. 5.
64. Groves, 'The case for the Aborigines of NSW'.
65. Groves, 'A condensed statement'.
66. Fay Gale, 'A study of assimilation', PhD thesis, University of Adelaide, 1960, pp. xxi–xxii, quoted in Kerin, 'Charles Duguid and Aboriginal assimilation', p. 85.11.
67. *Advertiser*, 26 October 1971, quoted in Kerin, 'Charles Duguid and Aboriginal assimilation', p. 85.12.
68. James Pierson, 'Aboriginality in Adelaide', PhD thesis, Washington University, 1972, p. 37, quoted in Kerin, 'Charles Duguid and Aboriginal assimilation', p. 85.12.
69. Peter Read, *Charles Perkins: a biography*, Viking, Melbourne, 1990, p. 61.
70. See, for example, Charles Perkins, 'The voice of the manager', *Irabina*, vol. 1, no. 8, 1965, p. 3; 'The Perkins proposals', *Aboriginal Quarterly*, vol. 1, no. 1, 1968, p. 10.
71. Native Welfare Conference, 1961, 'Verbatim record', pp. 7–8, 106.
72. 'Justice in Queensland', *On Aboriginal Affairs*, no. 10, September–December 1963, pp. 5–8.
73. Bain Attwood, 'Rights, racism and Aboriginality: critics of assimilation in the 1950s and 1960s', in Tim Rowse (ed.), *Contesting assimilation*, API Network, Perth, 2005, p. 277.
74. Stan Davey, *Genesis or genocide? the Aboriginal assimilation policy*, Federal Literature Committee of the Churches of Christ in Australia, Melbourne, 1963, p. 9.
75. See, for example, F Coaldrake, Chairman, ABM, to Hasluck, 5 December 1962, NAA, A452, 1962/7391.
76. *The Meaning of Assimilation*, NMC, Sydney, June 1963.
77. *Four Major Issues in Assimilation*, NMC, Sydney, June 1963.
78. Memo, Deputy Secretary, Territories, 20 June 1963, with handwritten annotations by Hasluck, NAA, A452 NT1963/3650. See also Judith Brett, 'Limited politics', in Tom Stannage, Kay Saunders & Richard Nile (eds), *Paul Hasluck in Australian history: civic personality and public life*, University of Queensland Press, Brisbane, 1998, pp. 186–9.
79. Quoted in Tim Rowse, *Obliged to be difficult: Nugget Coombs' legacy in Indigenous affairs*, Cambridge University Press, Cambridge, 2000, p. 22.
80. ibid.
81. *On Aboriginal Affairs*, no. 15, April 1966, p. 13.
82. VW Coombes, 'Aborigines as Australians', 29 January 1965, Elkin papers, box 65, item 1/12/102(k).
83. Colin Tatz, 'The politics of Aboriginal administration', in *We the Australians: what is to follow the referendum: proceedings of the inter-racial seminar held at the University College, Townsville, 2nd and 3rd December 1967*, Inter-racial Citizens Committee, Townsville, 1968, pp. 21–3.

84. CD Rowley, *The Remote Aborigines*, Penguin, London, 1972, pp. 212, 227.
85. CD Rowley, *Outcasts*, pp. 383–7; see also p. 35.
86. *Aboriginal Advancement and What It Takes*, Department of Territories, Canberra, 1967.
87. Commonwealth/State Aboriginal Welfare Conference 1967: Statement by the Minister, Hon. CE Barnes, MP, in the House of Representatives, FCAATSI records, box Y604.
88. 'Report from the Select Committee on Voting Rights of Aborigines: Part 1 — Report and Minutes of Proceedings', *CPP*, vol. 2, 1961, p. 1.
89. 'Extract from Second Reading Speech on Constitution Alteration (repeal of section 127) Bill', 1965, NAA, A406, E1967/30.
90. WC Wentworth, 'Aboriginals: the referendum and the future', 1968, AIATSIS PMS 2784.

Chapter 7

1. Mark Lopez, *The origins of multiculturalism in Australian politics 1945–1975*, Melbourne University Press, Melbourne, 2000, Pt. 1.
2. *Aborigines in the Community*, Department of Territories, Canberra, 1965, p. 2.
3. Jessie Street, 'Report on Aborigines in Australia', May–June 1957, Christophers papers, box 27.
4. Gordon Bryant, 'Aborigines Advancement League', *Smoke Signals*, vol. 1, no. 1, April 1960, p. 5.
5. Gordon Bryant, 'Editorial', *Smoke Signals*, vol. 1, no. 4, March 1961, p. 13.
6. J McGinness, 'FCAATSI President's Annual Report, 1964–65', FCAATSI records, box Y600.
7. Colin Tatz, 'Some Aboriginal thoughts', *Dissent*, no. 15, Spring 1965, p. 10.
8. 'The purpose and programme of NADOC', 25 August 1959, NADOC papers.
9. *What is N.A.D.O.C.?*, NADOC, Sydney, c.1967, NADOC papers.
10. See, for example, RP Greenish, NADOC, ACT, 'Australian participation in Expo '67', 7 September 1966, NADOC papers.
11. 'Minutes of the NADOC annual meeting', 18 March 1966, NADOC papers.
12. John Goodluck, 'Reconciling Australia's peoples', paper presented to the Aboriginal Scholarships National Conference, August 1960, Christophers papers, box 6.
13. Ian Spalding, 'Why be concerned', Christophers papers, box 6.
14. Spalding to PM, 12 May 1961, NAA, A463, 1961/5074.
15. 'Respect for our Aborigines', *Smoke Signals*, vol. 1, no. 7, March 1962, pp. 77–8.
16. Secretary, Territories, to Secretary, PM Dept, 22 October 1963, NAA, A463, 1961/5074.
17. Marie Reay, 'A Note on "Aborigines" and "aborigines"', in M Reay (ed.), *Aborigines now: new perspectives in the study of Aboriginal communities*, Angus & Robertson, Sydney, 1964, pp. 167–8.
18. 'Terminology: Black', *On Aboriginal Affairs*, no. 5, November–December 1962, p. 7.

Notes (pages 123–130)

19. Barry Christophers, 'Terminology is important', *Smoke Signals*, vol. 3, no. 3, September 1964, pp. 19–20.
20. Colin Tatz, 'Equal rights for Aborigines', *The Round Table: The Commonwealth Quarterly*, no. 228, October 1967, p. 444.
21. Colin Tatz, *Obstacle race: Aborigines in sport*, UNSW Press, Sydney, 1995.
22. Peter Corris, *Lords of the ring*, Cassell, Sydney, 1980, pp. 134–45; Richard Broome, 'Professional Aboriginal boxers in eastern Australia 1930–1979', *Aboriginal History*, vol. 4, 1980, pp. 48–71; Richard Broome, 'Sands, Dave', in *The Oxford companion to Australian sport*, 2nd edn, Oxford University Press, Melbourne, 1994, p. 373.
23. Colin Tatz, interview for *The Sports Factor*, ABC Radio National, 19 May 2006.
24. Quoted in Tatz, *Obstacle race*, p. 136.
25. Lionel Rose, *Lionel Rose: Australian: the life story of a champion*, Angus & Robertson, Sydney, 1969, pp. 16, 68, 124.
26. ibid., pp. 147–50.
27. Tatz, *Obstacle race*, p. 19.
28. ibid., pp. 238–40; Colin Tatz & Paul Tatz, 'Perkins, Charles', *Oxford companion to Australian sport*, p. 332.
29. Tatz, *Obstacle race*, pp. 201, 187–8; SJ Routh, 'Beetson, Arthur', in *Oxford companion to Australian sport*, p. 61.
30. Tatz, *Obstacle race*, pp. 149–80.
31. ibid., pp. 272–7, 281.
32. David Martin, 'Talking to Doug Nicholls', *Smoke Signals*, vol. 2, no. 1, October 1962, p. 8.
33. Tatz, *Obstacle race*, pp. 252, 260–1.
34. 'Aboriginal sports foundation suggested', *Age*, 23 October 1969, ARPNC.
35. Colin Tatz & Paul Tatz, 'Aboriginal Sports Foundation', *Oxford companion to Australian sport*, p. 3.
36. See, for example, 'Constitution of the AAF', 1956, Christophers papers, box 6; Lorna Lippman, 'Part-Aboriginal communities in Australia', c.November 1965, p. 3, Christophers papers, box 5; *One people*, Department of Territories, Canberra, 1961, p. 23.
37. *Origin*, vol. 1, no. 1, 7 August 1969, p. 1; *Origin*, vol. 1, no. 7, 30 October 1969, p. 2.
38. Tatz, *Obstacle race*, pp. 325–6.
39. 'Redfern All Blacks Football Club', statement by Ken Brindle, 31 October 1961, AAF records, box 14.
40. HC Coombs, 'Address to FCAATSI conference', 12 April 1968, p. 4, Simpson Papers, box 105, folder 302.
41. TGH Strehlow, *The sustaining ideals of Australian Aboriginal societies*, Hawthorn, Melbourne, 1956, pp. 6–7, 15–17.
42. ibid., pp. 15–20.
43. HH Penny, *Tribal Aborigines…an educated people: some thoughts on the meaning of education for Aborigines and other Australians*, AALSA, Adelaide, 1965, p. 2.

44. Langford to Hasluck, 2 August 1963, NAA, A452, 1962/2795; Hasluck to Langford, 8 August 1963, NAA, A452, 1962/2795.
45. E LeSueur, 'The Council of Aboriginal Women Travellers Aid Society in South Aus. Inc.', 10 September 1969, FCAATSI Records, box Y604.
46. Lamont West, 'The right to choose', *Outlook*, vol. 6, no. 4, July–August 1962, pp. 9–12.
47. 'Natives have lesson for us', *News* (Adelaide), 18 August 1969, ARPNC.
48. Minutes of the meeting of the 14th annual conference of FCAATSI, 10 April 1971, Townsville, Christophers papers, box 29.
49. Ronald Berndt & Catherine Berndt, *The first Australians*, Ure Smith, Sydney, 1952, p. 141.
50. Ronald Berndt & Catherine Berndt, *The first Australians*, 2nd edn, Ure Smith, Sydney, 1967, pp. xiii–xv.
51. HC Coombs, 'Address to FCAATSI conference', 12 April 1968, p. 5, Simpson Papers, box 105, folder 302.
52. Charles Rowley, 'The background of culture clash', in *We the Australians: what is to follow the referendum: proceedings of the inter-racial seminar held at the University College, Townsville, 2nd and 3rd December 1967*, Inter-racial Citizens Committee, Townsville, 1968, p. 12.
53. AW Reed, *Myths and legends of Australia*, AH & AW Reed, Sydney, 1965, p. 9.
54. Roland Robinson, *Aboriginal myths and legends*, Sun Books, Melbourne, 1966.
55. Charles Mountford, 'Introduction' to *The Dreamtime*, Rigby, Adelaide, 1965, pp. 14–15.
56. Peter Brady, *Whitefella Dreaming: the authorised biography of William Ricketts*, Preferred Image, Olinda, Victoria, 1994, pp. 7–11, 165–6.
57. ibid., pp. 199–202, 292–4.
58. Ian McLean, *White Aborigines: identity politics in Australian art*, Cambridge University Press, Cambridge, 1998, pp. 96–7.
59. Philip Jones, 'Perceptions of Aboriginal art: a history', in Peter Sutton (ed.), *Dreamings: the art of Aboriginal Australia*, Viking, Melbourne, 1988, p. 176.
60. JA Tuckson, 'Aboriginal art and the Western world', in RM Berndt (ed.), *Australian Aboriginal art*, Ure Smith, Sydney, 1964, p. 67; Roman Black, *Old and new Australian Aboriginal art*, Angus & Robertson, Sydney, 1964, p. xxi.
61. Catrina Vignando, 'Corroboree: Aboriginal inspiration in contemporary Australian ballet', in Julie Marcus (ed.), *Picturing the 'primitif': images of race in daily life*, LhR Press, Sydney, 2000, pp. 213–16.
62. *Sunday Telegraph* and *Daily Examiner* reviews, February 1954, quoted in Anna Haebich, *Spinning the dream: assimilation in Australia 1950–1970*, Fremantle Press, Fremantle, 2008 p. 334.
63. See Rex Butler (ed.), *What is appropriation? an anthology of writings on Australian art in the 1980s and 1990s*, 2nd edn, Institute of Modern Art, Brisbane, 2004.
64. See, for example, Brenda Factor, 'Marketing an Australian identity', in Marcus, pp. 188–92; Haebich, Ch. 8; Paul Carter, *The lie of the land*, Faber, London, 1996, pp. 68–9.

65. Nicholas Thomas, *Possessions: indigenous art/colonial culture*, Thames and Hudson, London, 1999, p. 141.
66. See, for example, 'Aborigines' Progressive Association: submissions to the select committee appointed by the New South Wales government', *Churinga*, February–March 1967, pp. 9, 11.
67. AP Elkin, 'Foreword' to Karel Kupka, *Dawn of art: painting and sculpture of Australian Aborigines*, Angus & Robertson, Sydney, 1965, p. x.
68. West, pp. 173–9.
69. See, for example, Haebich, p. 337.
70. Judith O'Callaghan, 'The Australian interior: the importance of being contemporary', in J O'Callaghan (ed.), *The Australian dream: design of the fifties*, Powerhouse Publishing, Sydney, 1993, p. 166; Bain Attwood, *Rights for Aborigines*, Allen & Unwin, Sydney, 2003, p. 198.
71. Haebich, Ch. 8; see also Julie Marcus, 'Introduction' to Marcus, p. 9.
72. Lambert to Simpson, 16 November 1961, NAA, A452, 1961/5590.
73. Denis Byrne, 'Deep nation: Australia's acquisition of an Indigenous past', *Aboriginal History*, vol. 20, 1996, pp. 97–101.
74. See, for example, Barrie Pittock, 'Compare overseas', *Smoke Signals*, vol. 6, no. 4, December 1967, p. 20; Tatz, 'Aboriginal thoughts', p. 10.
75. Beth Dean and Victor Carell, *Dust for the dancers*, Angus & Robertson, Sydney, 1955, p. ix.
76. ibid., pp. 3, 207–11; Beth Dean and Victor Carell, *Twin journey: an autobiography*, Pacific Publications, Sydney, 1983, pp. 145–7. See also Suzanne Spunner, 'Corroboree moderne', in Julie Wells, Mickey Dewar & Suzanne Parry (eds), *Modern frontier: aspects of the 1950s in Australia's Northern Territory*, Charles Darwin University Press, Darwin, 2005, pp. 155–8.

Chapter 8

1. *Sydney Morning Herald*, 19 May 1967, p. 6.
2. Horner to Cardinal Gilroy, 5 May 1967, FCAATSI records, box Y604.
3. *Australian*, 9 May 1967.
4. Charles Dixon, 'I want to be a human being', *Sun-Herald*, 21 May 1967, pp. 31, 56.
5. See, for example, the leaflet accompanying the National Petition: 'Towards Equal Citizenship for Aborigines', 1963, AAF records, box 7.
6. John Chesterman & Brian Galligan, *Citizens without rights: Aborigines and Australian citizenship*, Cambridge University Press, Melbourne, 1997, pp. 157–86.
7. John Chesterman, *Civil rights: how Indigenous Australians won formal equality*, University of Queensland Press, Brisbane, 2005, pp. 61–6.
8. 'Report from the Select Committee on Voting Rights of Aborigines: Part 1 — Report and Minutes of Proceedings', *CPP*, vol. 2, 1961, pp. 1, 2.
9. ibid., pp. 8, 38–41.
10. G Bryant, 'Editorial', *Smoke Signals*, vol. 1, no. 6, p. 13.
11. *CPD* Representatives, vol. 33, 19 October 1961, p. 2247.

12. *CPD* Representatives, vol. 35, 1 May 1962, p. 1771.
13. 'Report from the Select Committee on Voting Rights of Aborigines', pp. 8–9.
14. 'Report of the Special Committee enquiring into legislation for the promotion of the well-being of Aborigines and Torres Strait Islanders in Queensland', *QPP*, 1964–65, p. 3.
15. Quoted in Chesterman, p. 160.
16. Kath Walker, 'Voting in Queensland: an Aborigine's point of view', *Smoke Signals*, vol. 4, no. 3, 1965, pp. 22–3.
17. Information delivered to the Annual General Meeting of the CAR, 23 October 1964, Christophers papers, box 7.
18. Quoted in Chesterman, p. 160.
19. 'Racial discrimination: report of inter-departmental committee', 1964, NAA, A4940, C3371.
20. 'The student bus: SAFA interviewed', *Outlook*, April 1965, p. 7.
21. See Ruth Fink, 'The caste barrier: an obstacle to the assimilation of part-Aborigines in north-west New South Wales', *Oceania*, vol. 28, no. 2, December 1957, pp. 100–10.
22. 'The student bus', pp. 5–10; Ann Curthoys, *Freedom ride: a freedom rider remembers*, Allen & Unwin, Sydney 2002.
23. '"The dark people"', *Current Affairs Bulletin*, vol. 29, no. 4, 25 December 1961, p. 63; J Inglis, 'The right to drink', *Aborigines' Advancement League Newsletter*, no. 10, June 1961, p. 2; *News* (Adelaide), 21 January 1960, clipping in Christophers papers, box 1.
24. *CAR Bulletin*, no. 12, December 1959, Christophers papers, box 6.
25. 'Editorial: who are the savages?', *Guardian*, 26 November 1959, clipping in Christophers papers, box 1.
26. 'Liquor debases natives', *Age*, 27 November 1959, clipping in Christophers papers, box 1.
27. 'Citizen Bruce's case made them wild', *Sun* (Melbourne), 8 January 1961, clipping in Christophers papers, box 1.
28. NTCAR circular, 31 March 1962, Christophers papers, box 1.
29. Minutes of special meeting of AWB, 12 July 1960, Elkin papers, box 58, item 1/12/41.
30. Horner to leader, Country Party of NSW, 3 October 1960, AAF records, box 7; Horner to AJ Mulvihill, Acting Secretary, ALP, 29 August 1960, AAF records, box 7.
31. AAF letter to NSW parliamentarians, 18 October 1960, AAF records, box 7.
32. *Second-Class Citizens*, AAF, Sydney, c.1960, AAF records, box 7.
33. Petition to CA Kelly, Chief Secretary, c.1961, AAF records, box 7.
34. *Smoke Signals*, vol. 1, no. 7, March 1962, p. 79.
35. JH Bell, 'Liquor and the New South Wales Aborigines', c.January 1962, AAF records, box 7.
36. CD Rowley, *Outcasts in white Australia*, Penguin, Melbourne, 1972, pp. 358–9, 414.

37. Charles Duguid, 'Aborigines and alcohol: response to the Australian Temperance Council on the relationship of Aborigines to alcoholic liquors', 5 August 1959, Duguid papers, box 7.
38. Kim Beazley, *Dispossession and disease — or dignity*, Provocative Pamphlet no. 115, Federal Literature Committee of the Churches of Christ in Australia, 1964, p. 9.
39. AP Elkin, 'Hotel license at Gove', 1968, Elkin papers, box 110, item 1/17/86.
40. AP Elkin, 'Attitudes of Aborigines: 1929, 1969', Elkin papers, box 71 item 1/12/184; Elkin, 'Aboriginal policy — 1969 — facts and principles', Elkin papers, box 109, item 1/17/11; Elkin, 'Aborigines then and now', 1968, Elkin papers, item 1/17/27.
41. Russell McGregor, 'An absent negative: the 1967 referendum', *History Australia*, vol. 5, no. 2, 2008, pp. 44.1–44.2.
42. FCAATSI National Campaign Committee, 'The case for the referendum', 1967, Bryant papers, box 175.
43. Faith Bandler, *Turning the tide: a personal history of the Federal Council for the Advancement of Aborigines and Torres Strait Islanders*, Aboriginal Studies Press, Canberra, 1989, p. 97.
44. 'Awaking of conscience', *Churinga*, vol. 1, no. 6, April–May 1967, p. 5.
45. Chesterman, pp. 90–1; Bain Attwood & Andrew Markus, *The 1967 referendum: race, power and the Australian Constitution*, 2nd edn, Aboriginal Studies Press, Canberra, 2007, pp. 40–3.
46. *Australian*, 3 April 1967.
47. Queensland Vote Yes for Aboriginal Rights Campaign Committee, press release, May 1967, Bryant papers, box 175.
48. FCAATSI National Directorate, Vote Yes Campaign, 'Aboriginal rights and the referendum', May 1967, Christophers papers, box 27.
49. *Referendums to be held on Saturday, 27th May, 1967…The arguments for and against*, Government Printer, Canberra, 1967, p. 12.
50. Kay Keavney, 'Says a friend of the Aborigines…', *Australian Women's Weekly*, 10 May 1967, p. 7.
51. *Sydney Morning Herald*, 19 May 1967, p. 6.
52. For examples see Scott Bennett, 'The 1967 referendum', *Australian Aboriginal Studies*, no. 2, 1985, p. 30.
53. JRL Johnstone, 'Dangers in a yes vote', *Sydney Morning Herald*, 16 May 1967, p. 2.
54. SB Page, 'The case should have been put', *Australian*, 26 May 1967, p. 8.
55. 'Extract from second reading speech…' 1965, NAA, A406, E1967/30.
56. *Referendums to be held*, p. 12.
57. 'Natives: a yes vote', *West Australian*, 26 May 1967, document 50 in Attwood & Markus, *1967 Referendum*, p. 136.
58. Geoffrey Sawer, 'Between the lines', *Canberra Times*, 17 May 1967.
59. AP Elkin, 'A yes vote for Aborigines', *Sydney Morning Herald*, 16 May 1967 p. 2.
60. 'Some questions of morality and legality', *On Aboriginal Affairs*, no. 15, April 1966, pp. 2–3.
61. D Graham, FCAA NSW Publicity Officer, press statement, 17 May 1964, FCAATSI records, box Y600.

Notes (pages 156–162)

62. Bandler, p. 4.
63. *Daily Telegraph*, 20 April 1967, quoted in Lake, p. 114.
64. *Commonwealth laws against Aborigines*, FCAATSI leaflet, 1967, FCAATSI records, box Y600; Horner to Secretary, WEA, 1 May 1967, FCAATSI records, box Y604; *Petition for a referendum to remove discrimination…*, FCAA leaflet, 1963, AAF records, box 7.
65. Faith Bandler, 'What a yes vote means for Aboriginals', *Australian*, 17 May 1967.
66. ibid.
67. *Age*, 29 May 1967.
68. *Smoke Signals*, vol. 6, no. 2, May 1967, cover and p. 3.
69. S Andrews, 'Could legislation help instead of hindering the Aborigines', *Smoke Signals*, vol. 2, no. 3, 1963, pp. 19–21.
70. VAAL, 'Accepted policy re Victorian Aboriginal welfare', 30 October 1964, Christophers papers, box 5.
71. S Davey, General Secretary, FCAATSI, to Menzies, 14 November 1965, NAA, A452, NT1963/1447. See also Davey to Menzies, 5 April 1965, NAA, A1209/113, 1964/6244.
72. F Engel, 'Information paper on the federal referendum and Aborigines', 20 January 1966, Christophers papers, box 27.
73. Sue Taffe, 'The role of FCAATSI in the 1967 referendum: mythmaking about citizenship or political strategy?', in Tim Rowse (ed.), *Contesting assimilation*, API Network, Perth, 2005, pp. 291–3; Sue Taffe, *Black and white together: FCAATSI: the Federal Council for the Advancement of Aborigines and Torres Strait Islanders 1958–1973*, University of Queensland Press, Brisbane, 2005, pp. 117–24.
74. See for example J Horner, 'Radio broadcasts for station 2GZ', nos 2 and 3, May 1967, FCAATSI records, box Y604; FCAATSI National Campaign Committee, 'Yes vote information', no. 3, 31 March 1967, FCAATSI records, box Y604.
75. 'Annual report of NTCAR state secretary, Mr Davis Daniels, 15 June 1964, Christophers papers, box 7.
76. Taffe, *Black and white together*, pp. 119–20.
77. Tim Rowse, *Obliged to be difficult: Nugget Coombs' legacy in Indigenous affairs*, Cambridge University Press, Cambridge, 2000, p. 21.
78. See, for example, *Vote "Yes" for Aborigines*, leaflet authorised by K Walker, Queensland secretary, FCAATSI, 1967, Bryant papers, box 175; FCAATSI National Campaign Committee, 'Yes vote information', nos 1 and 3.

Chapter 9

1. Kevin Gilbert, *Because a white man'll never do it*, Angus & Robertson, Sydney, 1973, pp. 102, 104.
2. Kath Walker, 'Black–white coalition can work', *Origin*, vol. 1, no. 4, September 1969, p. 6.
3. Kath Walker, 'Voting in Queensland: an Aborigine's point of view', *Smoke Signals*, vol. 4, no. 3, 1965, p. 22.

4. *Koorier*, vol. 1, no. 8, 1969, p. 7; Kath Walker, 'Political rights for Aborigines', *Smoke Signals*, vol. 8, no. 1, April–June 1969, p. 11.
5. Walker, 'Black–white coalition', p. 6.
6. Kath Walker, 'The black commandments', *Koorier*, vol. 1, no. 10, 1969, p. 25.
7. See, for example, transcript of *Monday Conference*, ABC TV, 20 March 1972, pp. 12, 13, FCAATSI records, box Y599.
8. Russell McGregor, 'Another nation: Aboriginal activism in the late 1960s and early 1970s', *Australian Historical Studies*, vol. 40, no. 3, 2009, pp. 343–60.
9. *Age*, 25 May 1967.
10. Douglas Wilkie, 'Dream Time in Canberra', *Sun* (Melbourne), 29 May 1967, clipping in Bryant papers, box 175.
11. Holt, Cabinet submission no. 432, 14 August 1967, NAA A5619, C136 part 1; Cabinet decision no. 507 on submission no. 432, 15–16 August 1967, NAA A5619, C136 part 1.
12. Wentworth, Cabinet submission no. 92, 15 May 1968, NAA A5619, C136 part 1.
13. Cabinet minute, 2 July 1968, decision 314, NAA A5619, C136 part 1.
14. Tim Rowse, *Obliged to be difficult: Nugget Coombs' legacy in Indigenous affairs*, Cambridge University Press, Cambridge, 2000, pp. 26–7.
15. HC Coombs, 'Address to FCAATSI conference', 12 April 1968, pp.2, 4, Simpson papers, box 105, folder 302.
16. Rowse, p. 21.
17. FCAATSI, 'Memorandum to UN General Assembly', 1971, FCAATSI records, box Y600.
18. FCAATSI, 'Report on racism in Australia to the World Council of Churches, Geneva', [1971], pp. 1, 13, Christophers papers, box 19.
19. Peter Hastings, 'Can we break down our racist barriers?', *Australian*, 6 May 1970, clipping in ARPNC.
20. Ian Moffitt, 'Are Australians racist?', *Australian*, 19 May 1970, clipping in ARPNC.
21. *Australian Aborigines: Commonwealth policy and achievements. Statement by the prime minister, the Rt Hon. William McMahon*, Government Printer, Canberra, 1972, pp. 3–4.
22. 'Aboriginal Embassy land rights policy', c.February 1972, NAA, A6122, 2229.
23. Bain Attwood, *Rights for Aborigines*, Allen & Unwin, Sydney, 2003, pp. 215–53.
24. Frank Hardy, *The unlucky Australians*, Nelson, London, 1968.
25. William Stanner, 'After the Dreaming', 1968, in W Stanner, *White man got no Dreaming: essays 1938–1973*, ANU Press, Canberra, 1979, pp. 244–5.
26. *Land rights for Aborigines: answering your questions*, QCAATI leaflet, 1968, Christophers papers, box 3; FCAATSI Aboriginal land rights campaign, background material, fact sheet 5, 1968, Christophers papers, box 3.
27. Press statement, PJ Nixon, 9 August 1968, NAA, A1209, 1967/7512.
28. J McGinness, 'Aboriginal study in a contemporary situation', 14 November 1973, FCAATSI records, box Y604.

29. Neville Bonner, 'Aborigines require land, homes, work', *Newsletter on Aboriginal Affairs*, no. 2, July–September 1972, p. 6.
30. Kevin Gilbert, 'Letter of appreciation [to NADOC]', *Churinga*, vol. 1, no. 9, June–August 1968, pp. 19–21.
31. [Kevin Gilbert], 'When the thief is the judge...', *Alchuringa*, vol. 1, no. 2, March–May 1972, pp. 3–11.
32. 'Aboriginal policy', *Churinga*, vol. 1, no. 9, June–August 1968, p. 9.
33. 'The Gurindji blues', document 130 in Bain Attwood & Andrew Markus, *The struggle for Aboriginal rights: a documentary history*, Allen & Unwin, Sydney, 1999, pp. 237–9.
34. FCAATSI, fact sheet 5, 1968, Christophers papers, box 3.
35. FCAATSI/Abschol pamphlet, 1968, document 127 in Attwood & Markus, p. 232.
36. A Barrie Pittock, 'Land rights a way to equality and justice', *Origin*, vol. 1, no. 3, 4 September 1969, pp. 5, 7.
37. *Land Rights*, QCAATI leaflet, 1968; FCAATSI Aboriginal land rights campaign, background material: fact sheets 1, 4 and 6, 1968, Christophers papers, box 3.
38. Bain Attwood, *The making of the Aborigines*, Allen & Unwin, Sydney, 1989.
39. AP Elkin, 'The Australian Aborigines — their future', c.1957, Elkin papers, box 109, item 1/17/52; Ronald Berndt & Catherine Berndt, *The first Australians*, Ure Smith, Sydney, 1952, pp. xiii–xv.
40. Gilbert, *Because a white man'll never do it*, p. 7; see also Neville Perkins, ABC radio, *Fact and opinion*, 'Aborigines at the Centre', 19 April 1972, p. 10, FCAATSI papers, box Y600.
41. CARV, 'Report on FCAATSI conference, Easter 1969', Christophers papers, box 7.
42. Attwood & Markus, p. 249.
43. See, for example, Margaret Valadian, 'The case for a continuing partnership', *Smoke Signals*, vol. 8, no. 4, June 1970, pp. 23–4.
44. Sue Taffe, *Black and white together: FCAATSI: the Federal Council for the Advancement of Aborigines and Torres Strait Islanders 1958–1973*, University of Queensland Press, Brisbane, 2005, p. 266.
45. 'National Tribal Council policy manifesto', *Smoke Signals*, vol. 9, no. 1, September 1970, pp. 24–6.
46. 'The National Tribal Council holds its first conference', *Smoke Signals*, vol. 9, no. 1, September 1970, p. 23.
47. *Origin*, vol. 3, no. 1, 25 September 1970, pp. 1, 3.
48. Bob Maza, 'Tuesday 24th August, 1969', *National Koorier*, vol. 1, no. 9, 1969, p. 7.
49. 'Black power, Western Australia — an interview with Ken Colbung', *Newsletter on Aboriginal Affairs*, no. 3, 1972, pp. 8–13.
50. Bruce McGuinness, 'Black power, Victoria', *Newsletter on Aboriginal Affairs*, no. 3, 1972, p. 5.
51. Bobbi Sykes, 'Opening statement', in Ann Turner (ed.), *Black power in Australia: Neville Bonner versus Bobbi Sykes*, Heinemann, Melbourne, 1975, pp. 10–12.

52. 'Definition of black power', *Origin*, vol. 1, no. 4, 18 September 1969, p. 5.
53. Gilbert, *Because a white man'll never do it*, p. 104.
54. ibid., pp. 60–1; 'Editorial', *Alchuringa*, vol. 1, no. 2, March–May 1972, p. 1.
55. 'Black Panthers of Australia, platform and programme, 1970', document 139 in Attwood & Markus, pp. 252–4.
56. Bob Maza, 'The Koorie's disillusionment', *Smoke Signals*, vol. 8, no. 1, April–June 1969, p. 4.
57. [Bruce McGuinness], 'Stokely Carmichael on Black Power', *The Koorier*, vol. 1, no. 9, 1969, p. 23.
58. Bruce McGuinness, 'Don't go it alone!', *Smoke Signals*, vol. 8, no. 3, March 1970, p. 7; 'Editorial', *The Koorier*, vol. 1, no. 13, 1970, p. 4.
59. *Cook is bad news for Aborigines*, unattributed leaflet, 1970, Christophers papers, box 27.
60. Maza, 'The Koorie's disillusionment', pp. 3–4.
61. [Gilbert], 'When the thief', p. 5.
62. Gilbert, *Because a white man'll never do it*, p. 146.
63. *They're only gamin*, Black Rights Committee leaflet, c.1972, Bryant papers, box 174.
64. Anthony Smith, *Nationalism: theory, ideology, history*, Polity Press, Cambridge, 2001, pp. 140–1.
65. Maza, 'The Koorie's disillusionment', pp. 3–4.
66. 'National Tribal Council policy manifesto', p. 25.
67. Cooper to Minister, Interior, 15 June 1936, NAA, A1, 36/7014.
68. David Martin, 'Talking to Doug Nicholls', *Smoke Signals*, vol. 2, no. 1, October 1962, p. 10.
69. *Monday Conference*, ABC TV, 20 March 1972, p. 4.
70. Coe, quoted in Gilbert, *Because a white man'll never do it*, p. 184.
71. Workshop on Aboriginal culture and identity, January 1973, FCAATSI records, box Y604.
72. *Monday conference*, 20 March 1972, p. 6.
73. *Age*, 28 January 1972, clipping in NAA, A6122, 2229.
74. John Newfong, 'Captn Cook celebration protest', April 1970, FCAATSI records, box Y599.
75. *Monday Conference*, 20 March 1972, pp. 4–6.
76. *Official year book of Australia*, no. 59, 1973, p. 971.
77. Information sheet, Aboriginal Embassy, c.February 1972, NAA, A6122, 2229; Elizabeth Kwan, *Flag and nation: Australians and their national flags since 1901*, UNSW Press, Sydney, 2006, p. 119; Attwood, *Rights for Aborigines*, p. 345. I am unable to determine the provenance of the ochre, black and white flag; possibly it was designed by the Embassy protestors themselves.
78. Kevin Gilbert, 'To create a consciousness', *Alchuringa*, vol. 1, no. 1, December 1971–February 1972, p. 33.

Epilogue

1. Noel Pearson, *Up from the mission: selected writings*, Black Inc., Melbourne, 2009, pp. 239–40.
2. *Australian*, 2 January 2001, p. 5.
3. Peter Sutton, *The politics of suffering: Indigenous Australians and the end of the liberal consensus*, Melbourne University Press, Melbourne, 2009.
4. Gary Johns, *Aboriginal self-determination: the whiteman's dream*, Connor Court, Ballan, Victoria, 2011.
5. See Pearson, *Up from the mission*, especially 'Our right to take responsibility', 2000, pp. 143–71; 'On the human right to misery, mass incarceration and early death', 2001, pp. 172–80; 'White guilt, victimhood and the quest for a radical centre', 2007, pp. 219–62; 'Peoplehood', 2004, pp. 325–31; 'Layered identities and peace', 2006, pp. 332–43; and 'Over 200 years without a place', 2007, pp. 354–7.

Select Bibliography

Attwood, Bain, *The making of the Aborigines*, Allen & Unwin, Sydney, 1989.
—— *Rights for Aborigines*, Allen & Unwin, Sydney, 2003.
Attwood, Bain & Griffiths, Tom (eds), *Frontier, race, nation: Henry Reynolds and Australian history*, Australian Scholarly Publishing, Melbourne, 2009.
Attwood, Bain & Markus, Andrew *The struggle for Aboriginal rights: a documentary history*, Allen & Unwin, Sydney, 1999.
—— *The 1967 referendum: race, power and the Australian Constitution*, 2nd edn, Aboriginal Studies Press, Canberra, 2007.
Broome, Richard, *Aboriginal Australians: black responses to white dominance, 1788–2001*, 3rd edn, Allen & Unwin, Sydney, 2001.
Chesterman, John, *Civil rights: how Indigenous Australians won formal equality*, University of Queensland Press, Brisbane, 2005.
Chesterman, John & Galligan, Brian, *Citizens without rights: Aborigines and Australian citizenship*, Cambridge University Press, Melbourne, 1997.
Clark, Jennifer, *Aborigines and activism: race, Aborigines and the coming of the sixties to Australia*, University of Western Australia Press, Perth, 2008.
Ellinghaus, Katherine, *Taking assimilation to heart: marriages of white women and indigenous men in the United States and Australia, 1887–1937*, University of Nebraska Press, Lincoln, NB, 2006.
Gilbert, Kevin, *Because a white man'll never do it*, Angus & Robertson, Sydney, 1973.
Gray, Geoffrey, *A cautious silence: the politics of Australian anthropology*, Aboriginal Studies Press, Canberra, 2007.
Griffiths, Tom, *Hunters and collectors: the antiquarian imagination in Australia*, Cambridge University Press, Cambridge, 1996.
Haebich, Anna, *For their own good: Aborigines and government in the southwest of Western Australia, 1900–1940*, University of Western Australia Press, Perth, 1988.
—— *Spinning the dream: assimilation in Australia 1950–1970*, Fremantle Press, Fremantle, 2008.
Hall, Robert, *The black diggers: Aborigines and Torres Strait Islanders in the Second World War*, Allen & Unwin, Sydney, 1989.

Jacobs, Pat, *Mister Neville: a biography*, Fremantle Arts Centre Press, Fremantle, 1990.

Kerin, Rani, 'Charles Duguid and Aboriginal assimilation in Adelaide, 1950–1960: the nebulous "assimilation" goal', *History Australia*, vol. 2, no. 3, 2005, pp. 85.1–85.17.

Lake, Marilyn, *Faith: Faith Bandler, gentle activist*, Allen & Unwin, Sydney, 2002.

Markus, Andrew, *Governing savages*, Allen & Unwin, Sydney, 1990.

McGregor, Russell, *Imagined destinies: Aboriginal Australians and the doomed race theory, 1880–1939*, Melbourne University Press, Melbourne, 1997.

—— '"Breed out the colour" or the importance of being white', *Australian Historical Studies*, vol. 33, no. 120, 2002, pp. 286–302.

—— 'The necessity of Britishness: ethno-cultural roots of Australian nationalism', *Nations and Nationalism*, vol. 12, no. 3, 2006, pp. 493–511.

—— 'Another nation: Aboriginal activism in the late 1960s and early 1970s', *Australian Historical Studies*, vol. 40, no. 3, 2009, pp. 343–60.

Murphy, John, *Imagining the fifties: private sentiment and political culture in Menzies' Australia*, Pluto Press/University of NSW Press, Sydney, 2000.

Paisley, Fiona, *Loving protection? Australian feminism and Aboriginal women's rights 1919–1939*, Melbourne University Press, Melbourne, 2000.

Pearson, Noel, *Up from the mission: selected writings*, Black Inc., Melbourne, 2009.

Roshwald, Aviel, *The endurance of nationalism: ancient roots and modern dilemmas*, Cambridge University Press, Cambridge, 2006.

Rowley, CD, *Outcasts in white Australia*, Penguin, Melbourne, 1972.

—— *The remote Aborigines*, Penguin, London, 1972.

Rowse, Tim, *White flour, white power: from rations to citizenship in central Australia*, Cambridge University Press, Cambridge, 1998.

—— *Obliged to be difficult: Nugget Coombs' legacy in Indigenous affairs*, Cambridge University Press, Cambridge, 2000.

—— (ed.), *Contesting assimilation*, API Network, Perth, 2005.

Sawer, Marian, *The ethical state? social liberalism in Australia*, Melbourne University Press, Melbourne, 2003.

Smith, Anthony, *Nations and nationalism in a global era*, Polity Press, Cambridge, 1995.

—— *The nation in history: historiographical debates about ethnicity and nationalism*, University of New England Press, Hanover, 2000.

—— *Nationalism: theory, ideology, history*, Polity Press, Cambridge, 2001.

Stokes, Geoffrey, (ed.), *The politics of identity in Australia*, Cambridge University Press, Cambridge, 1997.

Sutton, Peter (ed.), *Dreamings: the art of Aboriginal Australia*, Viking, Melbourne, 1988.

Taffe, Sue, *Black and white together: FCAATSI: the Federal Council for the Advancement of Aborigines and Torres Strait Islanders 1958–1973*, University of Queensland Press, Brisbane, 2005.

Select Bibliography

Tatz, Colin, *Obstacle race: Aborigines in sport*, UNSW Press, Sydney, 1995.

Tavan, Gwenda, *The long, slow death of white Australia*, Scribe, Melbourne, 2005.

Tennant, Chris, 'Indigenous peoples, international institutions, and the international legal literature from 1945–1993', *Human Rights Quarterly*, vol. 16, 1994, pp. 1–57.

Thomas, Nicholas, *Possessions: indigenous art/colonial culture*, Thames and Hudson, London, 1999.

Thornberry, Patrick, *International law and the rights of minorities*, Clarendon, Oxford, 1991.

Wells, Julie & Christie, Michael, 'Namatjira and the burden of citizenship', *Australian Historical Studies*, vol. 31, no. 114, 2000, pp. 110–30.

Wells, Julie, Dewar, Mickey & Parry, Suzanne (eds), *Modern frontier: aspects of the 1950s in Australia's Northern Territory*, Charles Darwin University Press, Darwin, 2005.

Wise, Tigger, *The self-made anthropologist: a life of AP Elkin*, Allen & Unwin, Sydney, 1985.

Index

Abbott, CLA, 35
Aboriginal activism, 14, 31, 33–4, 37–54, 99–100
  see also under names of individual activists and activist groups
Aboriginal Affairs (lobby group), 109, 122–3, 156
Aboriginal–Australian Fellowship, 107–9, 142, 150
Aboriginal culture/society
  commercialisation of, 96–7, 137–9
  fragility of, 71–2, 76, 79–81, 92–3
  recovery of, 171, 173, 178–81
  resilience of, 28, 65–6, 72–3, 101–7
  value of, 21–2, 24–7, 114–8, 129–34, 171, 176
Aboriginal Embassy, see Tent Embassy
Aboriginal heritage
  maintenance of, 74–5, 93, 95–7, 119–20, 138–9
  popular interest in, 19, 23, 72–4, 133–4
  see also Appropriation, cultural
Aboriginal identity, 6, 38, 44–6, 93–7, 102–3 125, 163, 168, 171–2, 176–81, 184
  see also Nationalism, Aboriginal; Pan-Aboriginality)
Aboriginal people, legal definitions of, xxv
Aboriginal Sports Foundation, 127
Aboriginal state, advocacy of, 27–31, 168, 177, 181
Aboriginal Welfare Council, see Commonwealth–state conferences on Aboriginal affairs
Aborigines Advancement League (Victoria), 107–8, 110–11, 144, 150, 158–9

Aborigines' Friends' Association of South Australia, 31, 33
Aborigines Progressive Association, 13, 37–40, 49–50, 153, 171–2
Aborigines' Protection League of South Australia, 27, 30–1
Absorption, biological, 1–17, 110, 111
Acclimatisation, 12, 42–3
Africa/African people, xxi–xxiii, 100, 121, 153–4
  see also South Africa
Ahmatt, Michael, 127
Alcohol, 86, 100, 147–51
Anderson, Michael, 168, 181
Andrews, Shirley, 158
Anthropology, xvii–xviii, 20, 101, 173, 183
  see also under names of individual anthropologists
Antill, John, 135
Anti-Slavery and Aborigines Protection Society, 86
Apartheid, 100, 104
Appropriation, cultural, 23, 26, 135–40
Archer, JC, 86
Arnhem Land, 19, 52, 73, 137, 181
  see also Yolngu
Arrernte people, 69–70, 133, 185
Art, 132–4
  Aboriginal, 70–2, 132, 134–40, 183
  Aboriginal motifs in, 26–7
  bark painting, 134–5, 137, 169, 182
  see also under names of individual artists, and Design and decoration, Aboriginal motifs in
Asia/Asian people, xviii–xxiv, 7–8, 41, 60–2, 153–4
Assimilation, 25, 67–8, 80–1, 125, 138, 145, 146, 147, 150–1, 164–5, 172, 183, 185–6

Index

contested meanings of, xii, 40–1, 63–4, 98–9, 111–19
criticism of, 99–100, 107–11, 177–8
definitions of, 15–16, 77–8, 95–6, 101, 112–13, 115–16
government policies of, 15, 36, 77, 81–97, 166, 170–1
immigrant, 62–4, 90
promotion of, 59–60, 71, 89, 121–2
varieties of, 2, 14–17, 101–7, 131, 166–7
Association for the Protection of Native Races, 13, 31, 32
Attwood, Bain, 47, 48, 113, 169
Austin, Tony, 11
Australia, Peter, 149
Australian Aboriginal Progressive Association, 39
Australian Aborigines' League, 13, 37–40, 49, 52, 54, 180
Australian Board of Missions, 106–7
Australian Federation of Women Voters, 31
Australian Half-Caste Progressive Association, 84
Australian Rules (football), 125–6
Australian way of life, 63, 95, 97, 146

Baillie, Helen, 33
Bandler, Faith, 107, 153–4, 156–7
Bark petition, 169
Barnes, CE, 117
Basedow, Herbert, 8, 30
Beazley, Kim (Snr), 151
Beetson, Arthur, 126
Bell, JH, 150
Bennett, Elliott, 124, 127
Bennett, Mary, 9, 21
Bennett, Scott, 15
Berndt, Catherine, 72, 105, 131
Berndt, Ronald, 72, 105, 131
Birdsell, JB, 9
Black, Roman, 135
Black Panther Party, 176–7
Black power, 123, 127, 176–8
Blair, Harold, 74
Bleakley, JW, 6, 30
Board for Anthropological Research, University of Adelaide, 8–9, 22

Bonner, Neville, 163, 171
Borrie, WD, 64
Boxers/boxing, 38, 124–5, 127
    see also under names of individual boxers
Boy scouts, 23
Boyce, Milton, 23
Bracken, George, 124, 127
Breed out the colour, see Absorption, biological
British/Britishness, xx, 23–4, 33, 37, 42–4, 46, 48, 60, 63–4, 120, 138
British Empire Union in Australia, 55
Brown, HC, 4
Brown, Roosevelt, 176
Bryan, Cyril, 6
Bryant, Gordon, 120, 122, 144

Calwell, Arthur, 60
Capitalisation of 'Aboriginal', 122–3
Carell, Victor, 139
Carrodus, JA, 4, 5, 49, 68
Carroll, Alan, 11
Caucasian–Aboriginal race relatedness, 8–9, 12, 14
Chaseling, Wilbur, 105
Chesterman, John, xxiv
Chifley, Joseph, 54
Child removal, 2–3, 5, 8, 9, 63, 106
Chinnery, EWP, 35–6
Christophers, Barry, 123
Citizenship, xx, 16–17, 33–4, 36, 37–41, 46–7, 50–5, 64–9, 78, 81–8, 102, 108, 143–4, 151, 162
Civil rights, xix, 68, 108, 146, 159
Cleland, JB, 9, 10, 12, 15, 22–3
Coe, Paul, 180–1
Colbung, Ken, 176
Commonwealth–state conferences on Aboriginal affairs
    (1937) 5–6, 10–11, 13, 15–16, 78
    (1948) 16, 74, 78
    (1951) 16, 78, 81–3, 98
    (1952) 16, 83, 88
    (1961) 77, 95, 96, 112–13
    (1963) 122
    (1965) 115–16
    (1967) 117

224

Communism/communists, 29–31, 158, 165, 169
Coniston massacre, 19
Constitution, Australian, xviii–xx, xxv, 49, 68–9, 141–3, 151–2, 154–7, 159, 165
Cook, Cecil, 1, 4–7, 9, 11–12, 14, 18, 35
Coombes, VW, 116
Coombs, HC, 57, 64, 129, 132, 166–7
Cooper, William, 13, 37, 39–49, 51–4, 145, 158, 163, 180–1, 183–4, 186
Coorey, Tony, 168
Corroboree (ballet), 135, 139
Council for Aboriginal Affairs, 166–7
Council for Aboriginal Rights (Victoria), 101, 148
Craigie, Billy, 168
Cultural authenticity, 179–81
Curtis, Emily, 8

Dance, Aboriginal, 139, 180
Daniels, Davis, 149, 160
Davey, Stan, 113–14, 159
Day of Mourning, 34, 38, 39
Deakin, Alfred, xxi, xxv
Dean, Beth, 135, 139
Decolonisation, 58–9, 100
Defence, Aboriginal involvement in, 42–4
see also War
Delamothe, Peter, 146
Design and decoration, Aboriginal motifs in, 26–7, 72, 135, 137–8
Dexter, Barrie, 166
Dixon, Chicka, 142
Doomed race, *see* Extinction, Aboriginal
Duguid, Charles, 106, 111, 151
Durack, Mary, *see* Miller, Mary Durack

Education, Aboriginal, 74–5
Egan, Ted, 172
Elkin, AP, 9, 15–16, 21–2, 32, 34–5, 56, 57, 61–2, 64–71, 87, 98–9, 101–4, 107, 150–1, 155–6
Ellemor, Arthur, 87, 98–9
Engel, Frank, 159
Environmental stewardship, 23, 24–5, 131–4

Equality, legal, 46–7, 114, 157, 162, 173
Ernabella, 105–6
Eugenics/eugenicism, 1, 10–13
Evans, Ted, 107
Evatt, HV, 57
Exemption from Aboriginal legislation, 35–6, 82–3
Extinction, Aboriginal, xvii, xx–xxi, 5–6, 10, 13, 16, 26, 31–2, 74, 99

Farmer, Graham, 126
Farming, Aboriginal involvement in, 43–5, 49–50
Federal Council for Aboriginal Advancement/Federal Council for the Advancement of Aborigines and Torres Strait Islanders (FCAA/FCAATSI), xiv, 113, 120, 131, 141–3, 153, 156, 158, 160–1, 167, 171–5, 183
Federation, Australian, xvii–xxi, 28, 31, 185
Feminists, 20, 30, 33–4
Ferguson, Bill, xi, 13–14, 37–9, 49, 50, 51, 52, 67, 163, 183
Firebrace, Sharon, 127
Flags, Aboriginal, 181–2
Forrest River massacre, 19
Franchise, Aboriginal, xx, xxi–xxv, 68–9, 141, 143–7
Freedom Ride, 147

Gale, Fay, 111
Galligan, Brian, xxiv
Garran, Robert, xviii–xix, xxiii
Garvey, Marcus, 39
Geddes, WR, 104
Genders, JC, 27–31
Genocide, 108, 110–11, 113
Gibbs, Pearl, 51, 107
Gilbert, Kevin, 162, 171, 173, 177, 178, 182
Gillen, Frank, xvii, 181
Gilmore, Mary, 25
Good Neighbour Councils, 90, 92
Goodluck, John, 122
Goolagong, Evonne, 127
Green, TH, 81
Groves, Herbert, 107, 111, 163

225

Index

Gurindji, 169–70, 172

Haebich, Anna, 89–90, 138
Half-castes, xxv, 1–17, 35–6, 84–5
Hall, Robert, 53, 55–6
Hardy, Frank, 169
Harney, Bill, 72–3
Harris, William, 39
Harvard–Adelaide Universities Expedition, 1938–39, 9
Haskell, Arnold, 72
Hasluck, Paul, 68, 76–98, 103, 115, 117, 121, 130, 138, 145, 149
Hassen, Jack, 124
Hastings, Peter, 167
Hausfeld, RG, 105
Herbert, Xavier, 18–19
Hermannsburg artists, 69–71
Holocaust, 58
Holt, Harold, 153, 165
Horner, Jack, 141, 150

Immigrants/immigration, 43–4, 50, 57, 60–4, 119, 183
Ingamells, Rex, 24–6
Inglis, Judy, 148
Integration, 68, 100–1, 103–5, 114, 119, 159, 172, 183
 contested meanings of, 108–13
 promotion of, 107–11, 118, 128, 144–5, 176
 rejection of, 117, 177–8
International Labour Organisation (ILO), 59–60
 ILO Convention 107 of 1957, 100, 108

Jackson, Syd, 126, 127
Jago, John, 109
James, Shadrach, 54, 57, 67
Jindyworobak movement, 25–6, 73, 132
Johns, Gary, 185
Johnstone, JRL, 154–5
Jones, Frederic Wood, 22
Jones, Philip, 134

Kantilla, David, 126, 127
King, MF, 55
Kinsella, John, 127

Koppe, Margaret, 128
Kymlicka, Will, 77

Lake Tyers, 169
Lambert, CR, 86, 138
Land ownership, demands for, 47, 49–50, 106–7, 114
 see also Land rights
Land rights, 160–61, 164, 168–73
 see also Land ownership, demands for
Langford, ME, 130
League of Nations, 19, 29, 31, 32, 35, 57
LeSueur, E, 130–1
Liberalism, 77–81, 91–2, 144, 159
Little Rock, Arkansas, 100
Love, JRB, 105
Lyng, Jens, 1

Mahon, Hugh, xix, xxiv
Maori, xix, 28, 49, 104, 144–5
 see also New Zealand
Markus, 61–2
Marriage, regulation of, 3–4, 9
Marshall, Alan, 73
Martin, Jean, 105
Maynard, Frederick, 39
Maza, Bob, 176–9
McCaffery, RK, 93–5
McDonald, Norm, 126
McEwen, Jack, 13, 34–5, 37, 41, 42, 43
McGinness, Joe, 120, 171
McGrath, Ann, 26
McGuinness, Bruce, 176, 178
McLean, Ian, 27
McMahon, William, 167–8
McQueen, Humphrey, 26
Menzies, Robert, 37, 39, 52, 53, 55, 61, 118, 122, 153, 155, 159
Miller, Mary Durack, 71–2
Minority rights, 29, 30, 58
Miscegenation *see* Half-castes
Missions/missionaries, 4, 21, 37, 70, 101, 105–7
 see also under names of specific missions and missionaries
Mixed descent, *see* Half-castes
Modernisation of Aboriginal people, models for, 28, 32–6, 39–40, 44–5, 49–50, 65–7, 74–5, 115

Moffitt, Ian, 167
Morgan, Lionel, 126
Moriarty, John, 126
Morley, William, 13
Mountford, Charles, 132–3
Mullett, Cheryl, 126, 128
Myths and legends, Aboriginal, *see* Spirituality
Namatjira, Albert, 69–72, 74, 86, 100, 148–9
Naming of Aboriginal people, 93–5
National Aborigines Day, 89, 91, 121
National Aborigines Day Observance Committee, 121–2
National Missionary Council of Australia, 114–15, 121, 159
National Tribal Council, 174–6, 179
Nationalism
  Aboriginal, 30, 163–4, 168, 173–82, 184
  Australian, xiii, xx, 2, 13, 17, 23–7, 41, 63–4, 69, 119–20, 138–9, 148, 157–8, 172, 183
  see also White Australia policy/ideal
  civic and ethnic, xii–xiii, 7, 15, 42, 77–8
Nationality and Citizenship Act (1948), 83
Native Union of Western Australia, 39
Native Welfare Conferences *see* Commonwealth–state conferences on Aboriginal affairs
Neville, AO, 1, 3–6, 9–10, 13, 14, 18
New Deal for Aborigines, 1939, 34–7, 82
New Guinea, *see* Papua and New Guinea
New Zealand, xvii, xix, xxiii, xxiv, 28, 104, 144–5
  see also Maori
Newfong, John, 181
Newman, Tony, 131
Nicholls, Doug, 74, 125–7, 149, 158, 175, 176, 180
Nixon, PJ, 170–1
Noble, HW, 112–13
Northern Australia, development of, 27, 41–7, 49
Nott, Roger, 86

O'Connor, Richard, xxi–xxiii
Olympic Games, 127
One People of Australia League (OPAL), 130
Onus, Bill, 134, 137–8
Onus, Lin, 134
Oodgeroo Noonuccal, *see* Walker, Kath

Pacific Islanders, xix,
Page, SB, 154–5
Paisley, Fiona, 33
Pan-Aboriginality, 38, 46, 80, 173–4, 179
  see also Nationalism, Aboriginal
Papua and New Guinea, 20, 29, 32, 34–5
Pareroultja, Otto, 70
Parkes, Henry, xx
Parliamentary representation, Aboriginal, 28, 47–9, 54, 80, 144–6
Paterson, Thomas, 13, 42, 46
Patten, Jack, xi, 13–4, 37–9, 49, 50, 52, 183
Pearson, Charles, xviii
Pearson, Noel, 184, 186
Penny, HH, 130
Perkins, Charles, 112, 125–7, 147
Pierson, James, 111–12
Pink, Olive, 103
Pitjantjatjara, 105, 133
Pittock, Barrie, 172
Pluralism, cultural, 99, 102–4, 116, 119, 121, 175
Positive discrimination, 158–61, 165
Post War Reconstruction, 56–7
Pott, Bruce, 149
Preston, Margaret, 26–7, 72–3
Primitivity
  attribution to Aboriginal people, xvii–xviii, xx, 10, 22–3, 185
  changing evaluations of, 20–27, 129–31
Pritchard, Katherine Susannah, 18
Protection
  government policies of, xxiv, 45
  humanitarian advocacy of, 31–3
Public opinion on Aboriginal people
  campaigns to change, 88–93, 121–3, 141–2

Index

shifts in, xi, 19–20, 56, 120–2, 152–3, 183

Quick, John, xxiii

Racial discrimination, campaigns against, 38, 58, 88–9, 147
Racial mixing, *see* Half-castes
Racial purity, ideal of, 1, 7–8
Racism, 1, 13, 58, 61–2, 73, 112, 123, 164, 167, 183
Radcliffe-Brown, AR, 20–1
Read, Peter, 112
Reay, Marie, 105, 122–3
Reed, AW, 132
Referendum, 1967, 125, 140–4, 151–61, 162, 164–7, 183–4
Reid, Rex, 135
Religion, Aboriginal, 21, 66, 178–9
see also Spirituality, Aboriginal
Renan, Ernest, 6
Reserves, Aboriginal, 2, 10, 22–3, 170
Ricketts, William, 133–4
Roberts, Ainslie, 132
Robinson, Roland, 132
Rose, Lionel, 124–8
Rowley, CD, 17, 36, 109, 117, 132
Rowse, Tim, 63, 116, 160, 166
Rugby League, 126–8
Russell, William, xvii

Sands, Dave, 124
Saunders, Reg, 128
Sawer, Geoffrey, 155
Scougall, Stuart, 134
Segregation, xxiv, 10, 22–3, 41–2, 100, 110, 113
Self-determination, 29–30, 58–9, 167, 177, 182, 184–6
Separatism, 175, 177–8, 184
Sharpeville massacre, 100
Simms, Eric, 126, 128
Simpson, Colin, 73–4
Smith, Anthony, xiii, 77–8
Soccer, 125–7
South Africa, 100, 144, 152, 153, 154
Sovereignty, Aboriginal, 24, 168
Spalding, Ian, 122–3
Spencer, Walter Baldwin, xvii, 181

Spillman, Lyn, xviii
Spirituality, Aboriginal, 129, 133–4
see also Religion, Aboriginal
Sport, Aboriginal involvement in, 123–9, 184
Stanner, William, 166, 170
Stepan, Nancy, 11
Stephensen, PR, 23–4
Stereotypes, negative, xi, 49
of Aboriginal incompetence, 28, 31, 63, 73, 87–8, 92–3, 148
of Aboriginal ineffectualness, xviii, xxii, 12, 22–3
Street, Jessie, 120, 142–3
Strehlow, TGH, 70, 104–5, 129–130, 148
Sutton, Peter, 185
Sykes, Bobbi, 181

Taffe, Sue, 159, 175
Takiara, 19
Tatz, Colin, 116–17, 120–1, 124, 125, 146
Tennant, Chris, 59
Tennis, 127
Tent Embassy, 168, 177, 181–82
Thomas, Faith, 126, 127
Thomas, Harold, 182
Thomas, Nicholas, 136
Thomson, Donald, 22, 52
Thonemann, HE, 73
Tindale, Norman, 9–10, 12, 22–3
Torres Strait Islanders, xiv, 52, 112, 145–6, 175
Tuckson, Tony, 134, 135
Tudawali, Robert, 149
Turner, Robert, 23

Unaipon, David, 30, 33
United Nations 57–60, 76, 87, 146, 153, 167, 177
Declaration of Human Rights, 57–8, 106
Educational, Scientific and Cultural Organization (UNESCO), 58, 66, 134
United States of America, 11, 72, 100, 134, 176–7

Victorian Aboriginal Group, 31, 33
Victorian Aborigines Advancement League, *see* Aborigines Advancement League (Victoria)
Victorian Council for Aboriginal Rights, *see* Council for Aboriginal Rights (Victoria)

Walker, Alan, 61–2
Walker, Kath, 110, 145–6, 153, 162–3
War
  Aboriginal service in, 38, 50–6
  Cold War, 129
  First World War, 20, 29, 50–51
  Restrictions on Aboriginal enlistment, 53, 55
  Second World War, 17, 22, 36, 51–8, 60, 124, 129
  see also Defence, Aboriginal involvement in
Ward, Dick, 86
Wards of the state, Aboriginal status as, 82–8
Wave Hill, *see* Gurindji
Welfare benefits, 47
  Aboriginal entitlement to, 84, 143
  Aboriginal exclusion from, xxiv–xxv

Welfare dependency, 84
Welfare Ordinance, Northern Territory, 1953, 81–8, 93, 98–9
Wentworth, WC, 118, 131, 165–6
West, Lamont, 131
White Australia policy/ideal, xx–xxiii, 1, 10, 13, 18, 41–2, 89, 119
  affirmations of, 5–8, 12, 60
  questioning of, 61–2
  weakening of, 57, 61, 64, 120, 153
Wilkie, Douglas, 164–5
Williams, Bert, 168
Wise, FJS, 84
Women's Non-Party Association of South Australia, 31

Yirrkala, 105, 151, 169–70
Yolngu, 19, 72, 169–70
  see also Arnhem Land
Youth, Aboriginal, 163–4, 168, 177, 180
Yuendumu, 128
Yunupingu, Galarrwuy, 172